The Florentine florin

Manchester University Press

artes liberales

Series Editors

Carrie E. Beneš, T. J. H. McCarthy, Stephen Mossman, and
Jochen Schenk

Artes Liberales aims to promote the study of the Middle Ages – broadly
defined in geography and chronology – from a perspective that transcends
modern disciplinary divisions. It seeks to publish scholarship of the
highest quality that is interdisciplinary in topic or approach, integrating
elements such as history, art history, musicology, literature, religion,
political thought, philosophy and science. The series particularly seeks to
support research based on the study of original manuscripts and archival
sources, and to provide a recognised venue for increased exposure for
scholars at all career stages around the world.

To buy or to find out more about the books currently available in this
series, please go to: https://manchesteruniversitypress.co.uk/series/
artesliberales/

The Florentine florin

The politics and culture of money in the Middle Ages

Stefano Locatelli

MANCHESTER UNIVERSITY PRESS

Published by Manchester University Press
Oxford Road, Manchester, M13 9PL

www.manchesteruniversitypress.co.uk

British Library Cataloguing-in-Publication Data
A catalogue record for this book is available from the British Library

ISBN 978 1 5261 5813 0 hardback

First published 2025

EU authorised representative for GPSR:
Easy Access System Europe, Mustamäe tee 50, 10621 Tallinn, Estonia
gpsr.requests@easproject.com

Typeset by Newgen Publishing UK

To my family

D'ottobre nel contado a buono stallo
e' pregovi, figliuol', che voi v'andiate;
traetevi buon tempo e uccellate
come vi piace, a piede ed a cavallo.

La sera per la sala andate a ballo,
e bevete del mosto e inebrïate,
ché non ci ha miglior vita, in veritate;
e questo è ver come 'l fiorino è giallo.

E poscia vi levate la mattina,
e lavatevi 'l viso con le mani;
l'arrosto e 'l vino è buona medicina.

Alle guagnele, starete più sani
che pesce in lago o 'n fiume od in marina,
avendo miglior vita che cristiani.

Folgóre da San Gimignano, *Di ottobre*

Contents

Figures

The Inscription Numismatic Font used for coin legends on page 29 is provided courtesy of The Fitzwilliam Museum, Cambridge, United Kingdom.

Maps

Tables

Table 4.4 is available online via the manchesterhive:

Acknowledgements

I owe my sincerest gratitude to Georg Christ and Paul Oldfield. Their strong belief in this book, even when it was just a collection of scattered notes, coupled with their contagious enthusiasm and constructive comments, proved pivotal in the eventual fruition of this work. The example they set of how to be excellent scholars and kind human beings is a constant source of inspiration for my stay in academia.

I must also thank Lucia Travaini and Monica Baldassarri. Lucia introduced me to the intricacies of historical research with her incisive, original, and never-predictable comments, combined with rare intellectual honesty and genuine friendship. Under her careful mentorship, I learnt the patience and care essential to the craft of historical writing. Monica instilled in me a deep appreciation for asking questions rather than seeking answers. Her boundless curiosity and meticulous attention to detail in historical research are qualities I have tried to emulate, hopefully successfully, in this work.

I am deeply indebted to Barrie Cook for his unstinting support since we first met in 2012 at the Department of Coins and Medals of the British Museum (now Money and Medals). Barrie has always been there to discuss medieval money, and with exceptional humility and profound knowledge, he has dedicatedly commented on every page I have written, not just for this book.

David Abulafia and Philipp Rössner were among the first to read and provide constructive feedback on an early draft of this manuscript. Their suggestions allowed me to clarify some aspects and deepen others. I am grateful to both of them for their valuable insights.

Over the past few years, esteemed colleagues and friends, including Antonio Antonetti, Matteo Broggini, Jacopo Bruttini, Francisco Cebreiro Ares, Raffaele Danna, Ignazio Del Punta, Silvia Diacciati, Lorenzo Fabbri, Davide Fabrizi, Enrico Faini, Richard A. Goldthwaite, Lauren Jacobi, Alessio Montagano, Giuseppina Orobello, Jacopo Paganelli, Alma Poloni, Luca Scholz, Adolfo Sissia, Sergio Tognetti, Paolo Tomei, and Marco Vendittelli, have generously shared their ideas and work with me. I thank them all for their valuable time and assistance, particularly Antonio and Paolo, for helping collect some of the archival sources for this research.

In its final phase, this book benefitted greatly from two research fellowships I held, respectively, at the Italian Academy for Advanced Studies in America (Columbia University) and Queen Mary University of London as a Leverhulme Early Career Fellow. They provided me with the most precious resource a scholar needs: time to read, think, and develop ideas. Within the circle of colleagues encountered during these fellowships, I extend my sincere gratitude to Giovanni Ceccarelli, David Freedberg, Joel Kaye, Giorgio Lizzul, Filippo Petricca, Miri Rubin, Alan Stahl, and Francesca Trivellato.

I also thank Sarah White for her kind help in copyediting the text, as well as the series editors and the editorial staff of Manchester University Press, especially Meredith Carroll, Kate Hawkins, Siobhán Poole, and Laura Swift, for their guidance and patience. Any mistakes remain my responsibility alone.

I would like to remember and thank the late Professor Peter Spufford, a dear friend and 'marvellous' scholar, who was enthusiastic about this research from the very beginning. Peter was a constant source of advice and support, generously sharing his vast knowledge of medieval money and mercantile culture through signed copies of his publications, which he kept sending me by post. I am honoured to have made his acquaintance, and I jealously cherish the memory of our lunch at the Guildhall in Whittlesford in July 2017.

Finally, I would like to thank those colleagues who have always and foremost been close friends. These are Fabrizio Ansani, Simone De Cia, Michele Baitieri, Ambra Mazzelli, Maddalena Vaccaro, and Luca Zenobi. I deeply appreciate your full and unconditional support. A special mention should go to the Mancunian post-lads Marco Biasioli, Daniel Calderbank, Vitaly Kazakov, and Lewis

Ryder, as well as Eric Lepp and Ria Sunga Turner. Your good-for-the-soul company and countless pints together helped me navigate the precarity of the past years without losing heart. Gerardo Serra's fraternal friendship continues to enrich me both as a scholar and a human being.

My family has always been a constant source of love, present despite the geographical distance and time zones that too often kept us apart. This book is dedicated to Alberto, Giorgio, Giulia, and Mariarosa, but also to Gianangelo, Pietro, and Severina, wherever they are. My deepest gratitude is for Chiara. Her confidence in me surpasses my own, and she is my source of encouragement when I need it the most.

Abbreviations

£.s.d.	*Librae, solidi, denarii*
AAV	Archivio Apostolico Vaticano
Appendice	Pietro, Santini, *Documenti dell'antica costituzione del comune di Firenze: appendice* (Florence: L. S. Olschki, 1952).
ASDLu	Archivio Storico Diocesano di Lucca
ASF	Archivio di Stato di Firenze
ASI	*Archivio Storico Italiano*
ASPi	Archivio di Stato di Pisa
Bernocchi I–V	Mario Bernocchi, *Le monete della Repubblica fiorentina*, 5 vols (Florence: L. S. Olschki, 1974–85).
De Boüard I–II	Alain De Boüard, *Documents en française des archives angevines de Naples (regne de Charles Ier)*, 2 vols (Paris: E. De Boccard, 1933).
Documenti	Pietro Santini, *Documenti dell'antica costituzione del comune di Firenze* (Florence: G. P. Vieussuex, 1895).
EHR	*Economic History Review*
g	gram(s)
Grégoire IX	*Les Registres de Grégoire IX*, 4 vols, ed. L. Auvray, S. Clémencet and L. Carolus-Barré (Paris: A. Fontemoing/E. De Boccard, 1896–1955).
JMH	*Journal of Medieval History*

MEC 6   Miguel Crusafont, Anna M. Balaguer, and Philip Grierson, *Medieval European Coinage, with a Catalogue of the Coins in the Fitzwilliam Museum Cambridge, 6: The Iberian Peninsula* (Cambridge: Cambridge University Press, 2013).

MEC 12   William R. Day Jr., Michael Matzke, and Andrea Saccocci, *Medieval European Coinage, with a Catalogue of the Coins in the Fitzwilliam Museum Cambridge, 12: Italy (I) (Northern Italy)* (Cambridge: Cambridge University Press, 2016).

MEC 14   Philip Grierson and Lucia Travaini, *Medieval European Coinage, with a Catalogue of the Coins in the Fitzwilliam Museum Cambridge, 14: Italy (III) (South Italy, Sicily, Sardinia)* (Cambridge: Cambridge University Press, 1998).

NAC   *Quaderni Ticinesi di Numismatica e Antichità Classiche*

NC   *The Numismatic Chronicle*

o.t.gr.   Ounces, taris, grains

RCA   *I registri della Cancelleria angioina riscostruiti da Riccardo Filangieri con la collaborazione degli archivisti napoletani*, 50 vols (Naples: Academia Pontaniana, 1950–2010).

RIN   *Rivista Italiana di Numismatica e Scienze Affini*

RN   *Revue Numismatique*

RSI   *Rivista Storica Italiana*

Storia I–VIII   Robert Davidsohn, *Storia di Firenze*, 8 vols (Florence: Sansoni 1956–68).

Villani, *Nuova cronica*   Giovanni Villani, *Nuova cronica*, 3 vols, ed. Giuseppe Porta (Parma: Fondazione Pietro Bembo/U. Guanda, 1990–91).

Notes on dates, money, and terminology

Dates

Florence followed the so-called *Stile dell'incarnazione al modo fiorentino*, or the 'Style of the Incarnation in the Florentine way'. In this dating system, the new year began not on 1 January but on 25 March, the feast of the Annunciation. This meant that New Year's Day was delayed by two months and twenty-three days compared to the modern celebration. For this reason, we must add one year to the dates of Florentine documents redacted between 1 January and 24 March to convert them to the modern Gregorian calendar. Pisa also had its own *Stile dell'incarnazione al modo pisano*, or the 'Style of the Incarnation in the Pisan way'. The new year also began with the Annunciation on 25 March, but was nine months and seven days ahead of the modern celebration. Therefore, we must subtract one year from the dates of documents written in Pisa between 25 March and 31 December to translate them to the Gregorian calendar. I have used the modern Gregorian calendar in the text but have left the dates of documents in the notes and Figure 2.1 as they are written in the originals.

Money

I discuss two distinct medieval accounting systems in this book. The first is the system of *librae*, *solidi*, and *denarii* (£.s.d.), which was introduced by Charlemagne in the late eighth century and gradually became the most widespread monetary system in western Europe.

According to this system, 1 *libra* = 20 *solidi* = 240 *denarii*, and 1 *solidus* = 12 *denarii*. The second is the system of gold ounces, taris, and grains (o.t.gr.) in use in Sicily and southern Italy. Specifically, 1 ounce = 30 taris = 600 grains, and 1 tari = 20 grains. Although some of these denominations eventually manifested as actual coins during the Middle Ages, their primary role within these two accounting systems was as 'money' or units of account – standards of value for reckoning with and evaluating the many different coins involved in financial transactions.

Terminology

Carat: In antiquity, a carat was a very small unit of weight based on the seed of the carob tree (*ceratonia siliquia*) and used widely in the Near East and the Mediterranean to weigh gold. It was standardised differently from region to region, with weights ranging between 0.18 g and 0.21 g. With the introduction of the gold *solidus* of Emperor Constantine the Great (303–7), which weighed 24 carats (4.55 g), this term acquired a secondary meaning of 1/24th as a measure for the fineness of gold, divided into four fractions or grains (*c.* 0.05 g). In the modern metric system, the carat is retained by jewellers but rounded to 0.2 g.

Fineness: This is the proportion of precious metal used in an alloy in relation to its total weight. Today, it is expressed in percentages or in thousands. In the Middle Ages, it was expressed in carats (1/24ths) and fractions of carats or grains (usually 1/4th carats) for gold. Consequently, pure gold was described as 24 carats fine. For silver, ounces (1/12ths of the Roman pound) and *denarii* (1/24ths) were usually used. In the book, I have retained this medieval custom.

Weight: In medieval documents, weight was normally expressed in terms of the number of coins struck from a standard weight, usually a pound/*libra* (12 ounces) or a mark (8 ounces or 2/3 of a pound), but sometimes also from smaller units such as an ounce (24 *denarii*). These weights varied from time to time and place to place (in antiquity, they included carats and grains, as noted). Some of them, such as the marks of Cologne or Troyes, had a long and widespread use in the Middle Ages. The weights in the book are expressed in grams (g), according to the modern International System of Units (SI).

Introduction

Florence, November 1252. The Florentine army had just returned home from the successful war against Pistoia, as recounted by the fourteenth-century chronicler Giovanni Villani (1276–1348).[1] Emboldened by the victory, so the story goes, the city government acted on the request of the Florentine merchants to strike a new gold coin to honour the commune and its achievements: they called it the *florenus aureus* – the gold florin, as we know it today.

During the second half of the thirteenth century, the Florentine florin achieved such popularity that it became one of the most important and widely accepted gold currencies for the subsequent three centuries.[2] Thanks to its reputation, historians have traditionally referred to it as 'the dollar of the Middle Ages', emphasising its broad circulation in long-distance trade networks.[3] Yet, other sources, written closer to the events in question, tell a different but complementary story of the early life of the florin as money for diplomacy, funding for war, and part of the financial operations of the clergy. Three significant pieces of evidence stand out.

In a legal document from Parma, dated 23 March 1258, Guglielmo Beroardi, delegate of the Florentine government, compensated Matteo and his brother Guido, sons of the late Gherardo dei Denti da Correggio, with a sum of money. Although he was appointed *Podestà* of Florence between 1236 and 1251, for some unknown reason, Gherardo never took office.[4] The Florentine commune compensated his sons with 1,200 *libre* of *floreni parvi*, the Florentine money of account: £800 of this was paid in gold florins worth one *libra* of *floreni parvi* each.[5] Later, in a notarial act at Lucca dated 21 April 1258, two senior clergymen needed money for an obscure affair. The Lucchese moneychanger Gerardino Tacchi lent them £10, paid in ten gold coins of the types of Lucca and Florence, i.e., *grossi d'oro* and gold florins, respectively.[6] Lastly, in a fragmentary ledger of the Treasury of the commune of Florence, dated 27 July 1259, Benintendi di Guglielmo, an envoy of the local Council of Elders, consigned to Manente Uguccione da Jesi, ambassador of Manfred, King of Sicily and 'special friend of the Florentine commune and people', the sum of 50 gold florins in a large, pretty, red silk pouch, probably both as a diplomatic gift and as financial aid for his fight against the rival city of Pisa.[7]

These three documentary sources for the early history of the florin introduce the major themes of this book. Villani's fourteenth-century narrative firmly placed the context of the florin in the mercantile sphere and the rising power of Florence, and his assessment set the stage for decades of historiography on the florin. However, these three sources, which date back to 1258–59 and represent the earliest written evidence of the actual use of gold florins, point us in a different direction: toward the Florentine florin as a vehicle for the transfer of assets and thus power in other, namely ecclesiastical, political, and diplomatic, spheres.

Drawing on the research traditions and approaches of economic, political, social, and cultural history, as well as numismatics, and combining data from a large variety of sources, including archaeological material, such as coin hoards, and largely unpublished written documentation (e.g., detailed tax receipts, tithe registers, notarial documents, and so on) from seven different archives (Florence, Lucca, Pisa, Vatican City, Venice, Genoa, and Naples), this book provides a new perspective on the early life of the florin, significantly broadening the existing consensus around this coinage. Crucially, it offers an original approach that produces, for the first time, a comprehensive account and explanation of the patterns of the diffusion of the florin in commercial and non-commercial contexts and of its use by the agents of the time. Without denying Villani's merchants their due credit for the actual fabrication of the coin and the promotion of its success, this book will approach the early history of the florin from a more holistic perspective. It will demonstrate that it was not exclusively grand commerce that enabled its success but rather the simultaneous adoption of the florin and its permeation into networks of power within the political, diplomatic, military, and ecclesiastical spheres. Therefore, the early history of

the gold florin will be reconsidered in the context of the intersec-
tions between Florence and its merchants, the Angevin Crown in
the Kingdom of Sicily, and the papacy. Within this framework, the
florin will be presented as both an economic tool and a political
instrument. While the distinction between these spheres might seem
anachronistic for this time, the florin, as a creation of an economic
power with a strong political dimension, both reflected such distinction and transcended it, serving as a lynchpin between the two
spheres. The financial power it represented greatly enhanced the
political potential of an apparently lesser polity, the merchant city
of Florence, while offering improved financial power to other more
established, if less economically developed, polities that included the
Angevin Kingdom in southern Italy and the Roman Church.

Reassessing the florin

The early history of the florin and its diffusion in the decades immediately following its introduction have traditionally been subsumed
within the wider historical narrative of the resumption of gold coins
in western Europe and thus somewhat neglected. In 1933, Marc
Bloch was among the first to provide an early account of this return
to gold in his seminal study 'Le problème de l'or au moyen age'.[8]
Through a now famous metaphor that sees monetary phenomena
as 'the most sensitive [of] barometers' able to unveil 'the deeper
movement of an economy', Bloch considered the thirteenth-century
revival of gold coinage mainly as a result of the progressive growth
in the volume of commercial exchanges. According to him, the minting of the gold *genovino* of Genoa and the Florentine florin in 1252
was possible because of a growing quantity of gold from North
Africa and the Arabic East reaching Italy in exchange for weapons,
wood, grain, and cloth – a consequence of the increasingly favourable 'trade balance' of western Europe with those regions. The new
gold coins provided long-distance trade with a more effective means
of payment, given the severe debasement of both the silver *denarii*
and the foreign gold coins in circulation, which were 'a decidedly
inadequate instrument for purposes of trade'.[9]

In the 1950s, Bloch's theory found fertile soil in the work of
Roberto Sabatino Lopez. In his now famous article entitled

'Settecento anni fa: il ritorno all'oro nell'Occidente duecentesco', which first appeared in 1953, and later in a revised but much shortened English version with the title 'Back to Gold, 1252', Lopez concurred that gold was primarily minted to cater to the needs of grand commerce for a more stable 'supra-national tender', which would put an end to the 'chronic inadequacy' of the gold and silver coins then in circulation.[10] Lopez further refined Bloch's view by introducing the notion of a 'Commercial Revolution', which he regarded as the most significant economic movement of the period. His interpretation subsequently achieved a broad consensus among scholars.[11]

Carlo M. Cipolla, Andrew M. Watson, and Thomas Walker improved Lopez's thesis by providing a better understanding of particular aspects of or trends in the return to gold. Cipolla, for example, investigated the processes of currency depreciation or 'debasement', showing how progressive deterioration in the fineness and weight of the silver *denarii* in circulation generated an increase in the demand for money that could only be met either by the development of new forms of credit or else 'by resorting to new forms of money'.[12] Watson described the severe silver famine that affected the Muslim world and the Byzantine Empire in the eleventh and twelfth centuries, which corresponded to an intense gold famine in western Europe. It was in this context, he argued, that a redistribution of the supplies of gold and silver in the Mediterranean basin took place.[13] According to Walker, similar shifts in supply and demand for precious metals represented the 'basic cause' for the subsequent change from silver to gold coinage in the West and from gold to silver in the East.[14] More recently, Peter Spufford, Richard A. Goldthwaite, Enrico Faini, Sergio Tognetti, and William R. Day Jr. have tackled the subject, all reiterating the dominant narrative of the florin as a product of the contemporary intensification of long-distance trade.[15] Yet, the 'back-to-gold' theory alone cannot fully explain the early life of the florin and its subsequent affirmation.

To date, too much emphasis has been put on the year 1252 as a key moment in the return to gold in western Europe. Scholars have tended to see it as the culmination, or better yet, the endpoint of the so-called 'Italian gold revolution'. This approach has generated a twofold effect. On the one hand, all this emphasis has created a misleading myth around that historical event, which still appears to be popular within modern historiography. In the recent volume *Storia Mondiale dell'Italia*, which offers a world history of Italy from 3200 BC to 2015, a whole chapter has been devoted to the year 1252, and this is symptomatic of the importance that this date still holds.[16] On the other hand, the consequences of the introduction of gold coins in the historical context of the time have been largely ignored in scholarly literature.[17] With the exception of a few cases highlighted below, most scholars have focused primarily on the preconditions for the minting of gold, thus providing only a truncated explanation of the return to gold itself and one that does not thoroughly illustrate 'what happened next' or, in other words, the aftermath of these events.

Moreover, the majority of studies have investigated the early history of the florin from a purely macroeconomic perspective. Their focus on large structural economic features and processes, such as the 'Commercial Revolution', taking place over a long period of time and/or a large geographical range has hitherto prohibited historians from analysing the political, cultural, and social conditions that fostered the spread of the florin, together with the 'meso' and 'micro' history of this currency, understood here as its supra-regional and local – albeit limited – circulation. Lopez was probably the first to stress the necessity of looking more closely at the evidence from this period since those macro patterns, although familiar to the majority of modern economic and monetary historians, 'were hidden' to the very people who wanted the gold *genovino*, the Florentine florin, and the *grosso d'oro* of Lucca, as will be further illustrated.[18] Also, the severe lack of reliable data within the written sources at our disposal does not permit a conclusive assessment of any of those features.[19] This is not to say that the economic explanations mentioned above are wrong, but they do not take into consideration the particular historical and political contexts of the cities of Genoa, Florence, and Lucca, and of Italy and western Europe more generally, when the minting of gold was resumed, and the new gold coins entered the monetary circulation of the time. Lopez sought to tackle these issues, but his attention was primarily devoted to understanding the origins of the gold *genovino*, given its alleged 'primogeniture' over the florin.[20] The Florentine gold coin was relegated instead to the rank of mere imitation of the Genoese currency, albeit one with a strong political dimension, namely, as a statement of superiority by the city of Florence over other Tuscan centres.[21] Lopez also paid very little attention to the diffusion of the two currencies: in his attempt to explain why gold eventually conquered all of Europe, he referred once again to the long-term commercial development that had sustained the demand for new means of payment.[22] In other words, Lopez ascribed this conquest to the same 'macro' causes that had fostered the return to gold without really engaging with the actual context in which the new gold coins circulated. In this respect, not even the work of Mario Bernocchi, which is considered the standard numismatic reference for the Florentine coinage today, appears to be of much help.

Between 1974 and 1985, Bernocchi published five volumes on the Florentine mint and its coinage based on the analysis of the mint register or *Libro della zecca* – now kept at the State Archive of Florence – and on the examination of more than 800 Florentine gold and silver coins dating between 1252 and 1533.[23] Thanks to his extremely valuable study, we are currently in possession of a considerable amount of detail on, for example, the many types of coins issued in Florence and their respective chronology, the organisation of the Florentine mint, its technology, and the processes of minting. The coin series and their dating have recently been revised and updated by Alessio Montagano and Massimo De Benetti.[24] Although all of these works provide useful data on Florentine coinage, they do not fully integrate the numismatic evidence within the historical context of the period or engage with broader historiographical debates on Florence, Italy, and Europe more generally.[25] Moreover, the mint's records, as published by Bernocchi, do not assist the purposes of this study since the surviving *Libro* only begins in 1303, more than fifty years after the introduction of the florin, when the currency had already achieved its international reputation. Similarly, in 1982, Cipolla published *Il fiorino e il quattrino*, a seminal study on the monetary system and policies of fourteenth-century Florence. He adeptly redirected scholarly attention from the world of long-distance trade to the local dynamics of the florin, addressing significant issues beyond its origins, such as the banking crisis of Florence in the 1340s and the subsequent depreciation of gold and silver coinage. Yet, in this case, too, the chronological scope of his study precluded an analysis of the florin's role and impact in the preceding century.[26] Hence, none of these authors helps us understand the particular circumstances of the origins of the florin and its wide diffusion in the second half of the thirteenth century.[27]

The first important discussions on these earlier aspects appeared in Peter Spufford's seminal contributions. Following the geographical pattern suggested by the early exchange rates between the Florentine florin and other Italian and European currencies, Spufford showed that, although designed as a *libra* to fit in perfectly with the accounting and financial system of Florence, gold florins were being exchanged as early as 1263–64 along the commercial axis that ran from Florence to the Champagne Fairs, the major commercial centre of the time, and thence to Paris.[28] The early diffusion of the florin therefore mirrored the development of the commercial network of Florence and its merchant bankers into northern Europe.

It was along those lines that the history of the florin was also presented at a conference held in Florence in 2002 to celebrate the 750th anniversary of the coin's birth.[29] There, for the first time, the florin became the subject of an interdisciplinary discussion carried out by medieval numismatists and economic and monetary historians, such as Lucia Travaini, Philip Grierson, and Spufford himself. In his 'The First Century of the Florentine Florin', the latter provided the first account of the life of the florin, illustrating how by the 1270s, after a slow take-off following its minting, it was being used regularly throughout Italy, at the main fairs beyond the Alps, and along the Mediterranean littoral, and from the 1290s onward, the florin circulated widely in the East.[30]

In the following years, Spufford's theory found broad agreement among scholars: in his book, *The Economy of Renaissance Florence*, Richard A. Goldthwaite endorsed Spufford's argument by describing the florin as 'an international money', whose prestige 'followed on the success of the city's merchant bankers abroad'.[31] Indeed, one of the great merits of Spufford's work lies in his ability to provide important chronological and geographical details on the early diffusion of the florin. Even so, his research reinforced the established emphasis on the close relationship between the grand commerce and the Florentine coin. Spufford acknowledged that in the late Middle Ages, religious and political pressures, such as the needs of the papacy, pilgrimages, wars, or war preparations,

would have had a more immediate effect on the movement of bullion than trade balances in the short term.[32] This book will investigate the extent to which these elements also assisted the diffusion of
the florin.

However, in addition to the limitations outlined above, most of
the studies discussed so far suffer from a major conceptual drawback
that hindered their ability to provide a comprehensive understanding of what the florin actually was and represented. Crucially, they
display a propensity towards studying the Florentine currency and
medieval money more broadly, primarily as a medium of exchange,
a mere instrument of the market that had no other efficacy than to
facilitate commercial transactions between sellers and buyers. In
the case of the florin, these would be merchants engaged in long-
distance trade in need of a stable, high-quality gold currency, as
noted. Such a conception of money resonates deeply with the so-
called 'metallist' theory, as defined by Georg Friedrich Knapp in his
now famous book *The State Theory of Money*, first published in
German in 1905.[33]

According to this view, money arose 'naturally' from economic
exchanges between individuals to minimise transaction costs and
facilitate what could be done without it in a barter economy.
Defined exclusively by its function as a 'lubricator' of exchange,
money operates independently of the specific context of transactions and is governed by market principles. Treated as an exchange-
able commodity, it derives its value solely from the material used to
produce it, i.e., gold for the florin, although in the Middle Ages, any
precious metal or commodity (e.g., silver, pepper) that maintained
an exchange rate with other goods could perform that function.[34]
From this utilitarian perspective, money appears as a decontextual-
ised, ahistorical, and impersonal device, often compared to a 'veil'
that conceals the mechanisms of the 'real' economy. No reference
to politics is necessary to understand its nature within this framework: the state only has to produce coins and put a stamp on them
to certify the good quality and the correct quantity of their metal
content – any other public intervention is bound to fail.

Knapp opposed this interpretation by advocating what he called
a 'chartalist' theory.[35] In contrast to the metallist approach, he
emphasised the fundamental role played by political authorities in
the origin and evolution of money. In particular, he regarded money

as a creation of the law, a 'token' (*charta* in Latin) whose value has no connection to an underlying commodity. Whether it is gold, silver, billon, or anything else does not matter. Money is, first and foremost, a political instrument, an abstract unit of account chosen by the state, which also determines its nominal value, its characteristics as a means of payment, and the demand for it within society. In this framework, money does not arise from the market but precedes it, becoming a precondition for its development.

Both theories have been – and still are – at the centre of a lively debate on the nature and purposes of money. The metallist approach has been perpetuated by generations of thinkers, including mercantilists and neoclassical economists, and still constitutes the prevailing answer to the question 'what is money?' in the mainstream or orthodox tradition of modern economics. Conversely, chartalist arguments influenced the writings of Max Weber and John Maynard Keynes, to name a few, and have been gaining popularity among modern heterodox economists, sociologists, anthropologists, and those experts whose interest in money transcends the mere financial sphere.[36] Yet, by arguing in favour of one or the other, scholars have created and reinforced a clear-cut division between those two theories, thus establishing an unhelpful, artificial, and rather simplistic dichotomy that fails to fully grasp the complexity of money. In other words, despite the obvious classificatory benefits, 'much is also lost in this process of bifurcation'.[37]

In contrast, recent scholarship on the history of money and monetary thought, notably by Stefan Eich, Andrew Sartori, and Luca Fantacci, as well as Keith Hart's earlier but influential contributions, clearly demonstrate that the two theories were neither competitive nor mutually exclusive in their historical manifestation.[38] Aspects of both coexisted, and there is evidence of their interaction and influence both in the monetary policy of kings, governments, and money operators, as also illustrated by Constantina Katsari, Jotham Parsons, and Sebastian Felten in their studies on the monetary systems of the Roman Empire, sixteenth-century France, and the Dutch Republic, respectively, and in the thinking of many historical authors who otherwise 'fail to fit neatly in one of the two categories'.[39]

The Middle Ages were no different. In her study of the function of money in medieval England, Christine Desan has shown how, at the basis of commodity money, there was a monetary nominalism that tied denominations to the state authority. In order to make coins circulate, governments had to constantly regulate their metal content and bring it into congruence with their legal or nominal value.[40] Monetary alterations in the form of debasements, recoinages, and 'crying up' or 'crying down' decrees were common to many – if not all – medieval European monetary systems. Such interventions were often contested and became the subject of heated ideological disputes among medieval thinkers.[41]

Taken together, these studies suggest that if we overcome that bifurcated and compartmentalised view of money, the effective combination of metallist and chartalist theories and the constructive dialogue that can be established between them can offer a more capacious and nuanced understanding of its nature, purposes, and functioning throughout history, right up to the present day. Yet, earlier studies on the gold florin remain unaware of the potential of combining metallist and chartalist approaches as analytical tools in the study of medieval money. This book intends to fill this gap. Crucially, I will not discuss the metallist approach in detail, nor will I attempt to prove that the chartalist one is more consistent with the events narrated. In fact, rather than taking a side in favour of one or the other, I will demonstrate that by merging these two antithetical yet complementary theories to recount the early life of the florin, we can fully appreciate what that coin represented in its own historical context.

In the process of undertaking this study, I will also address a final drawback of the 'back-to-gold' narrative discussed so far. In 1933, Marc Bloch concluded his famous article by stating that the 'human history' of medieval coinage had not yet been written, although the time was already ripe for a 'frontal attack' on this issue. Specifically, he asserted:

> And this piece of economic history cannot be written without becoming a social history as well; we must remember that society consists of various groups whose opposing ways of life are expressed in their monetary habits. What would be the use of a statistical study of cheques today without giving precise information as to what kind of operations are carried out by these means and what classes make use of them? The same applies to the history of gold, silver, currency, ingots, and payments in kind during the Middle Ages.[42]

With these few words, Bloch paved the way for future investigations of not only medieval money but any means of payment throughout history. He underlined the paramount importance of linking such studies to the analysis of the people who adopted a given means of payment and their attitudes towards it, arguing that mere statistical or quantitative data on its use are worthless without considering the social dimension and its inherent values and norms. Bloch's insights found fertile ground in the significant scholarship of the so-called economic sociology of money. This field began to emerge in the 1980s and expanded considerably in the 1990s, largely due to pioneering and pivotal studies by Viviana A. Zelizer, Nigel Dodd, and Jane I. Guyer, among others, and continues to produce original contributions on money, such as those collected in the 2017 volume *Money Talks: Explaining How Money Really Works* edited by Nina Bandelj, Frederick F. Wherry, and Zelizer.[43] Underlying all these works is the idea that modern money is a social construct with its values and meanings defined by the very people who engage with it daily within their networks of social ties. Rather than merely exchanging it, individuals 'identify, classify, organize, use, manufacture, design, store, and even decorate money', transforming its most direct manifestation, i.e., coinage, into amuletic, symbolic, and ritual objects imbued with moral and emotional significance.[44]

However, ambivalent attitudes towards money existed in the past as much as they do in contemporary society. Besides being a means of payment at trade fairs, medieval coins were also placed in the foundations of new buildings or in tombs, worn as amulets, offered at holy shrines, or venerated as relics.[45] The transactional value of money was thus subjective and multifaceted: economics was but one element, political propaganda and symbolism another, and rituals linked to religious beliefs yet another.[46] In Rory Naismith's words, medieval money was not only 'deeply embedded in existing social relations', shaping itself around them, but also played a key role in articulating all kinds of human interactions.[47] Likewise, and vice versa, human agency was integral to every aspect of medieval money, from the accumulation of precious metals for minting to its production, diffusion, and iconography. The combination of images and inscriptions on coins was a deliberate 'human choice', making money a means of political and cultural communication and propaganda for the issuing authority. Hence, money in the Middle Ages was a 'connecting agent' between people, offering significant insights into the social, economic, and cultural dynamics of a society when analysed from this 'human' perspective.[48]

Although original, Bloch's voice has remained largely unheard among the many scholars studying the gold florin of Florence in its early life. Lopez described the gold florin as one of 'the dollars of the Middle Ages', together with the Byzantine gold bezant, the Muslim gold dinar, and the gold ducat of Venice, as noted.[49] All those currencies would, at different times, enjoy international supremacy over other coins of their period. Such success was identified as the effect of three specific characteristics common to all of them: to be a 'dollar', a currency had to have a high unit value, intrinsic stability over time, and be supported by a strong economy very active in long-distance trade.

Despite the implicit connection to medieval mercantile society, Lopez did not touch upon the potential contribution of other agents and institutions that used those international coins, especially in 'non-commercial' contexts, such as diplomacy, war financing, or papal finances. In Spufford's account, too, the success of the florin was closely intertwined with the mercantile class alone. Very little consideration was devoted to other and external agents (i.e., not Florentine) that adopted and relied on that currency for their own needs. However, if we go back to the premise of this introduction, the episodes recorded at Parma, Lucca, and Florence in 1258–59 signal a variety of potential actors and interactions that expand the florin's range considerably beyond long-distance trade. Yet, the ways in which these people and institutions animated the early life of the florin, motivated by their own needs, remain obscure. The existing influential narrative that explains the resumption of gold coinage in western Europe and its success does little to help in this regard. Thus, a comprehensive and contextualised analysis of the various uses of the florin by the many agents of the age and in different milieus, along with a full understanding of their contribution to the success of this currency, has – to my mind – yet to be achieved.

A set of relevant questions stands at the heart of my analysis: Who used the gold florin? Where and when did it circulate most? Which purposes of payment did it serve? Were there specific markets for its circulation? What were the benefits arising from its use for the money operators of the time? And what light does this use shed on the florin's own history?

By addressing these questions, this book undertakes an extensive study of the early life of the florin, one that brings the hitherto neglected interplay of human agents and political institutions more prominently into the history of this currency. I will show that the minting of the Florentine florin did not mark any 'revolutionary' return to gold per se. Other European cities before Florence – and indeed before Genoa and Lucca – either attempted to mint new gold coins or were counterfeiting foreign gold currencies to trade in the Mediterranean. This calls into question the primacy of the Italian cities and downplays the role of 1252 as a crucial date. Despite its common acceptance, the poor level of Florentine documentation for that year does not allow any certainty about this chronology.[50] By adopting a comprehensive approach that focuses on a longer period, i.e., covering the diffusion of the florin up to the early four-teenth century, it will be possible to better understand what the return to gold really meant in practical terms. This will eventually provide the first focused explanation of why it was the gold florin of Florence and not any of the other gold coins in circulation that won the day.

This book will therefore tell a new but complementary story of the gold florin, the narrative of which moves beyond the scope of the economic take-off of the city of Florence or the monetary neces-sities of long-distance trade. If we shift our attention away from the major themes of northern European and grand commerce to adopt an original perspective that takes account of the diffusion of the florin mainly in the Mediterranean region, unexpected outcomes that enrich our knowledge of the early life of this coin come to light. The present book shows that the simultaneous adoption of the florin in three different yet interrelated and entangled environ-ments fostered the early spread of the Florentine gold coin and its success in the second half of the thirteenth century: the world of the merchant bankers of Florence, with their commercial and political affairs, the Angevin monarchy in the Kingdom of Sicily, with its high military spending, and the papacy and its fiscal system.

Historians of thirteenth-century Florence have been well aware of the instrumental role that the alliance with the Angevin monar-chy and the papacy played in the economy and the development of Florence in the second half of the thirteenth century.[51] Yet, the questions of how these relationships, which were contemporary to the early diffusion of the florin, contributed to this and how the florin strengthened the creation of those political ties have not been explored.

Sources for what remains of the florin

The starting point for this analysis must be the surviving archaeological material, generally consisting of single or stray coin finds and coin hoards. The former are normally individual coins lost accidentally by the owner and discovered many centuries later. These are completely random samples of the coinage at a certain period and can potentially provide very useful details about the use, volume, and duration of single issues when a good range of specimens is available. Yet, they are normally dominated by coins of lesser value, i.e., petty coins, and thus mainly reflect the local circulation of a given area. This may explain why no gold florins are documented as single finds for the period in question. Further, single coin finds have not been systematically recorded in all countries, and, even when available, information may be either unreliable due to the lack of detail related to the discovery or hard to obtain, as it is usually disseminated in a wide range of publications – including local newspapers – if a publicly accessible online database is not available.[52]

Gold coins are more usually found in coin hoards – groups of coins concealed together and discovered as aggregates. To date, only six hoards with gold florins dating back to the second half of the thirteenth century have been discovered and published. The earliest hoard is the one found at the *Logge dei Banchi* in Pisa, presumably buried around 1269 and consisting of ninety-one Florentine florins out of 229 gold coins.[53] This is followed by the treasure recovered by the officials of Charles of Anjou, King of Sicily (1266–85), on the coasts of Trapani in November 1270, known today only through the reports from that time.[54] These are the only thirteenth-century coin hoards that can be connected to the circulation of the Florentine florin in the first decades after its minting. The hoards from Alberese (before 1290), Aleppo (1290–91), Acre (1290–91), and Pavia (1290–95) are too distant in time to provide any detail about the early life of the florin.[55]

Overall, however, this archaeological material is not adequate to assess the spatial and chronological distribution of the florin for the period in question. From a quantitative perspective, the hoards are too few to offer enough data on the florin's diffusion or a clear and comprehensive picture of it, although they do suggest an initial link between the Florentine coin to the monetary circulation of the Mediterranean region, which will be unfolded throughout this study. Also, caution must be exercised in interpreting such scant findings since coin hoards as historical sources are problematic in and of themselves. The quality of information they provide is normally affected by several factors, including their reliability as samples of what was really circulating, their association with other objects, and the context in which they were found.[56] This is especially true when assessing the role of any high-value currency, for which the number of finds available is commonly far more meagre than for any other level of coinage.[57] Moreover, on their own, these coin hoards remain silent on a number of important issues, such as their original owner(s), the economic or non-economic reasons for their accumulation and concealment, or the motives behind the function of the florins concealed and how general this practice was. Drawing conclusions from any of these aspects by relying solely on the archaeological evidence without analysing the archival documentation of the time creates problems. Due to similar limitations, the several thirteenth-century gold florins in museum collections are not considered in this book. These are necessary sources for a study on the florin's style and iconography; for example, they may help us solve certain issues related to the classification of the earliest specimens; yet, this kind of study is beyond the scope of the present work.[58] The analysis of the early life of the florin will therefore be addressed with a fresh approach, combining archaeological evidence from the few hoards available with the written sources of the period. I will refer to the few coin hoards presented above mainly when they offer details that would not otherwise be available from the surviving documentation.

Before introducing the array of sources this book will rest upon, it is important to point out the problems facing the interpretation of any reference to money in medieval documents. The general rule is that there is no exact correspondence between the currencies recorded in written sources and the actual coins used in payment. These do not necessarily, or even usually, coincide with each other. Such a discrepancy exists because, in the Middle Ages, there was no 'one concept' of money.[59] Medieval people distinguished between the coins actually paid in transactions and the so-called 'monies of account'.[60] The latter were denominations adopted in medieval documents to reduce the huge number of different types of coins in circulation to a common denominator, thus facilitating accounting. As such, monies of account were not visible or tangible coins but 'ghost monies', as Cipolla called them.[61] This implies that sums in the sources did not always consist of simple quantities of the specified currency.

For the gold florin, this scenario is even more complex, especially considering that, within the sources, the expression *florenos auri* or 'gold florins' could refer either to the actual coins or to money of account based on the Florentine currency. In the latter case, however, it could also be that other gold or silver coins were employed in the payment, while gold florins were being used purely to express the amount paid. To avoid any sort of ambiguity, I have decided to consider any reference to gold florins where the effective use of actual money is not clearly specified by further expressions within the text as 'money of account' and thus set these references aside. This is not to say that the use of the florin as money of account cannot reveal interesting details about its circulation. For instance, the adoption of a foreign coin, one not minted locally, as a money of account in a given monetary area usually occurred when that coin had been in circulation for some time, and local people had become familiar with it. Hence, the appearance of florins as money of account in contexts other than Florence, its district, and its people can potentially shed light on their actual use. Yet, in a study that aims at describing the diffusion of the florin 'in practice', i.e., how the gold coin physically entered the monetary circulation of the time, the volume of its spread, its demand and supply, as well as the actual use made by the agents of the time, references to money of account are of little help. This issue will be considered on a case-by-case basis while going through the sources.

However, on the whole, it is possible to distinguish between 'actual florins' and 'florins of account' when at least one of the following conditions applies. The first is a clear itemisation of the several monetary species used in payments. The second is the double recording of the sum both in actual money and money of account: the first reference normally expresses the amount in the local system of account, while the second one refers to the effective number of coins paid, usually linked together by Latin expressions such as '*videlicet*', literally 'namely' or 'that is'. The third is when there is a more detailed description of the florins in the source: thus, not just as '*florenos auri*', but with a clear reference to the quality of their gold, their fineness and weight, or to the dies adopted to mint the coins.[62] Also, the use of expressions such as '*manualiter*', '*ex mani*', '*in una manu*', and '*de propria manu*' indicates that the payment occurred literally 'by hand' and leaves little doubt about the actual involvement of Florentine coins.

This book is therefore based on written sources referring primarily to transactions in which Florentine florins were actually used alongside other coins. It draws mainly on fiscal records, such as detailed receipts, tax registers, and registers of deposits that offer a fragmentary but clear picture of the circulation of gold florins in the finances of the Angevin Crown and the papacy. More precisely, the collection and expenditure of gold florins by Charles of Anjou have been investigated through the records published in the twenty-seven volumes of the series of the *Registri della Cancelleria Angioina*.[63] They contain complete or partial transcriptions of administrative orders, letters, instructions, and fiscal accounts related to the economic and political business of the Crown. Due to their composite nature, they also provide interesting details of Charles's monetary and financial policy, which is crucial to understanding the motives behind the spread of the florin in the Angevin dominions.[64] The study of the florin in papal finances meanwhile draws on five unpublished registers devoted to the collection of the papal tithe in the Kingdom of Sicily for the years 1274–80, today kept at the Archivio Apostolico Vaticano.[65] This documentation has been supplemented by the published registers of papal letters, which also inform us of political relations between the popes, the Florentines, and the Angevins.[66]

The choice to turn to external archives to study the political life of the florin has also been dictated by the current status of the records at the State Archives of Florence. Public records such as statutes, acts, laws, edicts, and monetary ordinances, which could do much to recreate the different stages of the florin's issues and the monetary policy of Florence, are virtually absent for most of the period under investigation.[67] Information of this kind appears, for example, in the *Provvisioni* collection, consisting of the legal acts of the Florentine commune, but the majority of these sources date from the early 1280s. As can be seen, even the documentation produced by the local mint is of little help. Furthermore, the earliest books of account of the Florentine mercantile companies, which begin to appear with more frequency in the second half of the thirteenth century, are generally unhelpful due to their ambiguity: even if there are payments made in *floreni* as early as the year 1262, they do not always specify the kind of florins recorded in their transactions – whether they are gold, silver, actual coins, or money of account.[68]

Despite these limitations, this study still draws on a large number of notarial documents held mainly in the *Diplomatico* collection of the State Archives of Florence, as well as records from the Archivio Storico Diocesano of Lucca and published material from the State Archives of Pisa, Venice, and Genoa. The nature and the complexity of these collections as assemblages of documents related to the private business of medieval people make them a useful source through which to analyse the business of Florentine merchant bankers and their contribution to the minting of the florin, although they refer only incidentally to it. The picture is completed by references in narrative sources such as sermons or chronicles, although the latter must be approached cautiously.[69]

The book adopts an interdisciplinary methodology in order to deal with such a broad and original range of source material. Specifically, when applying modern frameworks, there is always the risk of distorting and manipulating historical facts to fit the theory. This could result in a stereotypical view of the past, disregarding the specificity and the distinctiveness of historical phenomena. Instead, this book draws from many research areas such as numismatics and monetary, economic, political, cultural, and social history to reach an in-depth and contextualised understanding of the early life of the florin in its own time. The analysis concentrates primarily on the years 1258–84 – thus on the period between the first appearance of gold florins in contemporary reliable written sources (i.e., not narrative ones, like Villani's chronicle) and the year of the introduction of the gold ducat, the Venetian response to the Florentine gold coin. Yet, to show the florin's full reach and influence, the chronological limits will be extended to the second half of the twelfth century in Chapters 1 and 2 and pushed to the first decade of the fourteenth century in Chapter 4. As for the agents, they have been chosen for more than just their central role in the politics and economics of Florence. When taken together, they also provide a comprehensive picture of the main political powers of the time, and each of them corresponds to a specific sector of the multifaceted market of the florin in the second half of the thirteenth century.

This book is split into four main chapters. Chapter 1 sets the stage by drawing attention to the period leading up to the 'back-to-gold' event, i.e., from the late twelfth century to the early 1250s. It discusses the key factors of this phenomenon, starting from a macro perspective that takes into account the economic revival of Europe and then looking at the monetary needs of the period. Other attempts to coin gold in Italy and Europe are discussed, and a comparison between the return to gold in Florence, Genoa, and Lucca is offered in light of the most recent historiographical debates. Against the backdrop of the economic and political context of the city of Florence in the years preceding the birth of the florin, the chapter offers a qualitative analysis of the conditions under which the gold florin was first conceived and eventually minted. It shows that the coin was the product of the city's economic development and commercial expansion and of the political upheaval following the death of Emperor Frederick II Hohenstaufen in 1250, which engendered the complete autonomy of the city and its government.

Each of the remaining chapters is dedicated to a specific agent or institution that contributed to the origins and affirmation of the Florentine coin. Chapter 2 concentrates on the contribution of the merchant bankers of Florence to the making of the florin and its early diffusion – an aspect that, although alluded to in current historiography, has not yet been systematically explored. The chapter challenges the traditional belief that the florin was simply the result of a request made by the mercantile class of the Florentine society, as narrated by Giovanni Villani in his fourteenth-century chronicle. Instead, it argues that the contribution of the mercantile elite was more complex, instrumental, and multifaceted: while merchants

were responsible for the supply of gold, they also provided the necessary *know-how* and *capacity*, thereby making the florin a con-
crete manifestation of their economic and political power at the
time of the so-called *Primo Popolo*.[70]

Chapters 3 and 4 examine the contribution of the Angevin
Crown and the papacy to the florin's early spread. They point
towards the importance of the financial requests and the military
spending of medieval rulers, including the popes, to explain the
enormous success of this currency. The two chapters share a similar
structure: they move from the study of the relations of each political
actor with Florence and its merchant bankers to the description of
the role played by the florin in their respective finances, with a focus
on the collection and expenditure of the gold coin. A final section
in each chapter attempts to clarify the contribution of each agent
to the diffusion of the florin and the benefits arising from its use. In
both cases, the florin is presented as an economic tool and a political instrument, crucial for the deployment of the political power of
these agents.

Through the analysis of the surviving registers of the Angevin
chancery for the reign of King Charles I of Anjou, Chapter 3 shows
that by the end of the 1270s, the Florentine florin was already
deeply rooted in the monetary system of the kingdom, in the service
of the administrative needs of the Crown, which included taxation,
payments to military personnel, and various local affairs involving the royal treasury. This is an extremely important and hitherto
unacknowledged facet of the early life of the florin, which was performing as a domestic gold currency in the Kingdom of Sicily on the
same level as the gold denominations minted there, despite its 'foreign' nature. The important role of Florentine currency in Angevin
finances, the origins of which may even date back to Charles of
Anjou's military venture in southern Italy (early 1260s), was also
the result of the contemporary demand for florins coming from
mercenary troops.

Chapter 4 analyses the diffusion of the florin within the financial
system of the papal curia. It begins with an overview of the relations
between the popes and Florentine merchant bankers, which became
increasingly important in the second half of the thirteenth century.
Then, the analysis of a remarkable set of hitherto neglected tithe
registers from southern Italy during Pope Gregory X's sexennial

tithe in the years 1274–80 reveals that gold florins were the prevailing currency collected by papal officials in the region at that time. The circulation of the florin in papal finances ultimately contributed to fostering its market.

Overall, this book offers new evidence for the early life of the Florentine coin that will complement and challenge accepted historiographical accounts of its origin and diffusion, thus advancing a hitherto unacknowledged understanding of the currency's significance in promoting certain aspects of social and political life. It refines the current interpretation of the 'Commercial Revolution' and of the 'back-to-gold' phenomenon by presenting them as historical processes – not just single events – with a social and political dimension and consequences that have thus far been disregarded. Most significantly, it will emphasise the role of human agents in the study of medieval coins while elucidating the role of gold coins as a lynchpin between economy and politics. From a methodological perspective, this book shows ways in which monetary history can be incorporated into the study of the Middle Ages more broadly, thus overcoming the existing boundaries between this subject, numismatics, and political, cultural, social, and economic history. Its findings will also show the inadequacy of the artificial separation between the economic and political dimensions to explain both the origins and early life of the florin and, more generally, of money in the Middle Ages. Finally, this book will speak to the now fashionable histories of materiality, which in the past have focused on different objects but not coinage, although coins probably represent the most obvious starting point for writing such histories, given their millennial tradition.[71] Thus, this book will provide a new perspective on the florin and establish a framework that reconceptualises the relationship between material culture and economic practice – a framework that further studies can follow.

Notes

1 Giovanni Villani, *Nuova cronica*, 3 vols, ed. Giuseppe Porta (Parma: Fondazione Pietro Bembo/U. Guanda, 1990–91), vol. 1, p. 345.
2 Philip Grierson, 'Il fiorino d'oro: la grande novità dell'Occidente medievale', *RIN* 107 (2006), 415–19 (at p. 415).

3 Roberto S. Lopez, 'The Dollar of the Middle Ages', *The Journal of Economic History* 11:3 (1951), 209–34 (at p. 211).

4 Jean-Claude Maire Vigueur (ed.), *I podestà dell'Italia comunale. Parte I: Reclutamento e circolazione degli ufficiali forestieri (fine XII sec.–metà XIV sec.)* (Rome: Istituto Storico Italiano per il Medio Evo– École Française de Rome, 2000), p. 536.

5 *Appendice*, p. 228, no. 74, and p. 242, no. 79.

6 Graziano Concioni, 'Le coniazioni della zecca lucchese nel secolo XIII', *Rivista di archeologia, storia, costume* 23:3/4 (1995), 35–88 (at p. 48). On the activity of Gerardino Tacchi, see also Pietro Guidi, 'Di alcuni maestri lombardi a Lucca nel sec. XIII (Appunti d'archivio per la loro biografia e per la storia dell'arte)', *ASI* 87:4 (1929), 209–31.

7 Ernesto Lasinio, 'Frammento di un quaderno di mandati dell'antica Camera del Comune di Firenze', *ASI* 35:238 (1905), 440–7 (at p. 445); *Storia* II, pp. 673–5.

8 Marc Bloch, 'Le problème de l'or au moyen age', *Annales d'histoire économique et sociale* 5:19 (1933), 1–34; translated by J. E. Anderson as Marc Bloch, 'The Problem of Gold in the Middle Ages', in *Land and Work in Medieval Europe: Selected Papers* (London: Routledge and Kegan Paul, 1967), pp. 186–229.

9 Bloch, 'The Problem', p. 211.

10 Roberto S. Lopez, 'Back to Gold, 1252', *EHR* New ser. 9:2 (1956), 219–40 (at p. 219); see also Roberto S. Lopez, 'Settecento anni fa: il ritorno all'oro nell'Occidente duecentesco', *Rivista Storica Italiana* 65 (1953), 19–55 and 161–98.

11 For more details on Lopez's 'Commercial Revolution', see Chapter 1.

12 Carlo M. Cipolla, 'Currency Depreciation in Medieval Europe', *EHR* 2nd ser. 15:3 (1963), 413–22; see also the most recent chapter by Martin Allen, 'Currency Depreciation and Debasement in Medieval Europe', in D. Fox and W. Ernst (eds), *Money in the Western Legal Tradition: Middle Ages to Bretton Woods* (Oxford: Oxford University Press, 2016), pp. 41–52.

13 Andrew Watson, 'Back to Gold – and Silver', *EHR* 2nd ser. 20:1 (1967), 1–34.

14 Thomas Walker, 'The Italian Gold Revolution of 1252: Shifting Currents in the Pan-Mediterranean Flow of Gold', in J. F. Richards (ed.), *Precious Metals in the Later Medieval and Early Modern Worlds* (Durham, NC: Carolina Academic Press, 1983), pp. 29–52.

15 Peter Spufford, *Money and Its Use in Medieval Europe* (Cambridge: Cambridge University Press, 1988); Richard A. Goldthwaite, *The Economy of Renaissance Florence* (Baltimore: Johns Hopkins

University Press, 2009); Enrico Faini, 'Prima del fiorino. Le origini del decollo economico di Firenze', in T. Verdon (ed.), *Firenze prima di Arnolfo: retroterra di grandezza. Atti del ciclo di conferenze (Firenze, 14 gennaio–24 marzo 2015)* (Florence: Mandragora, 2016), pp. 89–100; Sergio Tognetti, 'Il Mezzogiorno angioino nello spazio economico fiorentino tra XIII e XIV secolo', in B. Figliuolo, G. Petralia, and P. F. Simbula (eds), *Spazi economici e circuiti commerciali nel Mediterraneo del Trecento. Atti del Convegno Internazionale di Studi, Amalfi, 4–5 giugno 2016* (Amalfi: Centro di cultura e storia amalfitana, 2017), pp. 147–70; William R. Day Jr., 'Before the *Libro della Zecca*: Money and Coinage in Florence in the 12th and 13th Centuries, Part II (Silver and Gold Trade Coinages)', *ASI* 176:3 (2018), 431–84.

16 Franco Franceschi, '1252. Il fiorino di Firenze, il dollaro della crescita medievale', in A. Giardina (ed.), *Storia Mondiale dell'Italia* (Bari: Laterza, 2017), pp. 258–62.

17 Lopez seems to be an exception, but he focused on the gold *genovino* only, as discussed below.

18 Lopez, 'Back to Gold', p. 220.

19 Further details below and in Chapter 1.

20 Lopez, 'Back to Gold', p. 220.

21 Lopez, 'Settecento', p. 167. The counterargument that the first *genovino* imitated the florin of Florence recently appeared in *MEC* 12 and will be discussed in detail in Chapter 1.

22 Lopez, 'Back to Gold', p. 240.

23 Mario Bernocchi, *Le monete della Repubblica fiorentina*, 5 vols (Florence: L. S. Olschki, 1974–85).

24 Alessio Montagano, *Monete italiane regionali: Firenze* (Pavia: Numismatica Varesi, 2008); Massimo De Benetti, *I primi 100 anni del fiorino d'oro di Firenze (1251–1351): analisi e nuove prospettive di ricerca* (Rome: Istituto Poligrafico e Zecca dello Stato, 2024); William R. Day Jr. and Massimo De Benetti, 'The Willanzheim Hoard (1853) of Florentine Gold Florins', *RIN* 119 (2018), 101–62.

25 Similar comments have recently appeared in William R. Day Jr., 'Before the *Libro della Zecca*: Money and Coinage in Florence in the 12th and 13th Centuries, Part I (Petty Coinage)', *ASI* 175:3 (2017), 441–82 (at p. 446).

26 Carlo M. Cipolla, *Il fiorino e il quattrino. La politica monetaria a Firenze nel 1300* (Bologna: Il Mulino, 1982).

27 This is also the case with the detailed study of Richard A. Goldthwaite and Giulio Mandich on the development of Florentine monetary

system; Richard A. Goldthwaite and Giulio Mandich, *Studi sulla moneta fiorentina: secoli XIII–XIV* (Florence: L. S. Olschki, 1994).

28 Florentine florins have been documented at Marseille (1263–64), Provins (1265), and Paris (1267–68); Peter Spufford, *Handbook of Medieval Exchange* (London: Royal Historical Society, 1986), pp. 118 and 172; Spufford, *Money*, p. 177.

29 Lucia Travaini (ed.), 'Firenze 1252–2002: 750 anni del fiorino, Atti della Giornata celebrativa in ricordo del numismatico fiorentino Alberto Banti, Firenze, Palazzo Vecchio, Salone dei Cinquecento, 16 novembre 2002', *RIN* 107 (2006), 397–469.

30 Peter Spufford, 'The First Century of the Florentine Florin', *RIN* 107 (2006), 421–36.

31 Goldthwaite, *Renaissance Florence*, p. 48.

32 Spufford, *Money*, pp. 157–62.

33 Georg Friedrich Knapp, *The State Theory of Money* (London: Macmillan & Company Limited, 1924), chapter 1. See also Stephanie Bell, 'The Role of the State and the Hierarchy of Money', *Cambridge Journal of Economics* 25:2 (2001), 149–63 (at p. 151*ff.*); Keith Hart, 'Heads or Tails? Two Sides of the Coin', *Man* New ser. 21:4 (1986), 637–56 (at p. 643*ff.*); Geoffrey Ingham, *The Nature of Money* (Cambridge and Malden: Polity Press, 2004), chapter 1; Constantina Katsari, *The Roman Monetary System: The Eastern Provinces from the First to the Third Century AD* (Cambridge: Cambridge University Press, 2011), p. 245*ff.*

34 Philip Grierson, 'The Origins of Money', *Research in Economic Anthropology* 1 (1978), 1–35 (at p. 10).

35 Knapp, *The State Theory*, chapter 2. See also James Bonar, 'Knapp's Theory of Money', *The Economic Journal* 32:125 (1922) 39–47; Joseph A. Schumpeter, *History of Economic Analysis* (London: Routledge, 1987); Charles A. E. Goodhart, 'The Two Concepts of Money: Implications for the Analysis of Optimal Currency Areas', *European Journal of Political Economy* 14 (1998), 407–32; Ingham, *The Nature*, chapter 2; Larry Randall Wray, 'From the State Theory of Money to Modern Money: An Alternative to Economic Orthodoxy', in D. Fox and W. Ernst (eds), *Money in the Western Legal Tradition: Middle Ages to Bretton Woods* (Oxford: Oxford University Press, 2016), pp. 631–52 (at p. 632*ff.*); Bell, 'The Role of the State', p. 153*ff.*; Katsari, *The Roman Monetary System*, p. 245*ff.*

36 It is impossible to cite here the many scholars who have argued in favour of one theory or the other; further details can be found, for instance, in Ingham, *The Nature*, part I; Katsari, *The Roman Monetary System*, pp. 245–6; Goodhart, 'The Two Concepts', p. 408;

Jeffrey Y. F. Lau and John Smithin, 'The Role of Money in Capitalism', *International Journal of Political Economy* 32:3 (2002), 5–22.

37 Stefan Eich, *The Currency of Politics: The Political Theory of Money from Aristotle to Keynes* (Princeton and Oxford: Princeton University Press, 2022), p. 10.

38 Eich, *The Currency of Politics*; Andrew Sartori, 'Silver and the Social in Locke's Monetary Thought', *The Journal of Modern History* 93:3 (2021), 501–32; Luca Fantacci, 'The Dual Currency System of Renaissance Europe', *Financial History Review* 15:1 (2008), 55–72; Keith Hart, 'Heads or Tails?'.

39 Katsari, *The Roman Monetary System*; Jotham Parsons, *Making Money in Sixteenth-Century France: Currency, Culture, and the State* (Ithaca and London: Cornell University Press, 2014); Sebastian Felten, *Money in the Dutch Republic: Everyday Practice and Circuits of Exchange* (Cambridge: Cambridge University Press, 2022); quotation from Eich, *The Currency of Politics*, p. 10.

40 Christine Desan, *Making Money: Coin, Currency, and the Coming of Capitalism* (Oxford: Oxford University Press, 2014).

41 Adam Woodhouse, 'Who Owns the Money? Currency, Property, and Popular Sovereignty in Nicole Oresme's *De moneta*', *Speculum* 92:1 (2017), 84–116.

42 Bloch, 'The Problem', pp. 217–18.

43 Viviana A. Zelizer, *The Social Meaning of Money: Pin Money, Paychecks, Poor Relief, & Other Currencies* (New York: Basic Books, 1994); Nigel Dodd, *The Sociology of Money: Economics, Reason and Contemporary Society* (London: Continuum International Publishing Group, 1994); Nigel Dodd, *The Social Life of Money* (Princeton and Oxford: Princeton University Press, 2015); Jane I. Guyer (ed.), *Money Matters: Instability, Values and Social Payments in the Modern History of West African Communities* (Portsmouth, NH: Heinemann, 1995); Nina Bandelj, Frederick F. Wherry, and Viviana A. Zelizer (eds), *Money Talks: Explaining How Money Really Works* (Princeton and Oxford: Princeton University Press, 2017).

44 See, for example, Lucia Travaini and Namal Siedlecki, 'Branding Your Own Personal Offering: New Finds from the Trevi Fountain', *NAC* 49 (2020), 359–83; Ceri Houlbrook, *The Magic of Coin-Trees from Religion to Recreation: The Roots of a Ritual* (Cham: Palgrave Macmillan, 2018). Quotation from Zelizer, *The Social Meaning*, p. 1.

45 Lucia Travaini, *The Thirty Pieces of Silver: Coin Relics in Medieval and Modern Europe* (Abingdon and New York: Routledge, 2022); Rory Naismith (ed.), *Money and Coinage in the Middle Ages* (Leiden and Boston: Brill, 2018), especially part III; Nanouschka M. Burström

and Gitte T. Ingvardson (eds), *Divina Moneta: Coins in Religion and Ritual* (London and New York: Routledge, 2017).

46 Stefano Locatelli and Lucia Travaini, 'Objects for History: The Coins of South Italy, Sicily and Sardinia in the British Museum', in B. Cook, S. Locatelli, G. Sarcinelli, and L. Travaini (eds), *The Italian Coins in the British Museum. Vol. 1: South Italy, Sicily, Sardinia* (Bari: Edizioni D'Andrea, 2020), pp. 23–53 (at p. 23).

47 Rory Naismith, 'The Social Significance of Monetization in the Early Middle Ages', *Past & Present* 223 (2014), 3–39 (at p. 7).

48 Philipp R. Rössner, 'Money, Banking, Economy', in A. Classen (ed.), *Handbook of Medieval Culture: Fundamental Aspects and Conditions of the European Middle Ages. Volume 2* (Berlin and Boston: De Gruyter, 2015), pp. 1137–66 (at pp. 1139–40).

49 Lopez, 'The Dollar', p. 211.

50 On this issue, see Chapter 2.

51 See, for instance, Tognetti, 'Il Mezzogiorno'; David Abulafia, 'Southern Italy and the Florentine Economy, 1265–1370', *EHR* New ser. 34:3 (1981), 377–88, reprinted in David Abulafia, *Italy, Sicily and the Mediterranean 1100–1400* (London: Variorum, 1987), chapter 6; Giuseppe Petralia, 'I toscani nel Mezzogiorno medievale. Genesi ed evoluzione trecentesca di una relazione di lungo periodo', in S. Gensini (ed.), *La Toscana nel secolo XIV: caratteri di una civiltà regionale* (Pisa: Pacini, 1988), pp. 289–336; *Storia* VI, pp. 781–895. Further references and details can be found in Chapters 3 and 4.

52 This applies especially to Italy, where a national database of all archaeological findings, like the Portable Antiquity Scheme in the UK, is still lacking but particularly needed.

53 Monica Baldassarri, *Le monete di Lucca. Dal periodo longobardo al Trecento* (Sesto Fiorentino: All'Insegna del Giglio, 2021), p. 89; Monica Baldassarri, *Il tesoretto di Banchi. Un ripostiglio pisano di monete auree medievali* (Pontedera: Bandecchi e Vivaldi, 2000).

54 Louis Carolus-Barré, 'Objets précieux et monnaies retrouvés dans le port de Trapani, en 1270, dont 21 écus d'or de Saint Louis', *Revue Numismatique* 6:18 (1976), 115–18; *MEC* 14, p. 423.

55 On the Aleppo hoard, see Philip Grierson, *Later Medieval Numismatics (11th–16th Centuries)* (London: Variorum, 1979), chapters 11, 12, and 21; on the Acre hoard, see Robert Kool, 'A Thirteenth Century Hoard of Gold Florins from the Medieval Harbour of Acre', *NC* 166 (2006), 301–20 (at pp. 315–16); on the Alberese and Pavia hoards, see Massimo De Benetti, *Il tesoro di Alberese: un ripostiglio di fiorini d'oro del XIII secolo* (San Benedetto del Tronto: Numismatica Picena, 2015), especially pp. 71–2 and 82–107.

56 For a detailed account, see Philip Grierson, 'The President's Address: Session 1965–1966. The Interpretation of Coin Finds (I)', *NC 5* (1965), i–xvi.
57 See the case of the gold bezant in England; Barrie J. Cook, 'The Bezant in Angevin England', *NC 159* (1999), 255–75 (at p. 257).
58 On this aspect, see De Benetti, *I primi 100 anni.*
59 Rössner, 'Money', p. 1142*ff.*
60 Frederic C. Lane and Reinhold C. Mueller refer to a third concept of money called *'moneta numeraria'*, namely coins that in specific years and sectors of the economy constituted the basic coins of monies of account and thus another example of effective money; Frederic C. Lane and Reinhold C. Mueller, *Money and Banking in Medieval and Renaissance Venice* (Baltimore and London: John Hopkins University Press, 1985), p. 8.
61 Carlo M. Cipolla, *Money, Prices, and Civilization in the Mediterranean World: Fifth to Seventeenth Century* (Princeton: Princeton University Press, 1956), pp. 38–9.
62 See, for example, the expressions *'florenos auri bonos et legales et de bono et puro auro et boni ac ydoneus ponderis cum conio lilii Florencie'*, *'boni et puri auri et recte pondus florentino'*, *'de auro ad gilium ad rectum pondus et conium florentinum'*, *'iusti et veri ponderis'*, *'bonos et legales'*, *'ad rectum conium'*.
63 *RCA* I–XXVII.
64 For further details, see Chapter 3.
65 Vatican City, Archivio Apostolico Vaticano, Camera Apostolica, Collectoria 217. For a full description of this series, see Gaetano Ramacciotti, *Gli archivi della reverenda fabbrica Camera Apostolica* (Rome: Camera Apostolica, 1961).
66 See Chapter 4 for further details.
67 The first complete and intact version of the statutes of the commune of Florence only dates back to 1322–25; Romolo Caggese (ed.), *Statuti della Repubblica Fiorentina*, 2 vols (Florence: Tip. Galileiana, [then] E. Ariani, 1910–21); new edition, Giuliano Pinto, Francesco Salvestrini, and Andrea Zorzi (eds), *Statuti della Repubblica fiorentina editi a cura di Romolo Caggese*, 2 vols (Florence: L. S. Olschki, 1999); Giuseppe Biscione, *Statuti del Comune di Firenze nell'Archivio di Stato: tradizione archivistica e ordinamenti* (Rome: MiBAC, 2009).
68 Spufford, 'The First Century', p. 425. For an overall account of this documentation, see Sergio Tognetti, 'Mercanti e libri di conto nella Toscana del basso medioevo: le edizioni di registri aziendali dagli anni '60 del Novecento a oggi', *Anuario de Estudios Medievales* 42:2 (2012), 867–80.

69 Further details on these sources and their use for the study of the florin will be illustrated in Chapter 2.

70 When these words appear in italics, they encompass a range of meanings that will be elaborated in Chapter 2.

71 Philipp R. Rössner, 'From the Black Death to the New World (*c.* 1350–1500)', in Naismith (ed.), *Money and Coinage*, pp. 151–75 (at pp. 151–2).

1

The pre-history of the florin

Few currencies in the monetary history of medieval Europe can boast of success equal to that of the Florentine gold florin. First minted in Florence in November 1252, or so the story goes, the florin represented a 'great novelty' in the monetary context of the time, as it gave physical form to the pound or *libra*, which had until that moment been merely a unit of account in the £.s.d. monetary system introduced by Charlemagne in the late eighth century.[1] From the very beginning, the new coin bore on one side a stylised lily, the emblem of Florence, and the legend **✠ FLOR ‑ ENTIA** and, on the other side, the standing figure of St John the Baptist, patron saint of the city, facing forward and wearing a coat of animal hair, with a sceptre in his left hand and his right raised in benediction, surrounded by the legend **S · IOHA ‑ NNES · B ·** (see Figure 1.1).[2]

From the late thirteenth to the early decades of the sixteenth century, when it was eventually replaced by the Florentine gold *scudo* in 1533, the florin encountered such widespread success in Europe and the Mediterranean that it became, along with the Venetian ducat, one of the most important gold currencies of the time. Despite a minor change in its weight in 1422, it was minted to virtually the same standards throughout its entire lifetime, establishing itself as one of the most stable and trusted coins in circulation.[3] Given the florin's wide diffusion and lasting success, it is no wonder that other cities modelled their gold issues on its weight and fineness.[4] Moreover, from 1322, many rulers, beginning with Pope John XXII (1316–34) at the Avignon mint of Pont de Sorgues, began to strike their own florin imitations – gold coins bearing the same features as the Florentine specimen but with different inscriptions.[5]

Figure 1.1 The gold florin of Florence – specimen of the earliest issue, scale 2:1.

To present a more rounded picture of this coin as a major, although not revolutionary, monetary phenomenon of the Middle Ages and prepare the ground for further analysis, this chapter deals with the period before the introduction of the florin – its 'pre-history', as it were. It does so by moving from a 'macro' to a 'micro' perspective, that is, from the study of the broader economic and monetary conditions of Europe and the Mediterranean region as a whole to the economic and political contexts of Florence between the late twelfth and the mid-thirteenth centuries. The chapter opens with a detailed overview of the production and circulation of gold coins in those regions to show that since many foreign gold coins continued to circulate in western Europe, the minting of the Florentine florin was likely the most effective response to the contemporary decay of the other gold currencies in use rather than a revolutionary act per se. Several concomitant factors, ranging from the growing demand for stable money coming from the long-distance market and the decline in the intrinsic value of the gold coins then in circulation to the different levels of demand and supply placed on gold and silver in western Europe and the Muslim world, incentivised Florence, but also Genoa and probably Lucca, to strike new gold coins in the mid-thirteenth century. In the case of Florence, however, the minting of the florin coincided with an exceptional expansion of the urban population and manufacturing and political upheaval following the death of Emperor Frederick II Hohenstaufen in 1250, which together opened up unique opportunities for the introduction of the new gold coin. As will be shown, the Florentine florin furthered both the economic interests and political purposes of the so-called *Primo Popolo*, the new city-government dominated by merchants. From its very first issue, the florin was conceived of both as a financial innovation in a flourishing city set to become one of the major economic and financial powers of the late Middle Ages and a circumvention of an imperial privilege, i.e., the minting of a full-value gold currency, and thus a new political tool intended to redefine civic authority as a government of quasi-imperial power.

Gold money before the 'back to gold' movement

The minting of gold coins in western Europe came to an end in the final decades of the eighth century.[6] The increasing gold famine, which had been becoming more and more dire since the end of the fourth century, represented a major cause for the cessation of their production.[7] The Anglo-Saxon and Frankish kingdoms were the first territories to succumb, abandoning the minting of gold in the 670s. The shift in western Europe to a new monetary system based on the silver *denarius* as the only actual coin produced, together with the £.s.d. currency system for accounting purposes, emerged in the 790s as part of the monetary reforms of Charlemagne (774–814).[8] For nearly five centuries after the system was established, the silver *denarius* remained the highest denomination officially minted in Europe, exceeded in value only by its multiple, the new silver *grosso*, from the late twelfth century onwards.[9] Nevertheless, only western Europe was affected by this gold-to-silver transition. During the Middle Ages, gold never stopped being turned into coins in certain regions of southern Europe and the Mediterranean basin. Together with copper, it formed part of the monetary systems of territories under Muslim and Byzantine rule. Map 1 illustrates where gold coins were being produced in the first half of the thirteenth century, before the return to gold in the West.

Dinars and double dinars, the standard Muslim gold coins, were minted in southern Spain and North Africa, respectively, first by

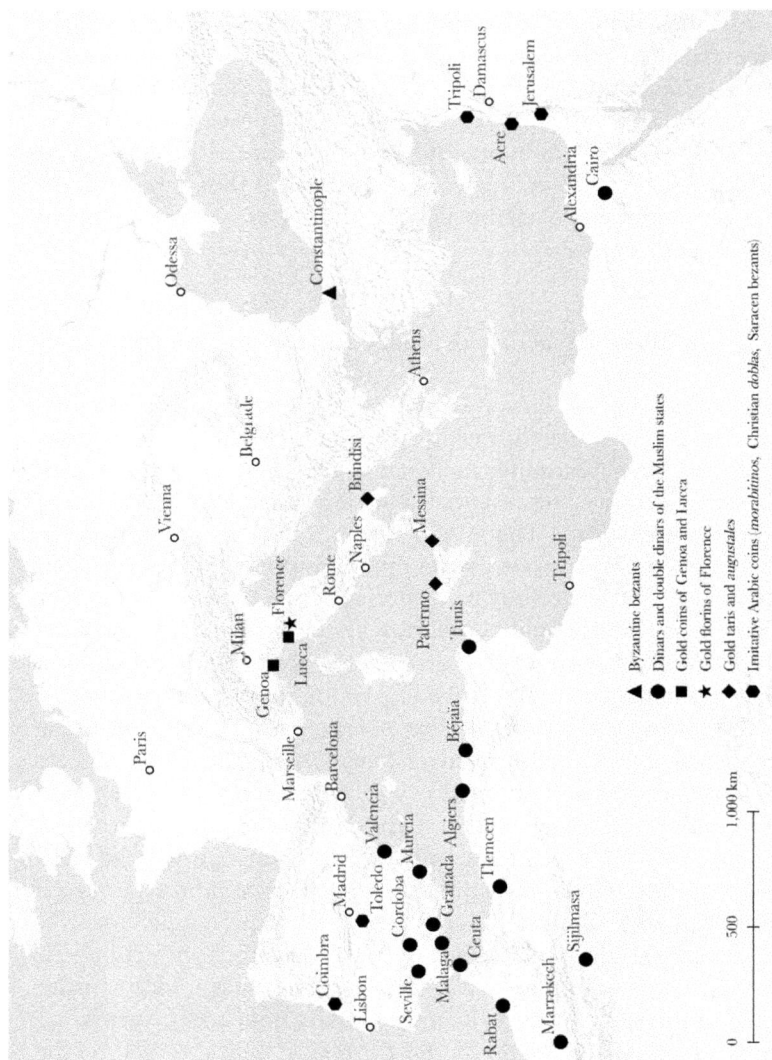

Map 1 Principal centres minting gold in the first half of the thirteenth century and their denominations.

Cities labelled on the map:
Paris, Coimbra, Lisbon, Madrid, Toledo, Seville, Malaga, Cordoba, Granada, Valencia, Murcia, Barcelona, Marseille, Genoa, Lucca, Milan, Florence, Rome, Naples, Brindisi, Vienna, Belgrade, Odessa, Constantinople, Athens, Messina, Palermo, Tunis, Algiers, Béjaia, Ceuta, Tlemcen, Rabat, Marrakech, Sijilmasa, Tripoli, Tripoli, Damascus, Jerusalem, Acre, Alexandria, Cairo

Legend:
▲ Byzantine bezants
● Dinars and double dinars of the Muslim states
■ Gold coins of Genoa and Lucca
★ Gold florins of Florence
◆ Gold taris and *augustales*
● Imitative Arabic coins (*morabitinos*, Christian *doblas*, Saracen bezants)

Scale: 0   500   1,000 km

the Almoravids (1094–1147) and then by the Almohads (1121–1269), in Tunisia and eastern Algeria by the Hafsids (1229–1574), and in the Arabic East.[10] The Almoravid dinars, or *morabitinos*, were made of 22-carat gold (91.6 per cent) with a theoretical weight of 4.10 g, although extant specimens are approximately 3.96–3.86 g.[11] The Almohad dinars, also known as *masmudini* or *massamutini* in Christian Europe, weighed only 2.30 g and were made of nearly pure gold (99 per cent), although not quite 24 carats.[12]

From 1173, King Alfonso VIII of Castile (1158–1214) began to strike imitative Almoravid dinars with Christian inscriptions circulating under the name of *morabitinos* or *maravedis alfonsis*.[13] Their weight and fineness remained constant at around 3.85 g and 20⅘ carats (86.6 per cent) for most of the duration of their production, which ceased in 1217.[14] Christian *morabitinos* were also used by King Alfonso IX (1188–1230) in the Kingdom of Leon, and by Sancho I (1185–1211), Alfonso II (1211–23), and Sancho II (1223–48) in the Kingdom of Portugal.[15] It is likely that Christian double dinars or *doblas* were issued by King Ferdinand III of Castile (1217–52) around the 1240s, but no actual specimen is known to date.[16] Under the Hohenstaufen dynasty (1194–1266), Sicily and southern Italy relied on gold quarter dinars known as *tarì* of 16⅓ or 16⅔ carats (68–69.4 per cent), usually sold by weight due to the wide variation in weights and shapes between individual specimens.[17] In 1231, the Emperor and King of Sicily, Frederick II Hohenstaufen (1220–50), created a new gold coin of 5.31 g and 20½ carats (85.4 per cent) called *augustalis*, struck at the royal mints of Brindisi and Messina.[18] In the East, the traditional currency of the Byzantine Empire was the gold *hyperpyra*, introduced by the Emperor Alexius I Komnenos (1081–1118) in 1092 to stop the dramatic debasement of the Byzantine gold *solidi* or *nomismata*.[19] Minted with a weight of 4.55 g and 20½ carats (85.4 per cent), the *hyperpyra* maintained these features until the reign of Emperor Andronikos I Komnenos (1183–35), when their fineness fell below 19 carats (79 per cent).[20] Their production ceased in the aftermath of the Fourth Crusade (1204), when the new Latin Empire supplanted the Byzantine Empire.[21] Between the 1190s and the Seventh Crusade (1248–54), in the Christian states of Syria and Palestine, the Crusaders adopted imitative Muslim (Fatimid) gold dinars called Saracen bezants of *c.* 3.44 g and 16.27 carats (67.8 per cent).[22]

Some of these gold coins circulated widely in western Europe before the so-called 'return to gold'.[23] Jean Duplessy dated the 'golden age' of the Muslim dinars between the beginning of the eleventh and the mid-thirteenth centuries, when Almoravid and Almohad gold dinars, as well as Iberian imitations, entered the monetary circulation of England, France, and Italy through trade or tributes, also acting as money of account on occasion.[24] Byzantine gold coins made their appearance in several administrative and financial transactions between the English Crown, its officials, and its subjects and formed part of the treasure amassed by King Henry III (1216–72) in the 1240s and 1250s.[25] A similar monetary circulation is attested in the Kingdom of France, too, where a large number of gold *oboles* (another name for the Almohad dinars in Christian Europe), as well as their Iberian imitations, *hyperpyra*, and Sicilian *augustales* were purchased locally to be sent overseas to Alphonse of Poitiers (1220–71), the brother of King Louis IX, who was in captivity in Egypt during the Seventh Crusade.[26] In the first half of the thirteenth century, many of those foreign gold coins also circulated among the merchants of the major Italian trading cities, such as Genoa, Pisa, and Venice – places that were perfectly accustomed to using them in their commercial transactions and to reckoning in those foreign gold currencies. The surviving archival documentation suggests that Sicilian taris, Muslim dinars, and Saracen bezants were more common among the Genoese and the Pisans, and gold *hyperpyra* and Saracen bezants among the Venetians.[27] It was also due to the presence of so many gold denominations that, by the end of the 1220s, the Venetian government had to appoint Pietro Nani and Iacopo Miani as 'gold estimators' – officials in charge of the quality of gold circulating in Venice in the form of coins, ingots, or bars.[28] Despite the few earlier documented cases of counterfeited Muslim and Byzantine gold coins discussed below, the minting of gold in western Europe only fully resumed in the early 1250s, when the cities of Genoa, Florence, and probably Lucca began to mint their new gold currencies.

Genoa, Florence, and Lucca compared

The earliest written evidence documenting the new production of gold coins in thirteenth-century Genoa comes from the commune's annals, known as the *Annales Ianuenses*.[29] Started around 1100 on the personal initiative of Caffaro di Rustico of Caschifellone (*c.* 1080–1166), a local politician and urban chronicler, and formalised by the city consuls in 1152, the *Annales* narrate the history of Genoa for almost two centuries, from 1099 to 1294. Caffaro was the sole author of the events described until 1163, which he recalled from his own memory, notes, and experience. His work was then continued for another 130 years by other chancery scribes, notaries, and chroniclers, all adhering to Caffaro's model. The *Annales* are regarded as the first communal chronicle in Italy.[30]

Among the events recorded for the year 1252, one can read '*eodem anno nummus aureus Ianue fabricatus*'.[31] This most likely occurred some months before the introduction of the gold florin, which Villani placed in November of the same year, as noted. Although simple and brief, especially when compared to the bombastic description of the florin's birth, this sentence is still subject to speculation and debate. This is mainly due to the use of the expression '*nummus aureus*'. The term was probably chosen to recall the prestige of the Roman gold coin issued from the first century BC to the beginning of the fourth century AD when it was supplanted by the gold *solidus* of Constantine the Great (303–7), as it did not correspond to any of the gold denominations minted in Genoa from the mid-thirteenth century onwards.[32]

In *MEC* 12, Michael Matzke argued that the earliest gold coin produced in the city was the small *quartarola*, with a theoretical weight of 0.88 g and 23.7 carats. This was followed almost twenty years later, i.e., around 1270, by the so-called gold *genovino*, a larger gold coin of the same weight and fineness as the florin.[33] In support of his claim, Matzke observed that the inscriptions, symbols, and style of the earliest gold *genovino* did not resemble those of the supposedly contemporary silver *grossi* and billon *denari* of Genoa. Instead, he wrote, the symbol at the centre of the gateway on its obverse 'always forms a small fleur-de-lis', which 'can only be interpreted as a reference' to the larger lily on the Florentine florin.[34] In other words, the first gold *genovino* was nothing but a Genoese florin.

Despite its originality, this interpretation clashes with the information we find in the surviving documentation. Matzke based his analysis exclusively on the iconographical and stylistic features of the few specimens of Genoese gold coins available today. He made no attempt to engage with the archival sources of the time or even acknowledge their existence. His choice is quite surprising, especially considering that written evidence documenting the circulation of heavier Genoese gold coins beginning in 1253 has long been known. I am referring here to a notarial act recording a payment of four '*denariis grossis aureis ianuensis*' made by the commune of Genoa to the Turin jurists Guidorcio del Pozzo and Ruggero Pavaroli, first published by Lopez in 1936.[35] Monica Baldassarri has recently put forward a new interpretation of this source by integrating lexical analysis with new data derived from the non-destructive analytical technique of X-Ray Fluorescence (henceforth XRF), which uses the interaction of x-rays with the metal of surviving coins to ascertain their elemental composition without causing damage.[36] The result is a more rounded picture of the return to gold in the city of Genoa.

Baldassarri accepts that the *quartarola* predated any other Genoese gold coin but, contrary to Matzke, dates the minting of the *genovino* to the same period. As she correctly points out, the adjective *grossus*, which also appears in the written source mentioned above, was typically used in Latin to describe the dimension of something 'larger, thicker, and/or heavier' than normal.[37] This is also how it began to be employed in thirteenth-century Italian territories to name, qualify, and thus distinguish the newer, bigger, and heavier silver coins known as *denarii grossi* from the older and lighter ones, which, by contrast, were called *denarii parvi* or little deniers. For this reason, the adjective *grossus* would hardly fit a coin like the gold *quartarola*, which was only 0.88 g and 11–12 mm, i.e., no larger than a half *denaro*. Instead, it seems to be more suited to a bigger and heavier denomination, most likely the first gold *genovino*, which was 3.52 g (theoretical weight) and 20 mm. It is worth mentioning in this regard that the same adjective also formed the Latin name of another Italian gold coin in circulation at the time, whose size and features were more similar to those of the *genovino* than the *quartarola*: the *'denarius grossus de auro'* or *grosso d'oro* of Lucca, which was 3.50 g (on average) and 21 mm and will be discussed below. In light of these considerations, the argument that the *genovino* was minted around the same time as the *quartarola*, i.e., a quarter of it in the local monetary system, and perhaps as part of a wider monetary reform that also included the silver coinage of Genoa, proves to be better supported and more convincing.[38]

Despite the similar weight, the first *genovino* was not as pure as the gold florin and therefore cannot be called such. This is explicitly documented in the lists of coins preserved in both abacus manuals and merchants' notebooks dated between the 1250s and 1300, the nature and characteristics of which will be examined later. For now, suffice it to say that the compilers often differentiated between gold florins of exactly 24 carats and two types of gold *genovini*, namely the *'vecchi'* or 'old' ones of 23¼–23½ carats, minted from 1252 and the *'nuovi'* or 'new' ones of 24 minus ⅕ or ⅟₁₅ carats, probably issued by the early 1270s.[39] Further documentary evidence can be found in the register of the Genoese notary Angelino de Sigestro: on 12 March 1274, he recorded that Pino, son of Guidone Medici from Florence and procurator of the Florentine citizens and merchants Duccio Davicini and Giacomo Manetti, received from Simone Rondana an unspecified sum of *genovini* – a term most likely used here as money of account – with the promise to return by Easter '100 ounces of gold of the alloy of the mint of Genoa of carats 23 ½', namely, the fineness of the old *genovini* in the lists of coins mentioned above.[40] Those values are now also confirmed by the results of the XRF analyses conducted on the gold content of these denominations, where the florin had a fineness of 99.1 per cent, while the 'old' *genovino* had 98.7 per cent.[41]

Such a discrepancy in the quality of gold between these two currencies can be seen as additional proof that the Genoese gold coinage predates the Florentine one. It seems more plausible that Genoa minted its first or 'old' *genovino* a few months before the florin, with no regard for what was happening in the Tuscan city. Yet, due to the growing popularity of the Florentine coin, which was also preferred to the other gold coins in circulation for its unparalleled fineness, the Genoese government soon had to adjust the fineness of its old *genovino* so as not to fall behind a major competitor like Florence. Adopting the Florentine standards as the international benchmark for the issue of new gold coins was, after all, a common practice among the many Italian and western European cities that minted gold – or at least tried to – from the second half of the thirteenth century onwards.[42] In Genoa, this led to the introduction of a second or 'new' *genovino*, with a gold content closer to the Florentine standard, as noted.[43]

Finally, since the surviving documentation is completely silent on the style and iconography of the *genovino*, the alleged presence of a stylised Florentine lily in the gateway portrayed on the side usually regarded as its obverse – which is in itself a minute detail difficult to spot and recognise at first glance – is purely speculative. Instead, Matzke failed to acknowledge the striking resemblance between the style of the legends (letterform and distribution of punctuations) and the type (city image or gateway, with a dot or dots around the central arches) of the 'old' *genovino* and the first *quartarola*.[44]

Compared to Genoa and Florence, the contours of the return to gold in Lucca are certainly more blurred. Unlike its counterparts, no known civic chronicles or written sources of any kind narrate the first minting of the *grosso d'oro*. This has sparked a lively and ongoing debate among scholars as to whether or not Lucca was the first of the three cities to strike gold. Drawing on the works of nineteenth-century Italian numismatists such as Giulio Cordero di San Quintino and Domenico Massagli, Luciano Lenzi dated the introduction of the *grosso d'oro* to 1246, six years before the traditional chronology of the return to gold.[45] However, this early start is not reflected in the archival documentation available today. Lenzi obtained that information from Cordero di San Quintino, who had simply indicated that year in one of the plates with images of Lucchese coins at the end of his work without specifying its provenance.[46] Massagli, who also agreed with that chronology, cited the seventeenth-century Lucchese nobleman Daniello de Nobili as a possible source. Yet, he referred to a notarial deed from 1264 instead of 1246 in support of his claim.[47] There is no way of knowing whether this was a typo in Massagli's work, but Lenzi's search for the 1246 document did not yield the desired results. Details in favour of an early minting of the *grosso d'oro*, closer to 1250 and thus only a couple of years before the gold *genovino* and the florin, eventually emerged from an analysis of a list of gold coins in the abacus manual known as the *Liber habaci* of *c.* 1310, which Gino Arrighi attributed to the Florentine master Paolo Gherardi.[48]

Abacus manuals were manuscripts of practical arithmetic written and used by lay 'abacus masters' to teach the forms and methods of Hindu–Arabic mathematics to pupils aged eleven to thirteen. They covered a whole range of topics, usually organised in thematic sections, ranging from operations with Arabic numerals and fractions to mercantile problems concerning monetary systems, weights and measures, interest rates, and so on.[49] To assist pupils with their calculations, abacus manuals might also include lists of coins sorted by metal (gold, silver, and billon, usually in that order) and their relative fineness expressed in carats for gold and in ounces or *denarii* for silver and billon specimens. These works, however, are 'shifting quicksand as far as the dating of their information is concerned'.[50]

Abacus masters often incorporated parts of previous manuals into theirs – the most popular being Leonardo Fibonacci's *Liber Abaci* of 1202 – with occasional updates and annotations. Moreover, as they were 'teaching aids' during lessons, manuals were often handed down from one generation of abacus masters to the next, enabling them to reach a vast plethora of students. It was therefore not uncommon for those volumes to contain data and information that had been circulating for decades. Consequently, the end date of the original compilation rarely corresponded to the dating of the material in the various parts of the same manual. This is also the case with the coin list in Gherardi's *Liber habaci*.

As Lucia Travaini illustrates, the information it contains can be divided into two distinct parts composed at different times – one for gold and one for silver coins. The former offers a snapshot of the circulation of gold coinage in the Mediterranean around 1250, even if the manual was only completed around 1310, as noted. It includes Byzantine *hyperpyra*, *morabitinos*, *doblas*, and Sicilian *augustales* and taris, but there is no mention of either the *genovino* or the florin. The only western European gold coin in the list is the '*lucchese d'oro*' – another name for the *grosso d'oro* of Lucca – of 23½ carats. On the basis of these elements and considering what has been said about the preparation of abacus manuals, Travaini left open the possibility that Lucca's first gold coin was minted only a couple of years before the return to gold in 1252.[51] The latest studies on its iconography and gold content further corroborate this view.

According to Monica Baldassarri, both the Holy Face of Christ depicted on its obverse 'in an unprecedented and never repeated fashion', that is, with a left profile and draped bust, and the arrangement of the inscription all around it, would strongly recall the imperial bust on the gold *augustalis* of Frederick II, minted from 1231 on. If this was a deliberate choice, the *grosso d'oro* would have represented not only Lucca's political response to the imperial yoke of the Hohenstaufen, who in the 1240s was waging a strenuous battle against the Guelph party in the Italian peninsula, but also a challenge to his authority, considered inferior to that of Christ. To make sense, such a propaganda operation would have to have taken place before or shortly after the emperor's death in 1250.[52]

The choice of minting the *grosso d'oro* with a fineness of 97.1 per cent detected by XRF analysis and equivalent to the 23½ carats on Gherardi's list – thus not quite 24 – would also reinforce the hypothesis of an early birth for this coin, either before the florin or, in any case, before Florentine standards became the benchmark in the monetary scene of the time.[53] More specifically, the production of the *grosso d'oro* would have started on the autonomous initiative of the city of Lucca that, just like Genoa with its *genovino*, was then forced to adapt the fineness of its gold coinage to Florentine standards in order to keep up with the competition. As narrated by the fourteenth-century chronicler Giovanni Sercambi, it was only from around 1269 that the local mint began to strike a new gold coin with a fineness practically equal to that of the florin of Florence, i.e., 'carats 24 minus ⅛' in an almost contemporary coin list; it is no accident this coin was called the '*fiorino*' or Lucchese florin.[54]

However convincing, all these chronologies are characterised by considerable uncertainty, especially in the absence of overwhelming evidence in support of one or the other. In fact, the first written reference to Lucchese *grossi d'oro* spent together with other local silver coins dates back only to 1257. On 19 January, Master Benencasa, canon of the urban cathedral, contributed £200 '*denariorum lucensium in denariis grossis de auro et argento tante valentie ad parvos denarios*' to the commercial partnership created with Gottifredo of the late Conetti Bonostri and Bartolomeo of the late Orlando Bettori.[55] Thomas W. Blomquist, who also found this document, referred to it to date the birth of the Lucchese *grosso d'oro* to 1256, four years after Genoa and Florence had introduced their gold coinage. In light of the above, this year should instead be regarded as the *terminus ante quem* of the return to gold in Lucca, which would therefore have occurred sometime between about 1250 and 1256.

However, none of these brand-new gold coins could have been produced without a series of favourable economic and historical conditions that, from a macroeconomic perspective, constitute the driving factors for the western European 'back to gold' phenomenon.

The decay of the 'old' gold coins

A primary factor that led to the minting of the new gold coins was the contemporary demand for a reliable and stable gold monetary standard to suit the peak of the so-called 'Commercial Revolution' of western Europe. Originally coined by Raymond de Roover in the early 1940s, this expression was adopted some thirty years later by Roberto Sabatino Lopez to refer to a period of socio-economic expansion that started in the late tenth century when, following the acceleration of agricultural and craft production, the resumption of population growth, the revival of towns and urban life, and the rapid development of trade and markets, the Old Continent evolved into a dynamic trading region.[56] As part of this transformation, a new economic system heavily based on monetary exchange was established: payments in kind became rarer, while money developed into the habitual medium of exchange of a rapidly commercialising society.[57] The opening of new (silver) mining centres at Freiberg (Meissen), Friesach (Carinthia), and Montieri (Tuscany), as well as the contemporary rise of new trading centres like fairs, ports, and towns acting as central hubs of expanding commercial networks in Europe and the Mediterranean, enhanced the volume of money in circulation and thus the frequency of money payments and transactions.[58] At the heart of all these changes, there was an unprecedented demand for money that could barely be met by the contemporary money supply when the 'Commercial Revolution' reached its apex in the thirteenth century.[59] In the attempt to increase the volume of money in circulation, new and lighter silver *denarii* of only 0.20 g, 0.10 g, or even 0.08 g, thus with a reduced content of precious metal compared to the original Carolingian *denarius* of 1.70 g, were produced in the northern Italian mints of Pavia, Verona, and Venice.[60] These became such a weak and unsuitable means of payment for the monetary and financial needs of an ever-growing economy that merchants were soon forced to use silver bars or ingots, uncoined gold dust or *paiola* gold, foreign gold coins and, later, silver *grossi* for large payments within and outside Europe.[61] Due to their higher value and stability, these alternative means of payment were more convenient and portable than the circulating *denarii*, as they did not need to be counted out as thousands of individual coins to pay large sums of money.

However, by the middle of the thirteenth century, many of the gold coins in circulation underwent significant transformations as they either suffered from debasement in their fineness, which never thereafter recovered the high standards of their earlier issues, or else they stopped being minted altogether. The Almoravid dinars, although in use until the end of the twelfth century or shortly after, ceased to be issued between 1147 and 1172, when the Almohads succeeded in conquering the Almoravid territories and introduced their own gold dinars.[62] The *maravedis alfonsis* suffered reductions in their gold content, dropping from 87 to 83 per cent until 1217, when their production stopped.[63] No Christian *morabitinos* are known to have been minted either in the Kingdom of Leon or in Portugal after 1230 and 1248, respectively.[64] The gold *augustalis* of Frederick II only lasted two decades, until the death of the emperor in 1250 or at the latest up to 1266 if minted by his successors, although no pieces in their names have ever been found.[65] In the East, the production of Byzantine *hyperpyra* came to an end in 1204, but their fineness had already fallen from the original 20½ to 19 carats in the final years of the twelfth century, as noted. Among the Byzantine successor states that emerged after 1204, gold was coined only in Nicaea, but its production was very limited at first.[66] Under Emperor John III Vatatzes (1222–54), new and significant quantities of *hyperpyra* were minted at Magnesia in western Anatolia, but with only an average fineness of 16–17.6 carats (66.6–73.3 per cent).[67] Latin imitations of John III Vatatzes' *hyperpyra*, called *perperi latini d'oro*, of only 16½ carats (68.75 per cent), were in circulation at least from the 1230s onwards.[68] Saracen bezants continued to be produced in the Crusader states with the same fineness of 16.27 carats (67.8 per cent) up to *c.* 1270, but that was already the consequence of a twelfth-century decline.[69] Except for the Almohad *massamutini* of almost pure gold, the majority of gold coins in circulation in the first half of the thirteenth century did not surpass 21 carats in fineness.[70]

This decline and the restricted availability of existing gold coins were also a result of the political turmoil affecting the territories where they were produced, such as the Christian *Reconquista* in the Iberian peninsula, the decline of the Almohad Empire and the rise of other dynasties in North Africa, the crisis and subsequent conquest of the Latin Empire of Byzantium in 1204, and the military campaigns of Frederick II in northern and central Italy followed by his death in 1250. Together, these events added crucial factors that intensified the need for new gold coins of better quality to assist long-distance trade. The retention of a stable and high-value currency must have been a matter of great concern, especially among the Italian merchants, given their significant economic involvement in the Mediterranean and the Levant at that time.[71] Thus, the introduction of the new gold coins of Genoa, Florence, and Lucca met these needs in the first instance. However, such a significant change in the monetary landscape of western Europe would not have occurred had there not been changes in the gold supply.

Gold in motion: where and when

The gold for minting the new coins did not come from the direct exploitation of contemporary European mines, affected as they were by 'the unluckiest poverty'.[72] Western Europe had to rely mainly on imported gold, sources for which were located outside the Mediterranean region. The yellow metal was to be found primarily in West Africa, in the historical region of western *Sudan*, meaning 'the Land of the Blacks', a large plain south of the Sahara Desert stretching from the Atlantic Ocean to Lake Chad. The Muslim geographer Muhammad al-Idrīsī (1100–65), writing in the twelfth century, reported to Roger II, King of Sicily, that gold came from two major sources, 'the town of *Takrūr*' and the unspecified 'island of *Wangara*.[73] Geographers, archaeologists, and historians have long speculated about these places and their possible locations on the basis of often contradictory sources.[74] They have usually been associated with two of the most important gold-producing regions of the time, Bambouk, at the confluence of the Senegal River and its tributary Falémé, and Bure, on the upper Niger.[75] However, Susan K. McIntosh argued that *Wangara* might correspond to the Inland Niger Delta or refer to the ethnic group of Soninke merchants who traded in gold in West Africa in the first millennium.[76] According to Amar S. Baadj, other gold deposits could be found in the south-eastern regions of Lobi, on the upper Volta in Burkina Faso, and further east, in the tropical forests of present-day Nigeria.[77] Yet, strong doubts remain as to whether these sites were already being exploited.[78] Conversely, the East African gold mines in lower Nubia, in use since the time of the pharaohs, were unproductive by the twelfth century.[79]

The precious metal was primarily obtained from auriferous quartz-gravel deposits transported downstream along rivers in periods of heavy rainfall. Once washed and pounded, it was ready for transit to Christian Europe in the form of specks, nuggets, and *paiola* gold.[80] By the tenth century, large quantities of gold began to flow northwards as a result of the trans-Saharan trade that had developed along three main axes stretching over three distinct commercial and cultural zones, namely western Sudan, the Sahara Desert, and the Maghreb. These consisted of a western route, passing through Aoudaghost (Mauritania) and Sijilmasa (Morocco); a central route, running through Tadmakka (Mali) and Ouargla (Algeria); and an eastern route, passing through Fezzan (Libya).[81]

Historical and political events determined their changing prosperity and importance throughout the centuries. A significant impetus to this trade certainly came from the eighth-century conquest of the Maghreb by the Arabs, attracted as they were by Sudanese gold to mint their own dinars and finance their military campaigns. Other incentives were the spread of the camel for the transportation of goods through the desert, the role of the Berbers as commercial intermediaries between north and sub-Saharan Africa, and the rise of powerful Sudanic empires such as the Kingdom of Ghana (*c.* 700–*c.* 1240) and the Kingdom of Mali (*c.* 1240–1670), which acquired gold through barter or tributes and traded it in their capitals with foreign merchants from the north under carefully regulated conditions.[82]

At the core of the trans-Saharan trade, there stood the exchange of salt for gold.[83] Salt was such a rare commodity in western Sudan that the Sudanese people living close to the goldfields would exchange it for an equivalent weight of gold.[84] However, salt was quite abundant south of the Maghreb, where the salt-mining centre of Taghaza (Mali) was located. There, Arab and Berber merchants active mainly along the western routes supplied their caravans with salt, which was then transported south – with other goods – to be exchanged for Sudanese gold.[85] The consolidation of this gold-salt exchange ensured the supply of gold from the Sudanese goldfields to North Africa and beyond.

Once in the Maghreb, some of the metal went to North African and Iberian Muslim mints to be turned into Arabic dinars; another part reached Sicily and southern Italy for the production of local gold coins.[86] An extraordinary description of gold being taken to Sicilian mints survives today in one of the *fatwās* – judicial rulings on specific aspects of Islamic law issued in response to questions posed by private individuals – of the Muslim jurist Abū 'Abd Allah al-Māzārī (d. 1141).[87] It is said that a group of Tunisian merchants formed a partnership in Mahdia to buy grain in Sicily, which they intended to pay for with Almoravid and Tripolitan gold dinars. After receiving the coins from the merchants, however, the head of the Sicilian mint melted them down, added a quarter of their weight in silver, and used the new alloy to strike Sicilian gold taris, which could then be used to purchase the grain.[88]

From the main port cities located along the North African coast, such as Tangier and Ceuta (Morocco), Oran and Béjaïa (Algeria), Tunis and Mahdia (Tunisia), and Tripoli (Libya), gold was eventually bought as a commodity by Italian traders who extended their maritime hegemony from the quays of Amalfi in the tenth century, and from those of Pisa and Genoa in the early eleventh to the southern coasts of the Mediterranean by means of trade agreements with Islamic authorities.[89] They sold finished cloth, textiles, foodstuffs, glass, copper, and silver in return for raw materials such as hides, leather, and wool, goods like honey and ivory, as well as enslaved people and, of course, gold.[90]

Economic historians have traditionally described the movement of gold from the Muslim world to Christian Europe as the result of changing balances of trade between these different economic areas.[91] Since the value of European imports hardly matched the value of African exports, for the most part composed of bulk goods, the balance of trade from North Africa – excluding Egypt – to western Europe in the twelfth and thirteenth centuries was characterised by a constant deficit.[92] The sale of gold was therefore intended to even things out. According to Watson, it was usually the metal with a lower value at home than abroad that would be chosen to redress the imbalance.[93] His analysis of gold–silver ratios between western Europe and the Muslim world, namely the quantity of silver required to buy a unit of gold, suggests that by the mid-thirteenth century, gold had a higher price in Europe than elsewhere.[94] This generated a constant flow of silver moving from Europe to North Africa, matched by a complementary shipment of gold and thus a direct exchange of one metal for the other.

However, this is essentially a modern economists' formulation to describe what might have occurred, and quite an anachronistic one. The balance of payment is a statistical convention and thus assumes the existence of a 'national economy' and a fully developed money–goods/services dualism. It presupposes two defined and separate economic areas, which did not exist, and implies that late medieval traders dealt with each other along similar lines to today's monetary and economic syntax, which does not match the historical evidence.[95] As Harry A. Miskimin rightly pointed out, the relative growth in the proportion of gold as a commodity in western Europe was made possible by trade and commerce rather than monetary arbitrage. The choice of the metal that the merchants brought with them, along with their commodities, depended on both the actual availability of gold or silver and the 'utility' of a given metal at the place of destination, i.e., not different from any other good.[96] From Iraq to southern Spain and the western part of North Africa, via Asia Minor and the Levant, it seems that it was silver that was most in demand. Indeed, a severe dearth in the eleventh and twelfth centuries put a stop to its minting.[97] This was probably triggered by the outflow of silver to neighbouring regions, including India and China to the east, and certainly Europe to the west, as well as by the simultaneous closure of some silver mines for technical or political reasons.[98] For about a century, gold and copper formed the main metals minted in those territories, with gold as the basis of any monetary system in place.

The striking of silver coins was resumed in the final quarter of the twelfth century when the Ayyubids began to mint new *dirhams* in Damascus in 1174–75. In the thirteenth century, a number of other centres in modern Turkey, Armenia, Georgia, Iraq, Uzbekistan, and Turkestan followed suit.[99] The necessary quantity of silver did not come from 'local' mines, but from abroad, in particular from western Europe and the Khwarazm and Khorasan regions in central Asia.[100] Silver also circulated in the Middle East in the form of western European coins used by the Crusaders or as counterfeited *miliarenses* – square Almohad *dirhams* or half-*dirhams* minted in a number of Christian mints in southern Spain, France, and Italy and exported by European merchants for trade purposes across the Mediterranean.[101] The return to silver minting in the Muslim world generated such a new and significant demand for this metal that its value in commerce became higher there than in Europe. Hence, for the sake of profit, it made more sense for Western merchants to carry their silver to the Levant or North Africa rather than sell it in Europe, especially if prices were lower in silver than in gold in those territories.[102]

Nevertheless, since medieval trade hardly followed a fixed pattern, it would be wrong to assume that gold completely ceased to flow from Europe to the Levant, even though it was silver that was most requested there. The Latins, for instance, needed it to strike their Saracen bezants up to *c.* 1270, as was seen.[103] Moreover, gold was not necessarily traded for silver in a direct and complementary exchange. In this regard, it cannot be ruled out that gold increased its value as a monetary metal in western Europe without actually being imported, but simply because more and more silver had been drained away.[104]

Indeed, the large-scale trade in luxury goods and other commodities with the Mediterranean and the Islamic world imposed a strain on the European economy, facilitating the movement and exchange of precious metals. However, gold could also reach Europe through channels disconnected from long-distance commerce: for instance, some came as booty through the crusades and some by way of tributes to Christian rulers, such as the payment of 34,330 gold dinars from the Hafsid Emir of Tunis to Emperor Frederick II as King of Sicily.[105] Further gold might have entered Europe as part of the salaries of Christian mercenaries serving in the armies of African sultans in Marrakech, Béjaïa, and Tunis, regarded as a *corps d'élite* since the twelfth century.[106]

Therefore, in light of all these considerations, the 'overly subtle calculation of gold–silver ratios' as an explanation for the monetary phenomena of the return to gold in western Europe carries less conviction. And yet, these ratios have also been used to explain the resumption of gold minting in Italy precisely in 1252.[107] Between the second half of the twelfth and the middle of the thirteenth century, gold–silver ratios in Genoa and Florence would have fallen from 1:10 to 1:8.16 and 1:8.451, respectively.[108] These values, the lowest ever recorded, and the unprecedented decline in gold prices of that year made it more convenient for Genoa and Florence to produce new currencies in gold rather than silver, thus relieving the strain placed on the latter in support of the western European 'Commercial Revolution'.

Although possible, excessive emphasis has been placed on those numbers in recent years. The gold–silver ratios may indeed be of some help in understanding the general patterns and development of the medieval monetary economy, but caution must be exercised when dealing with these figures, as it is tricky to calculate them. First, different kinds of ratios existed at that time, e.g., market ratios for uncoined or coined metals, ratios used in account books or by tax collectors for official accounting purposes, and so on.[109] A comparative study is possible only between homogeneous data referring to the same type of transaction, although in many cases, one can only guess at the nature of the affair involved. Yet, scholars have too often failed to specify the nature of the ratios referred to in their analyses.[110] Second, not only did those values fluctuate significantly over time and with respect to where they were recorded, but they may also have included a hidden rate of interest that is hard to discern. Third, Italian data are not sufficient 'to draw even the roughest diagram'.[111] This is particularly true for Florence, given the significant lack of commercial documentation prior to the second half of the thirteenth century. Such calculations require a great deal of data, usually provided by a series of prices on a daily basis, but nothing like this survives for Florence in the years before the florin was issued. The current status of Florentine sources does not even allow us to be entirely sure that the introduction of the florin really took place in 1252, even though this chronology is generally accepted.[112]

At any rate, the return to gold was neither revolutionary nor unexpected. As was seen, foreign gold coins continued to circulate in western Europe, and people used them in their affairs. Genoa, Florence, and Lucca might have been the first cities to produce gold currencies with their own symbols and iconography, yet there are documented cases of many other western European cities with a strong economic background, including Genoa itself, that were already tinkering with gold and might have had the opportunity to produce their own specimens up to a century before the canonical year of 1252.

In 1149, for instance, in order to raise money for the repayment of debts incurred during the victorious siege of Tortosa, the Genoese authorities leased out the administration and collection of a whole series of revenues held by the commune to a consortium of twelve citizens, who would retain them for the next twenty-nine years for a lump sum of £1,200. Alongside tolls on goods loaded and unloaded in the port (*redditus de ripa*), on anchorage (*redditus de scariis*), and other customs duties, Genoa also ceded the revenues on 'gold coinage' (*redditus de moneta auri*).[113] Yet, it would be a mistake to think that the Genoese issued gold coins at such an early date. This reference to *moneta auri* shows instead that Genoa treated minted gold as a commodity on which the commune collected tolls.[114]

In the case of Venice, Gustave L. Schlumberger referred to a lost treaty between the Venetian *Podestà* in Constantinople and Theodore Laskaris, Emperor of Nicaea, in 1219, in which both sides agreed not to mint gold *hyperpyra* – and other coins – by imitating each other.[115] Instead, it was the city of Marseille that concluded a secret treaty with Thomas, Count of Savoy (1189–1233) and Imperial Vicar of Lombardy, for the proclamation of its autonomy as an independent commune on 8 November 1226.[116] Although the agreement did not work out, the minting of new silver and gold coins under its name was among the rights the city claimed for itself. In 1237, counterfeited Almohad gold dinars were illegally produced in Lucca by certain members of the mercantile company

of Ricciardi to be exchanged on the market.[117] Archival sources
from 1244–46 show that counterfeit *'morabotinos et bisantios et
masmutinos'* were also being minted in the city of Montpellier.[118]

Collectively, all those episodes downplay the role of the year
1252 as a major date for the return to gold. They suggest that a
definite need for gold coins was clearly felt and widespread among
Europeans and well before that date. Furthermore, the fact that
Genoa, Venice, Marseille, Lucca, and Montpellier were among
the major trading centres of the time, and all of them either had
a chance to mint gold or managed to do this by illegally imitating
other gold coins in circulation speaks volumes about the relevance
of their gold supply.

Nevertheless, all the aspects, patterns, and dynamics described
so far today form part of the grand narrative of the 'back to gold'
event of western Europe. Despite some reservations, they provide a reasonable context for the introduction of the florin, but
one that looks at the phenomenon mainly from a Europe- and
Mediterranean-wide perspective. The decline of gold coins, the
gold supply, and the gold–silver ratios all represent 'macro' phenomena occurring over a long period and across a large geographical scope, which do not say much about the situation in each city,
especially in Florence. They answer, to an extent, why minting gold
coins became a more attractive option and when this happened, but
they do not provide strong clues as to where it would happen (i.e.,
why Florence) nor how (i.e., why a brand-new type of gold coin
rather than an imitation, for instance). To answer these questions,
I will adopt a 'micro' perspective that investigates the economic and
political conditions of Florence in the years before the florin.

Economic Florence: from just agricultural
to a more diversified economy

The city of Florence was a 'latecomer' to the economic revival
of western Europe.[119] In the twelfth century, it was arguably the
least important of the major centres of Tuscany, overshadowed by
the more prosperous cities of Pisa, Lucca, and Siena. Owing to its
active port and extensive trade networks, Pisa had emerged as one
of the leading maritime republics of the Italian peninsula by then,

and was a direct competitor to Venice and Genoa for commercial supremacy from west to east of the Mediterranean.[120] Lucca, on the other hand, built its wealth and fame on its silk industry, becoming the major producer in Europe, with no equals in the sector until the fourteenth century. Lucchese merchants were also among the first Italians documented at the Champagne Fairs, and soon expanded into banking, serving monarchs and popes.[121] The financial sector, however, was dominated by the merchant bankers of Siena. Their city's close ties with the papacy enabled them to serve as the principal and official bankers to the popes, establishing a vast financial network that made them indispensable to clerics and rulers for the collection and transfer of money to the Holy See. Siena's economic growth was further bolstered by the activities of its mercantile companies along the trade routes to the Champagne Fairs and beyond to northern Europe.[122]

Nevertheless, from the last decades of the twelfth century, Florence joined these three cities at the forefront of the 'Commercial Revolution', to become the largest of them by the end of the thirteenth century. This was possible thanks to a comprehensive structural transformation of the Florentine social and economic fabric, fuelled by a significant demographic expansion buttressing an abrupt and intense economic development. The florin came into being in this context, but providing a quantitative study of Florence's growth and an uncontroversial chronology proves very problematic due to the inadequacy of the surviving documentation. I will therefore limit myself to a more qualitative analysis of the economic conditions that paved the way for the new gold coin.

An extraordinary increase in population stimulated the economic development of Florence between the last decades of the twelfth and the mid-fourteenth century. In 1172–75, the Florentine government ordered the construction of a new circuit of walls intended to enclose *c.* 10,000 inhabitants, but the population must have been at least 15,000 by the end of the twelfth century. Due to the ever-increasing number of residents, the walls necessitated the first extension in 1258, when the so-called *Oltrarno*, the southern suburbs of today's Florence, became part of the urban enclosure. In 1284, less than thirty years later, the walls were expanded a second time to include an area of approximately 630 hectares, which hosted *c.* 105,000 residents by 1300. The Florentine urban population increased almost sevenfold throughout the thirteenth century.[123]

This rapid and considerable demographic expansion was the effect of intense immigration of people from the surrounding *contado* or countryside, although the reasons for this remain unclear.[124] Johan Plesner argued that most of those immigrants were wealthy landowners because of their predominance within the surviving documentation, but this suggestion is problematic.[125] More recent studies convincingly show that the vast majority were undocumented landless peasants and poor farmers in search of new sources of profits no longer related to the exploitation of the land.[126] However, it is hard to say what Florence had to offer to them or when the migration began.

It can be assumed that Florence attracted so many immigrants because of significant industrial development within the city. Those people constituted a major source of manpower in emerging labour sectors such as construction, urban manufacture, and eventually the woollen industry.[127] Enrico Faini has dated this economic upturn back to the 1120s–30s when more and more immigrants began to leave the Florentine *contado* to work in the nascent cloth industry.[128] However, it is only from the last quarter of the twelfth century that the first clear signs of an emerging textile industry in Florence appear in the surviving documentation. Details become more frequent in the early decades of the thirteenth century when the contours of the Florentine economic take-off seem more precise.[129]

References to *Arti* or guilds in the extant sources provide an initial confirmation of the economic dynamism of Florence in those years. These were associations of artisans and merchants controlling various sectors of urban economic life. The *Arte di Calimala* is the first guild to be documented, appearing in 1192.[130] It consisted of merchants involved in the import of unfinished northern textiles from Brabant, Flanders, and France, which were dyed and refined in Florence before being sold abroad. They also provided textile workers with foreign models to be imitated.[131] The presence of a guild with similar activities not only means that Florentine textile production began in this context but also that Florentine merchants were already actively participating in the contemporary cloth trade. Other guilds appear for the first time in the subsequent years. The judges' and notaries' guild, or *Arte dei giudici e notai*, is documented in 1212,[132] as is the wool guild or the *Arte della Lana*, although there may be archival evidence of its activity as early as 1193.[133] The *Arte di Por Santa Maria*, the guild that brought together the urban goldsmiths and the Florentines involved in the production and trade of silk cloth, is recorded a few years later, in 1218 – about the same time that the guild of bankers and moneychangers or *Arte del Cambio* came into existence.[134] Their appearance in such a short time span further corroborates Florence's economic vitality and positive trend. This is also supported by a series of trading arrangements between Florence and other neighbouring centres, which expanded the Florentine commercial network.

In the final decades of the twelfth century, for example, Florence signed treaties with Pisa (1171), San Miniato (1172), Siena (1176), Lucca (1184), Colle Val d'Elsa (1201), and San Gimignano (1201).[135] Among these, the forty-year agreement with Pisa of 1171 played a key role, as it allowed the merchants of Florence to access Mediterranean trade and expand their commerce far beyond the local framework.[136] On that occasion, the Florentines were granted free movement and protection within Pisan territory, as well as official permission to use the Pisan port and its sea routes for only half the tax on the exploitation of waterways (*ripaticum*). They could also trade in the Mediterranean as 'Pisans', thus under a flag of convenience, meaning they would benefit from all the commercial privileges usually granted to Pisan merchants in foreign ports. For their stay in Pisa, the Florentines obtained a hostel (*domus*) and two workshops (*bottega*), which together formed the Florentine *fondaco* there. The treaty also included specific military and monetary requirements: Florence would receive 400 horsemen from Pisa as military aid in the event of an attack, as well as half of the Pisan *logorie monete* or debased coins, which would form the local currency of Florence in the absence of Florentine coin production at that time.[137]

In the early decades of the thirteenth century, new treaties were signed with many other centres, most of them located outside the Tuscan region and presumably corresponding to the early destinations of the Florentine inter-regional trade. Those were the cities of Bologna (1203), Faenza (1204), Prato (1212), Perugia (1218 and 1235), Imola (1228), and Orvieto (1229).[138] These agreements bear witness to the growing involvement of Florence and its merchants in many marketplaces and to the contemporary expansion of Florentine business on the mainland. The majority of them, however, merely formalised previously existing commercial relations without offering any specific details on the goods involved. Only the cases of Faenza and Perugia provide useful information in this regard. According to William R. Day Jr., the language adopted in the treaty with Faenza strongly implies that as early as 1204, woollen textiles were among the main articles purchased by the Faentini merchants in their commercial travels to Florence, and vice versa.[139] A vibrant trade in textiles is also attested to in the city of Perugia a few years later. The 1218 commercial agreement set custom duties to be paid by the merchants of each city upon the export of cloths and furs of different qualities from the respective centres.[140] The variety of textiles documented (*panni lane, panni lini, selvaticume, torscia cuniculorum*, etc.) is a clear outcome of the productivity of the Florentine industry and its diversified production.

From the mid-1220s, Florentine cloth circulated widely in Italy and beyond. Hidetoshi Hoshino has collected references to Florentine cloth purchased in Venice (1225), Palermo (1237), Macerata (1245), Lucca (1246), Genoa (1253), and Dubrovnik (1253) during the first half of the century, but the contemporary spread of Florentine merchants into northern Europe and the Mediterranean discussed below points to a broader market.[141] At this stage, however, it seems that Florentine textile products were not of the highest quality. In Lucca, where transport costs from Florence would be lower than to other more distant destinations, they were sold at a much lower price than the luxury cloth from northern Europe known as the *panni franceschi* of Arras and Ypres.[142] Yet, there is little doubt that the Florentine wool industry already enjoyed some popularity, considering that Florentine workers were lured to towns intending to start up their textile production. In 1231, for example, the commune of Bologna hired forty-nine foreign workers to build there an export industry in woollen textiles: a quarter of them came from Florence.[143] The fact that the Bolognese government decided to rely on Florentine workers as skilled labour to develop their cloth industry is an indicator of the positive reputation of the Florentine textile sector by that time, likely the result of a long tradition of production and trade.

As anticipated, such widespread distribution of Florentine cloth was fostered by the concomitant diffusion of the merchants of Florence in all the major trading centres of the period, at least from the second half of the twelfth century onwards. In 1169, for example, a certain Ugolino the Florentine was negotiating a maritime loan for some business in Constantinople at the port of Armiro, on the north-west coast of the peninsula of Mani in the Peloponnese, where the Venetians might have had a *funduq* by then.[144] In 1193, a street in Messina was recorded as the *Ruga Florentinorum*, 'the street of the Florentines'.[145] Although already significant in terms of expansion, little more can be said about Florentine merchants at this early stage. The picture becomes clearer in the first decades of the thirteenth century, when Florentines emerge in a greater number of cities and marketplaces, engaging in commercial and financial activities within and beyond the Italian peninsula. They appear in Genoa (1200), Bologna (1211), Milan (1211), Rome (1219), and Lucca (1248). In Rome, in particular, they acted mainly as money lenders for clerics from all over Europe, as will be seen in Chapter 4. At the Champagne Fairs, they carried out commercial and exchange operations, negotiating an insurance policy in Provence for the dispatch of wool cloth (1215), lending money to King Henry III in England (1223), and purchasing leather in Marseille (1248). They were also active in the Mediterranean, selling clothes in Acre (1224), trading in Tunis on behalf of certain Genoese citizens (1225), and lending money to the French army fighting in Damietta during the Seventh Crusade (1249).[146] The genuine contribution of such a network to the rise and success of the gold florin will be illustrated in the next chapter. For now, what is clear from all these references is that trade and banking represented key activities for the Florentines in the decades before the florin and were often interrelated.

Two major forces pushed the merchants of Florence beyond the city walls: the urge to feed an ever-growing population and the needs of the nascent cloth industry.[147] We have already mentioned the dramatic demographic expansion of the Florentine population from the late twelfth century onwards. In his memoirs, written in a much later period between 1320 and 1335, the Florentine grain merchant Domenico Lenzi reported that the city of Florence could only feed its inhabitants for five months per year if it had to rely exclusively on the limited grain supply

coming from its countryside.[148] Florentine merchants were therefore compelled to venture outside the region to provide the necessary quantity of grain for such a vast mass of people. Supply
problems might have existed even before then since there is evidence of grain coming from the Pisan Maremma, an agricultural
region in south-western Tuscany and northern Lazio, as early
as 1182.[149] Large grain reserves were also to be found in Sicily,
Sardinia, and southern Italy, in the cities of Barletta (Apulia),
Manfredonia (Apulia), and Naples, where the Florentines had
had a *fondaco* since 1243.[150] Moreover, according to Day, many
of the aforementioned cities that entered into commercial agreements with Florence, including Bologna, Faenza, Orvieto, and
Perugia, were 'net exporters of grain', although precise figures
are unobtainable today.[151]

Despite the lack of data, however, there is little doubt that
grain represented one of the major imported products of Florence
during the thirteenth century. As illustrated by Edwin S. Hunt,
the so-called Florentine 'super-companies' of Bardi, Peruzzi, and
Acciaiuoli were able to build their economic and financial empires
in late thirteenth-century southern Italy thanks to a 'two-way trade
of grain and cloth'.[152]

Merchants of Florence venturing abroad were also motivated by
contemporary developments in textile production. The Florentine
industry needed to import large quantities of wool to work properly.
To this end, raw material and semi-finished cloth were purchased at
the Champagne Fairs by the *Calimala* merchants, manufactured in
Florence, and traded northwards at the Fairs or southwards in the
Mediterranean. Wool also came to Florence from southern Spain
and North Africa.

Taken together, these two dynamics and the concomitant activities of Florentine merchants described above helped to form the
economic prerequisites for the minting of the florin and its further
success. As illustrated in the next chapter, they gave Florence an
international dimension, familiarity with the international circuits
of money, finance, and commerce, an awareness of its monetary
needs, and all the necessary resources (i.e., gold, expertise in minting, etc.) that were crucial to the introduction of its brand-new gold
coinage. The opening of the civic mint around 1236 marked a further and fundamental step toward that goal.[153]

Until the mid-twelfth century, Tuscany had only one mint, that
of Lucca, which had been operating almost uninterruptedly since
the Lombard rule of the seventh–eighth centuries.[154] Starting in the
1150s, due to the increasing demand for money and the progressive
debasement of the circulating *denari*, other Tuscan centres began to
produce their own coinage: new mints were opened first in Pisa in
1155, followed by Siena and Volterra between 1186 and 1189, and
eventually Arezzo and Florence in the second and third decades of
the thirteenth century.[155] Except for Florence, which never received
such a privilege, these cities had all previously been granted the
right to mint coins (*ius cudendi*) by the emperors.[156] The Florentine
delay in operating a mint, however, should not be regarded as a
sign of weakness in the urban economy of the time, but rather the
opposite.[157] Before 1236, the city depended on the output of other
mints to satisfy its demand for money. Between the late twelfth
and early thirteenth centuries, in particular, it was the Pisan *denaro*
that dominated the Florentine currency, as attested by the above-
mentioned treaty with Pisa of 1171 and by later evidence from the
Florentine archives.[158] If, on the one hand, Florence waited until
c. 1236 to build its mint and produce its own coinage, this could
imply that the contemporary supply of Pisan money was enough
to meet the local demand. On the other hand, if one considers the
rapid and significant economic growth described so far, the opening of the urban mint in the 1230s could also be an effect of the
ever-expanding economy of Florence, by then in need of additional
money to sustain its thriving business.

The lack of consistent evidence makes it impossible to verify
these or other hypotheses. However, one fact is certain and worthy
of note: by the time Florence began minting coins, its relations with
Pisa had soured, leading to open warfare in 1220–22 and again
in the early 1230s. The Florentine coinage thus originated on the
autonomous initiative of its city as a gesture of rupture from the
hitherto 'friendly' Pisa – as well as from imperial authority, as will
be discussed below.

This political situation, which likely played a crucial role in the
opening of the Florentine mint, offers the opportunity for us to
question whether the political context of the time was also decisive
for the minting of the gold florin. The analysis carried out so far
has addressed the 'where' of the origin of the florin, showing that

by the mid-thirteenth century, Florence had emerged as a flourishing economic centre with the potential and resources to strike gold,
including a mint. However, many of these features were also common to the Tuscan cities of Siena and Pisa, which had a longer
minting tradition than Florence but never issued gold coins in the
thirteenth century. It therefore remains unclear why it was the latter
that minted gold coinage and why the Florentine government opted
for a new gold specimen rather than a silver one or an imitation.

Political Florence: from 'imperial town' to 'city commune'

Roberto S. Lopez was probably the first to stress the political
dimension of the minting of the florin, embodying the 'municipal
pride' of the city that took its 'last and most fateful step' in its
political and economic emancipation from Pisa, given the long-term
rivalry between the two centres.[159] Other historians, such as Marco
Tangheroni and Monica Baldassarri, agreed on the importance of
the political context to explain the minting of the florin but placed
much more emphasis on the contemporary weakness of imperial
authority, especially after the death of Emperor Frederick II in 1250
and the conflict between the Guelph and the Ghibelline parties.[160]
Both of these interpretations constitute complementary aspects of
the more general process of affirmation of autonomy and power
undertaken by the city of Florence in those years. Specifically, the
main political factors that prepared the ground for the florin were
(i) the antagonism with Pisa, (ii) the imperial weakness/void, and
(iii) the building of civic identity.[161]

Between the last quarter of the twelfth and the early years of the
thirteenth century, Florence was involved in a growing number of
military conflicts, first with rural nobles to establish its control over
the nearby *contado*, then with other Tuscan cities such as Siena
and Pistoia to expand its power and authority. A period of peace
followed in the 1210s, during which no external conflicts seem to
have occurred.[162] Around the 1220s, the situation worsened again,
with Florence becoming involved in three successive wars against
Pisa (1222), Pistoia (1228), and Siena (1228–35). It was in Rome
in 1220, during the coronation ceremony of Frederick II as Holy

Roman Emperor, that the conflict between the Florentines and the Pisans erupted. On that occasion, the latter obtained important commercial privileges from the emperor, including total exemption from taxes in the empire's territories, thus becoming Frederick's first allies.[163] This was a severe blow to Florence and its thriving economy, now overshadowed by the dominant power of Pisa. A military reprisal of the Florentines against the Pisans in Rome followed soon after and had serious implications for Florence's business, as many of its merchants trading in Pisa were imprisoned, their goods confiscated, and all the previous commercial treaties between the two cities were revoked. This marked a clear break in relations between the two centres, precipitating a new war a couple of years later (1222).

A new pattern of alliances among Tuscan cities came into existence during this and the following conflicts against Pistoia and Siena: on the one side were Florence, Lucca, and Arezzo, and on the other side, Pisa, Siena, and Pistoia. At this early stage, however, these two sets of allies had not yet aligned with the later antagonism between Guelphs and Ghibellines, the supporters of the pope and the emperor, respectively, which affected many regions of the Italian peninsula. On the contrary, these wars generated a progressive decline in stability and an atmosphere of intense violence and civic discord in Tuscany that turned into a 'general confrontation' between the two parties only after the 'increasing interference' of Emperor Frederick II in northern Italian affairs following his victory over the Milanese army at Cortenuova (1237).[164]

The escalation of the conflict between Guelphs and Ghibellines forced Frederick II to appoint his illegitimate son Frederick of Antioch imperial vicar of Tuscany and *Podestà* of Florence in 1246 to restore peace. Initially, Frederick was relatively tolerant towards the Guelphs in the town. Yet, his decision to abolish local institutions dominated by papal supporters, such as the *Capitani del Popolo*, marked an outbreak of hostilities that culminated in February 1248, when the Guelphs were exiled and their possessions confiscated.[165] A few years before the return to gold, Florence therefore appeared as a Ghibelline centre ruled by Frederick of Antioch, vicar of the Holy Roman emperor. But this did not last long.

The year 1250 was a turning point for the political situation of Florence, Italy, and western Europe in general. On 21 September,

Frederick of Antioch and his Ghibelline troops were defeated near Figline by the exiled Guelphs. This episode marked the end of Frederick's power as *Podestà* of Florence and imperial vicar of Tuscany. On 20 October, the Florentine *Popolo* rose up against the Ghibelline regime, expelled Frederick's representatives, and took control of the city.[166]

In addition, on 13 December, the emperor died in Castel Fiorentino (Apulia). Conrad, the second-born son of Frederick II, who succeeded him with the title Conrad IV, never managed to reassert imperial power over Tuscany and Florence. The Holy Roman Empire entered a period of political uncertainty, also known as the 'interregnum', marked by the absence of a strong and powerful figure to take the lead.[167] In the wake of these events, Florence embarked on a process of affirming its power, authority, and independence inside and outside its walls.

As regards its external policy, it was soon involved in new wars against its Ghibelline neighbours to take possession of the *contado* and establish its power in Tuscany. The conclusion of a new military alliance between Pisa, Siena, and Pistoia in 1251, also secretly signed by Ghibelline families in Florence, led to the temporary resumption of the clash between the Guelph and Ghibelline parties in Tuscany. Once discovered, the Florentine government forced the Ghibelline families into exile and, on 20 October, established a three-party agreement with Genoa and Lucca to create a ten-year league with the sole purpose of destroying the rival city of Pisa through a war 'by sea and land'.[168] To them, Pisa represented the last imperial Ghibelline threat after Frederick's death, as well as a strong competitor in the market. Hence, the widespread anti-Ghibelline and anti-imperial sentiments common to these three cities, together with their economic interests, eventually shaped the nature of this successful alliance. The peace agreement of 1254 between Florence and the cities of Pistoia, Siena, and Pisa, following a series of successful wars in 1252–54, marked the temporary victory of Florence and its leading role in the political landscape of Tuscany at that time.

Within the Florentine walls, meanwhile, the above-mentioned uprising against the Ghibellines in 1250 coincided with the rise of a new government known as the *Primo Popolo*.[169] This consisted mainly of members of classes that had recently become wealthy through their economic and financial transactions, such as merchants, bankers, craftsmen, notaries, and judges, and thus were not related to the previously dominant aristocratic families.[170] This new leading group maintained the peace between the Guelphs and Ghibellines and introduced important reforms in several areas of public life. The city provided itself with new constructions such as bridges and churches, new institutions such as the *Consiglio degli Anziani*, a new military organisation, a new fiscal administration, and a new identity.[171] In this context, the florin can be regarded as a propaganda device for Florence, which was now determined to assert its autonomy and authority independent of any external power. Specifically, the florin was the product of a 'double' appropriation of the imperial authority. First, it was minted without any formal authorisation. In the twelfth century, the right to open a mint and strike coins (*ius cudendi*) was usually part of the privileges or *regalia* dispensed by the emperor. Unlike many other Tuscan cities of the time, Florence did not hold any imperially granted right of coinage when its mint went into operation, as already noted. That occurred around 1236, during the war against Siena and Pisa, following the conviction of the imperial court in 1232, which banned Florence for its refusal to pay for any damage caused to the latter. It was therefore in such a condition of open rebellion against the emperor and Pisa that Florence decided to open its mint and produce coins in its own name. The iconography of the new silver *grosso* of Florence, first struck on that occasion with the images of the lily on one side and the bust of the patron saint John the Baptist on the other, and with no reference to any imperial authority in its inscriptions, is a clear statement of the Tuscan city's independence (see Figure 1.2).

According to Robert Davidsohn, however, this was only the first step in the process of self-determination since the same message and iconography – but with the saint standing – were re-proposed a few years later on the gold florin.[172] A second appropriation occurred on that occasion.

Until then, gold had traditionally been associated with the idea of sovereignty.[173] In the first half of the thirteenth century, as illustrated, foreign gold coins in circulation belonged only to kings and emperors, while minor authorities or communes produced silver or billon coins. The gold *augustalis* minted by Emperor Frederick

Figure 1.2 The silver *grosso* of Florence, *c*. 1235, scale 2:1.

II in Sicily in 1231, for example, was an imperial creation in all respects: with the laureate bust of the emperor on one side and the classical eagle on the other, this coin was issued to accommodate contemporary monetary needs while also celebrating Frederick's *imperium* through its symbols.[174] Against this background, the decision of a 'simple' commune like Florence to adopt gold for its new coin constituted something extraordinary, yet in line with the political situation of the period. This appropriation must be seen as an act of power by Florence in the process of political affirmation that the city undertook in the 1240s–50s. Specifically, by taking over an imperial task like the minting of gold coins to produce the florin, not only was Florence reclaiming its new political status as an autonomous city free from the imperial overlordship, but it was also acting as a *'civitas sibi princeps'*, or 'an emperor in its own territory' that recognised no superior, as theorised by the fourteenth-century jurist Bartolus of Sassoferrato (1314–57).[175] This was possible only in the absence of a strong and intrusive authority like the Holy Roman Emperor, who would quite possibly have prevented the new minting. On this basis, the florin was a powerful instrument supporting the contemporary sovereignty of Florence and a carrier of a new political image of the city, now free from the imperial yoke.

All these implications therefore explain why Florence opted for a new and original coin made of gold rather than striking another silver denomination or imitating foreign currencies in circulation. None of these solutions were as powerful as the gold florin in conveying its new political message. This also could clarify why other

Tuscan cities such as Pisa or Siena never tried to mint their own gold coins before Florence, subjected as they were to the political authority of the emperor and his allies. For this very reason, moreover, the Florentine florin differed from the other contemporary gold coins of Genoa and Lucca, which still retained references in their iconography to the imperial power that granted them the *ius cudendi*. With the gold florin, Florence marked instead a total break with its political past and the beginning of a new era.

Conclusions

The florin was the result of favourable economic and political conditions converging at both macro and micro levels. At a macro level, its minting was made possible by a combination of factors, ranging from the thirteenth-century decline of other gold coins in circulation, also associated with the political instability of the regions where they were minted, to the need for a new and stable gold currency coming from merchants involved in long-distance trade. Commerce and trade, rather than monetary arbitrage, led to a greater concentration of gold in Europe, to the point that striking gold – in addition to silver – became cheaper and more convenient, although the reasons for the European return to gold are still debated, as is its chronology. If, for Genoa, the annals of the city government report that the gold *genovino* was produced in 1252, the same cannot be said with certainty for Florence, and even less so for Lucca, for which there is no documentation contemporary with the introduction of their gold specimens. However, while the minting of the Genoese, Florentine, and Lucchese gold coins would have occurred almost simultaneously, both the introduction of the *genovino* and the *grosso d'oro* were soon followed by political and financial crises that hindered the innovative impact of these currencies, resulting in less successful and widespread coinages than the florin.[176] At any rate, the year 1252 should not be considered a revolutionary date since other cities in Italy and Europe more generally were minting gold, or at least had the right to do so.

On a micro level, the florin came into being in a period of economic revival and political renewal. Unlike other Tuscan cities such as Pisa, Lucca, and Siena, Florence was a latecomer in the

'Commercial Revolution', as it began to grow into an important trading centre in the Italian peninsula only at the turn of the twelfth and thirteenth centuries. Driven by swift population growth that led to the creation of new urban walls in the late twelfth century, Florence developed its commercial network by concluding treaties with other Italian marketplaces. Florentine merchants thus began to venture abroad, driven by the need for grain for their fellow citizens and the trade in textiles and wool between northern Europe and the Mediterranean, where they also provided financial services. The late opening of the Florentine mint around 1236 represented a direct consequence of the need for additional money due to the expansion of Florentine business. Besides economic purposes, however, political reasons also contributed to the minting of the florin: these included anti-Ghibelline and anti-imperial sentiments, which were common to Genoa and Lucca but were not reflected in the iconography of their own gold coins. Both the death of Emperor Frederick II in 1250 and the weakness of Conrad IV, his successor, offered the perfect occasion for Florence to claim quasi-imperial authority and independence. From this perspective, the minting of gold represented a political opportunity to redefine the Florentine commune led by the *Primo Popolo* as an autonomous proto-state in the absence of the emperor. The story of the florin was therefore, essentially, also a political one, highlighting (usurped) Florentine autonomy and sovereignty and the rise to power of a new mercantile class, whose fundamental contribution to the origin and early life of the coin will be illustrated in the next chapter.

Notes

1 Grierson, 'Il fiorino', p. 415.
2 The side with the name and symbolic representation of the issuing authority, i.e., the lily and the related inscription, has tended to be considered as the 'obverse', meaning the most important side, although it is not clear whether contemporaries regarded it as such. For a different interpretation based on technical considerations in the making of the florin, see Lucia Travaini and Matteo Broggini, 'San Giovanni sull'incudine. Fondatori cristiani e fondatori mitici sulle monete italiane medievali e moderne', in L. Travaini and G. Arrigoni

(eds), *Polis, urbs, civitas: moneta e identità. Atti del Convegno di studio del Lexicon Iconographicum Numismaticae (Milano 25 ottobre 2012)* (Rome: Quasar, 2013), pp. 165–76. 'Stylised lily' is preferable to 'fleur-de-lis', which might anachronistically suggest the slightly different form on French coinage.

3 Philip Grierson, 'The Weight of the Gold Florin in the Fifteenth Century', *NAC* 10 (1981), 421–31.

4 Denominations of a similar gold standard were minted, for example, in England (1257), France (1266), Rome (1271), Naples (1278), and Venice (1284); Marc Bompaire and Pierre-Joan Bernard, 'Le retour à l'or au treizième siècle: le cas de Montpellier (…1244–1246…)', in N. Holmes (ed.), *Proceedings of the XIVth International Numismatic Congress Glasgow 2009* (Glasgow: International Numismatic Congress, 2011), pp. 1392–400.

5 Between the fourteenth and fifteenth centuries, around 160 varieties of florin imitations were issued in fifty different mints across western and central Europe; *Bernocchi* V, and more recently William R. Day Jr., 'Early Imitations of the Gold Florin of Florence and the Imitation Florin of Chivasso in the Name of Theodore I Paleologus, Marquis of Montferrat (1306–1338)', *NC* 164 (2004), 183–99; Lucia Travaini and Matteo Broggini (eds), *Il tesoro di Montella (Avellino): ducati e fiorini d'oro italiani e stranieri occultati nella metà del Trecento* (Rome: Quasar, 2016), pp. 35*ff.*

6 Philip Grierson, *The Coins of Medieval Europe* (London: Seaby, 1991), pp. 20–8.

7 Spufford, *Money*, p. 18.

8 Spufford, *Money*, pp. 20–1; William R. Day Jr., 'The Monetary Reforms of Charlemagne and the Circulation of Money in Early Medieval Campania', *Early Medieval Europe* 6:1 (1997), 25–45.

9 Monica Baldassarri and Daniele Ricci, 'I grossi d'argento e la monetazione di Genova tra Due e Trecento: nuovi dati e osservazioni per vecchi problemi', *NAC* 42 (2013), 275–99. Gold coins were occasionally minted by Louis the Pious King of the Franks (814–40) and by King Offa of Mercia (757–96), among others, but those were not always intended for normal circulation; Spufford, *Money*, pp. 50–1.

10 *MEC* 6, pp. 62–3 and 287; Raymond J. Hebert, 'The Coinage of Islamic Spain', *Islamic Studies* 30, 1:2 (1991), 113–28 (at pp. 114–22); Harry W. Hazard, *The Numismatic History of Late Medieval North Africa* (New York: American Numismatic Society, 1952).

11 *MEC* 6, p. 289; Hebert, 'The Coinage', p. 124. See also Corinne Roux and Maria F. Guerra, 'La Monnaie Almoravide: de l'Afrique à l'Espagne', *Revue d'Archéométrie* 24 (2000), 39–52; Ronald A.

Messier, 'The Almoravids: West African Gold and the Gold Currency of the Mediterranean Basin', *Journal of Economic and Social History of the Orient* 17:1 (1974), 31–47.

12 *MEC* 6, p. 63; Hebert, 'The Coinage', p. 126. See also Alexandra Gondonneau and Maria F. Guerra, 'The Circulation of Precious Metals in the Arab Empire: The Case of the Near and The Middle East', *Archaeometry* 44:4 (2002), 573–99.

13 *MEC* 6, pp. 286–90; Bompaire and Bernard, 'Le retour', p. 1393.

14 The final issues would have been of a lower standard of weight and fineness; *MEC* 6, p. 435.

15 *MEC* 6, pp. 272–3 (Leon), and pp. 430–5 (Portugal).

16 *MEC* 6, pp. 294–5; Spufford, *Money*, pp. 168–9. Regular issuances only began under King Alphonse X (1252–84) between 1252 and 1272; *MEC* 6, pp. 307–8.

17 *MEC* 14, pp. 141–93.

18 *MEC* 14, p. 167; Heinrich Kowalski, 'Die Augustalen Kaiser Friedrichs II', *Schweizerische Numismatische Rundschau* 55 (1976), 77–150.

19 Cécile Morrisson, 'Byzantine Money: Its Production and Circulation', in A. E. Laiou (ed.), *The Economic History of Byzantium: From the Seventh through the Fifteenth Century* (Washington, DC: Dumbarton Oaks, 2002), pp. 909–66 (at p. 932); Alan Stahl, 'The Mediterranean Melting Pot: Monetary Crosscurrents of the Twelfth through Fifteenth Centuries', in M. S. Brownlee and D. H. Gondicas (eds), *Renaissance Encounters: Greek East and Latin West* (Leiden and Boston: Brill, 2013), pp. 241–62 (at p. 243).

20 Morrisson, 'Byzantine Money', p. 933.

21 Alan Stahl, 'Coinage and Money in the Latin Empire of Constantinople', *Dumbarton Oaks Papers* 55 (2001), 197–206.

22 David M. Metcalf, *Coinage of the Crusades and the Latin East in the Ashmolean Museum Oxford* (London: Royal Numismatic Society, 1995), pp. 43–51.

23 For further details, see Marc Bompaire, 'Le Mythe du Bezant?', in *Mélanges Cécile Morrisson* (Paris: Association des Amis du Centre d'Histoire et Civilisation de Bysance, 2010), pp. 93–116 (at pp. 94–6).

24 Jean Duplessy, 'La circulation des monnaies arabes en Europe occidentale du VIIIᵉ au XIIIᵉ siècle', *RN* 5:18 (1956), 101–63 (at pp. 115–16 and 120).

25 Cook, 'The Bezant', p. 256; David A. Carpenter, 'The Gold Treasure of King Henry III', in P. R. Coss and S. D. Lloyd (eds), *Thirteenth Century England I. Proceedings of the Newcastle-upon-Tyne*

Conference, 1985 (Woodbridge: The Boydell Press, 1986), pp. 61–88; David A. Carpenter, 'Gold and Gold Coins in England in the Mid-Thirteenth Century', *NC* 147 (1987), 106–13.

26 Bompaire, 'Le Mythe', pp. 98–101. For the term '*oboles*', see Philip Grierson, 'Oboli de Musc', *The English Historical Review* 66:258 (1951), 75–81.

27 For Genoa, see Monica Baldassarri, 'Coniazioni ed economia monetaria del Comune di Genova: dalle origini agli inizi del Trecento', *NAC* 45 (2016), 283–306 (at p. 289); for Pisa, see Monica Baldassarri, *Zecca e monete del comune di Pisa: dalle origini agli inizi della seconda repubblica. XII secolo–1406*, vol. 1 (Ghezzano: Felici, 2010), p. 80; Monica Baldassarri, 'Tarì e altre monete normanno-sveve in area alto tirrenica: un quadro tra fonti scritte e materiali (X-XIII secolo), in A. M. Santoro and L. Travaini (eds), *Il Tarì moneta del Mediterraneo. Atti del Convegno, Amalfi, 20–21 maggio 2022* (Amalfi: Presso la Sede del Centro, 2023), pp. 239–64. For Venice, see Louis Buenger Robbert, 'Money and Prices in Thirteenth-Century Venice', *JMH* 20:4 (1994), 373–90 (at p. 384, note 47).

28 Riccardo Predelli (ed.), *Il Liber Communis detto anche Plegiorum del R. Archivio Generale di Venezia: Regesti* (Venice: Tipografia del commercio di Marco Visentini, 1872), p. 144, no. 604. To date, the activity of these officials has only been documented from 1262 and thus after the return to gold in Italy and western Europe; Alan Stahl, *Zecca: The Mint of Venice in the Middle Ages* (Baltimore and London: The Johns Hopkins University Press, 2000), pp. 136–9 and 413–14.

29 Richard D. Face, 'Secular History in Twelfth-Century Italy: Caffaro of Genoa', *JMH* 6 (1980), 169–84.

30 Chris Wickham, 'The Sense of the Past in Italian Communal Narratives', in P. Magdalino (ed.), *The Perception of the Past in Twelfth-Century Europe* (London and Rio Grande: The Hambledon Press, 1992), pp. 173–89.

31 'In the same year the gold *nummus* of Genoa was fabricated'; Cesare Imperiale di Sant'Angelo, *Annali Genovesi di Caffaro e de' suoi continuatori dal MCCLI al MCCLXXIX*, vol. 4 (Rome: Tipografia del Senato Palazzo Madama, 1926), p. 10, lines 4–5. Author's translation.

32 On the choice of the term '*nummus*', see Monica Baldassarri in Monica Baldassarri and Stefano Locatelli, 'Genoa, Florence and the Mediterranean: New Perspectives on the Return to Gold in the 13th Century', *RN* 178 (2018), 433–75 (at p. 445, note 59).

33 *MEC* 12, pp. 267 and 269.

34 *MEC* 12, p. 267.

35 'Large/thicker/heavier Genoese gold *denarii*'; Roberto S. Lopez, 'Un "consilium" di giuristi torinesi nel Dugento', *Bollettino Storico-bibliografico Subalpino* 38:1–2 (1936), 143–50; later quoted by Philip Grierson – see Baldassarri in Baldassarri and Locatelli, 'Genoa, Florence', p. 446, note 62. Author's translation.

36 Monica Baldassarri *et al.*, 'X-Ray Fluorescence Analysis of XII–XIV Century Italian Gold Coins', *Journal of Archaeology* (2014), 1–6.

37 Baldassarri in Baldassarri and Locatelli, 'Genoa, Florence', p. 446, note 63.

38 On the possible reform of the Genoese silver coinage, see Baldassarri and Ricci, 'I grossi d'argento', pp. 280 and 286.

39 Baldassarri in Baldassarri and Locatelli, 'Genoa, Florence', pp. 449–50.

40 '*100 onze d'oro di lega della zecca di Genova di carati 23 ½*', Arturo Ferretto, *Codice Diplomatico delle Relazioni fra la Liguria, la Toscana, la Lunigiana ai Tempi di Dante (1265–1321). Parte prima: dal 1265 al 1274* (Rome: Tipografia Artigianelli di San Giuseppe, 1901), p. 340, no. DCCCXLVIII. Author's translation. A further piece of evidence from 1276 can be found in Giovanni Pesce and Giuseppe Felloni, *Le monete genovesi. Storia, arte ed economia nelle monete di Genova dal 1139 al 1814* (Genoa: Cassa di Risparmio di Genova e Imperia, 1975), p. 348.

41 Baldassarri in Baldassarri and Locatelli, 'Genoa, Florence', p. 451.

42 See, for instance, the case of Perugia discussed below.

43 This could also explain why, later on, Genoese notarial records began to refer to gold *genovini* as *floreni Ianuensium* or 'Genoese florins', as noted in *MEC* 12, p. 269.

44 Baldassarri in Baldassarri and Locatelli, 'Genoa, Florence', p. 447, note 65.

45 Luciano Lenzi, 'Il grosso d'oro di Lucca: 1246?', *Memorie dell'Accademia Italiana di Studi Filatelici e Numismatici* 6:1 (1995), 73–91.

46 Giulio Cordero di San Quintino, *Della zecca e delle monete di Lucca nei secoli di mezzo. Discorsi*. Memorie e documenti per servire alla storia di Lucca. Tomo XI (Lucca: Tipografia di Giuseppe Giusti, 1860), plate VIII.

47 Domenico Massagli, *Introduzione alla storia della zecca e delle monete lucchesi*. Memorie e documenti per servire alla storia di Lucca. Tomo XI, parte seconda (Lucca: Tipografia Giusti, 1870), p. 53.

48 Gino Arrighi, 'Due trattati di Paolo Gherardi matematico fiorentino. I codici magliabechiani cl. XI, nn. 87 e 88 (prima metà del Trecento) della Biblioteca Nazionale di Firenze', in F. Barbieri, R. Franci, and L. Toti Rigatelli (eds), *Gino Arrighi. La matematica dell'età di mezzo.*

Scritti scelti (Pisa: Edizioni ETS, 2004), pp. 81–98. For a full edition of the *Liber habaci*, see Gino Arrighi (ed.), *Opera matematica. Libro di ragioni – Liber habaci. Codici Magliabechiani Classe XI, nn. 87 e 88 (sec. XIV) della Biblioteca Nazionale di Firenze* (Lucca: Maria Pacini Fazi editore, 1987).

49 Further details can be found in Raffaele Danna, 'Figuring Out: The Spread of Hindu-Arabic Numerals in the European Tradition of Practical Mathematics (13th–16th Centuries)', *Nuncius* 36 (2021), 5–48 (at p. 13*ff.*) and its rich bibliography.

50 Peter Spufford, 'Lapis, Indigo, Woad: Artists' Materials in the Context of International Trade before 1700', in J. Kirby, S. Nash, and J. Cannon (eds), *Trade in Artists' Materials: Markets and Commerce in Europe to 1700* (London: Archetype Publications, 2010), pp. 10–25 (at p. 21).

51 Lucia Travaini, *Monete mercanti e matematica. Le monete medievali nei trattati di aritmetica e nei libri di mercatura. Seconda edizione ampliata con nuove liste inedite* (Milan: Jouvence, 2020), pp. 114–15.

52 Baldassarri, *Le monete di Lucca*, pp. 87–8.

53 Baldassarri *et al.*, 'X-Ray Fluorescence Analysis', p. 2.

54 Baldassarri, *Le monete di Lucca*, p. 90.

55 'Lucchese *denarii* [i.e., money of account] (paid) in gold and silver *grossi* of such value in little deniers'; Thomas Blomquist, 'The Second Issuance of a Tuscan Gold Coin: The Gold Groat of Lucca, 1256', *JMH* 13:4 (1987), 317–25 (at p. 318). Author's translation.

56 Raymond de Roover, 'Discussion of Gras's paper "Capitalism: Concepts and History" ', *Bulletin of the Business Historical Society* 16 (1942), 34–9; Roberto S. Lopez, *The Commercial Revolution of the Middle Ages, 950–1350* (Englewood Cliffs, NJ: Prentice Hall, 1971); Franco Franceschi, 'La crescita economica dell'Occidente medievale: un tema storico non ancora esaurito. Introduzione', in Centro Italiano di Studi di Storia e d'Arte (eds), *La crescita economica dell'Occidente medievale: un tema storico non ancora esaurito, Pistoia, 14–17 maggio 2015* (Rome: Viella, 2017), pp. 1–24 (at pp. 14–17); Francesca Trivellato, 'Renaissance Florence and the Origins of Capitalism: A Business History Perspective', *Business History Review* 94 (2020), 229–51 (at pp. 232–5). The narrative of the 'Commercial Revolution' has recently been the subject of a major revision by Chris Wickham, but his analysis offers minimal consideration of the history of money, despite the many monetary innovations and transformations of the time; Chris Wickham, *The Donkey and the Boat: Reinterpreting the Mediterranean Economy, 950–1180* (Oxford: Oxford University Press, 2023).

57 For the monetisation and monetary consciousness of the medieval
   society in the thirteenth and fourteenth centuries, see the fundamental
   work by Joel Kaye, *Economy and Nature in the Fourteenth Century:
   Money, Market, Exchange, and the Emergence of Scientific Thought*
   (Cambridge: Cambridge University Press, 2004), pp. 15–36. See also
   Jim L. Bolton, *Money in the Medieval English Economy: 973–1489*
   (Manchester: Manchester University Press, 2012), Part II.
58 It has been estimated that the volume of coinage in circulation in
   England increased from *c.* 37,500 pounds in 1086 to *c.* 1,100,000
   pounds after 1300; Nicholas J. Mayhew, 'Modelling Medieval
   Monetisation', in R. H. Britnell and B. M. S. Campbell (eds), *A
   Commercialising Economy: England 1086–1300* (Manchester:
   Manchester University Press, 1995), pp. 55–77 (at pp. 62–5).
59 Carlo M. Cipolla, *Le avventure della lira* (Bologna: Il Mulino, 1975),
   pp. 38–9. In this regard, Peter Spufford has referred to a 'long thir-
   teenth century' stretching from the 1160s to the 1330s; Spufford,
   Money, p. 240.
60 Peter Spufford, 'The Provision of Stable Moneys by Florence and
   Venice, and North Italian Financial Innovations in the Renaissance
   Period', in P. Bernholz and R. Vaubel (eds), *Explaining Monetary and
   Financial Innovation: A Historical Analysis* (Berlin: Springer, 2014),
   pp. 227–51 (at pp. 231–3).
61 On silver ingots, see Spufford, *Money*, pp. 209–24; Marcus Phillips,
   'The Monetary Use of Uncoined Silver in Western Europe in the
   Twelfth and Thirteenth Centuries', in M. Allen and N. J. Mayhew
   (eds), *Money and Its Use in Medieval Europe: Three Decades On.
   Essays in Honour of Professor Peter Spufford* (London: Royal
   Numismatic Society, 2017), pp. 1–18. On silver *grossi* and their circulation in western Europe and the Mediterranean, see Baldassarri and
   Ricci, 'I grossi d'argento', p. 286; Monica Baldassarri, 'Miliarenses
   and Silver Grossi in the Western Mediterranean: New Documents
   and Perspectives', in M. Caccamo Caltabiano (ed.), *XV International
   Numismatic Congress Taormina 2015: Proceedings*, 2 vols (Rome
   and Messina: Arbor Sapientiae, 2017), vol. 2, pp. 1052–7.
62 The Almoravid Kingdom of Murcia minted *morabitinos* until 1170;
   MEC 6, p. 286.
63 *MEC* 6, p. 289.
64 In the Kingdom of Castle-Leon, regular issues of gold *doblas* and their
   fractions restarted under Alphonse X between 1252 and 1272. In
   Portugal, there is no further numismatic evidence of gold issues until
   King Ferdinand I (1367–83); *MEC* 6, pp. 307–8 and 450–3, respectively.
65 *MEC* 14, p. 176.

66 So far, only a single *hyperpyron* of Theodore I Laskaris (1204–22) has been found; Lucia Travaini, 'La quarta crociata e la monetazione nell'area mediterranea', in G. Ortalli, G. Ravegnani, and Peter Schreiner (eds), *Quarta crociata: Venezia, Bisanzio, Impero Latino* (Venice: Istituto veneto di scienze, lettere e arti, 2006), pp. 525–53 (at p. 530).

67 Robert D. Leonard, 'The Effects of the Fourth Crusade on European Gold Coinage', in T. F. Madden (ed.), *The Fourth Crusade: Events, Aftermath, and Perceptions* (Burlington: Ashgate, 2008), pp. 75–88 (at p. 80).

68 Ernest Oberländer-Târnoveanu, 'Les hyperpères de type Jean III Vatatzès. Classification, chronologie et évolution du titre (à la lumière du trésor d'Uzunbair, dép. de Tulcea)', in M. Iacob, E. Oberländer-Târnoveanu, and F. Topoleanu (eds), *Istro-Pontica, Muzeul Tulcean la a 50-a Aniversare 1950–2000* (Tulcea: Consiliul Județean, 2000), pp. 499–562 (at pp. 506–8). On their chronology and their attribution, see, for instance, Travaini, 'La quarta crociata', p. 537; Leonard, 'The Effects', pp. 81–3. On stylistic grounds, Michael Hendy suggested that the revival of gold *hyperpyra* began shortly after the year 1204, but there is no documentary evidence for that; Michael Hendy, *Coinage and Money in the Byzantine Empire 1081–1261* (Washington, DC: Dumbarton Oaks, 1969), p. 208.

69 Adon A. Gordus and David M. Metcalf, 'Neutron Activation Analysis of the Gold Coinages of the Crusader States', in D. M. Metcalf and W. A. Oddy (eds), *Metallurgy in Numismatics I* (London: The Royal Numismatic Society, 1980), pp. 119–50.

70 Baldassarri in Baldassarri and Locatelli, 'Genoa, Florence', p. 444.

71 Walker, 'Gold Revolution', p. 43.

72 Bloch, 'The Problem', p. 191. The Hungarian gold deposits around Kremnica in Slovakia, which later became the main source of gold in Europe, did not open until *c.* 1320; Spufford, *Money*, p. 267. Before then, it seems that an alloy of gold and silver could be found in the mines of what are today Bosnia and Serbia, but these sites only appear in the sources from 1254 onwards, after the 'return to gold' in western Europe; Desanka Kovacević, 'Dans la Serbie et la Bosnie medievales: les mines d'or et d'argent', *Annales. Économies, Sociétés, Civilisations*, 15:2 (1960), 248–58 (at pp. 249 and 253).

73 Idrīsī, *La première géographie de l'Occident*, ed. H. Bresc and A. Nef (Paris: Flammarion, 1999), pp. 71 and 76–7.

74 For possible identifications, see Edward W. Bovill, *Golden Trade of the Moors* (London: Oxford University Press, 1958), pp. 119–31; 'Umar Al-Naqar, 'Takrur: The History of a Name', *The Journal of*

African History 10:3 (1969), 365–74; Nehemia Levtzion, *Ancient Ghana and Mali* (London: Methuen, 1973), p. 155.

75 Interestingly, Bambouk is still known today as *Gangaran*, whose assonance with *Wangara* is striking. In the Maninka language, *gba-gara* or *ga-gara* mean 'hole in the ground'; Marco Aime, *La carovana del sultano. Dal Mali alla Mecca: un pellegrinaggio medievale* (Turin: Einaudi, 2023), pp. 134–5.

76 Susan K. McIntosh, 'A Reconsideration of Wangara/Palolus, Island of Gold', *The Journal of African History* 22 (1981), 145–58 (at pp. 146 and 153*ff.*); François-Xavier Fauvelle, *The Golden Rhinoceros: Histories of the African Middle Ages* (Princeton and Oxford: Princeton University Press, 2018), pp. 121–2.

77 Amar S. Baadj, *Saladin, the Almohads and the Banū Ghāniya: The Contests for North Africa (12th and 13th Centuries)* (Leiden and Boston: Brill, 2015), p. 19.

78 Katja Werthmann, 'Gold Mining and Jula Influence in Precolonial Southern Burkina Faso', *The Journal of African History* 48:3 (2007), 395–414.

79 Walker, 'Gold Revolution', p. 39; Baadj, *Saladin*, pp. 117 and 121.

80 Ian Blanchard, *Mining, Metallurgy and Minting in the Middle Ages. Vol 3: Continuing Afro-European Supremacy, 1250–1450* (Stuttgart: Franz Steiner Verlag, 2005), p. 1129; Lauren Jacobi, 'Reconsidering the World-system: The Agency and Material Geography of Gold', in D. Savoy (ed.), *Globalization of Renaissance Art: A Critical Review* (Leiden and Boston: Brill, 2017), pp. 131–57 (at p. 146).

81 Further details in Baadj, *Saladin*, pp. 15–18 and 117, also the map 4 at p. 215.

82 For a full account of these aspects, see Levtzion, *Ghana*, pp. 124–32. On the role of the camel in North Africa, see Richard W. Bulliet, *The Camel and the Wheel* (Cambridge, MA: Harvard University Press, 1975), chapter 5.

83 On the pivotal role of salt in trade and its regulation, see Jean Claude Hocquet, *Le sel et le pouvoir: de l'an mil à la révolution française* (Paris: Albin Michel, 1985).

84 Levtzion, *Ghana*, p. 171.

85 Jean Devisse, 'Routes de commerce et échanges en Afrique occidentale en relation avec la Méditerranée. Un essai sur le commerce africain médiéval du XIe au XVIe siècle', *Revue d'histoire économique et sociale* 50:1 (1972), 42–73 (at pp. 61–2).

86 For a detailed account of the main destinations of gold and mints in North Africa, see Spufford, *Money*, pp. 165–6. For Sicily and its gold circulation/supply, see David Abulafia, *The Two Italies: Economic*

Relations Between the Norman Kingdom of Sicily and the Northern Communes (Cambridge: Cambridge University Press, 1977), p. 271*ff.*

87 On Islamic *fatwās* and monetary issues, see Russel Hopley, 'Aspects of Trade in Western Mediterranean During the Eleventh and Twelfth Centuries: Perspectives from Islamic Fatwās and State Correspondence', *Mediaevalia* 13 (2011), 5–42.

88 David Abulafia, 'Maometto e Carlomagno: le due aree monetarie dell'oro e dell'argento', *Storia d'Italia, Annali 6* (1983), 223–70; reprinted in David Abulafia, *Italy, Sicily and the Mediterranean 1100–1400* (London: Variorum, 1987), chapter 4 (at p. 242 and note 21); Hady Roger Idris, *La Barbérie orientale sous les Zīrīdes. Xᵉ–XIIᵉ*, 2 vols (Paris: Adrien-Maisonneuve, 1962), vol. 2, pp. 666–7.

89 This is a gross simplification; for more details, see Romney David Smith, 'Calamity and Transition: Re-imagining Italian Trade in the Eleventh-Century Mediterranean', *Past & Present* 228 (2015), 15–56.

90 Spufford, *Money*, p. 163.

91 Lopez, 'Back to Gold', p. 233; Watson, 'Back', p. 14; Spufford, *Money*, chapter 7; Lane and Mueller, *Money and Banking*, pp. 16–21.

92 Egypt should be considered part of the Middle East; Eliyahu Ashtor, *Les métaux précieux et la balance des payements du Proche-Orient a la Basse Époque* (Paris: SEVPEN, 1971), chapter 4.

93 Watson, 'Back', p. 21.

94 The ratio in most parts of Europe was generally between nine and ten before the return to gold in the mid-thirteenth century, compared to the 5:1 ratio of the Muslim world; Watson, 'Back', pp. 23–5 and 27.

95 This well-accepted narrative around the 'back to gold' event needs clarifications, if not an entirely new study that cannot be developed here. Some reservations also appeared in David Abulafia, 'Maometto e Carlomagno'; Harry A. Miskimin, 'The Enforcement of Gresham's Law', in A. Vannini Marx (ed.), *Credito, banche e investimenti, secoli XIII–XX. Atti della quarta Settimana di studio (Prato, 14–21 aprile 1972), Istituto Internazionale di Storia Economica 'F. Datini'* (Florence: Felice le Monnier, 1985), pp. 147–161, reprinted in Harry A. Miskimin, *Cash, Credit and Crisis in Europe, 1300–1600* (London: Variorum, 1989), chapter 9; Harry A. Miskimin, 'Money and Movements in France and England at the End of the Middle Ages', in J. F. Richards (ed.), *Precious Metals*, pp. 79–96 (especially p. 83); Jacques Le Goff, *Money and the Middle Ages: An Essay in Historical Anthropology* (Cambridge: Polity Press, 2012); Wickham, *The Donkey*, p. 624.

96 Miskimin, 'Gresham's Law', pp. 155–6.

97 In Tunisia, this occurred at the end of the century, while in Spain
   and North Africa, not until the year 1164; Watson, 'Back', p. 3. Yet,
   David Abulafia has pointed out that some silver remained in circulation since there are traces of it in gold coins of the period, such as the
   Sicilian gold taris; Abulafia, 'Maometto e Carlomagno', p. 253.
98 Ashtor, *Les métaux précieux*, chapter 2.
99 Watson, 'Back', pp. 5–6. In Iraq, Egypt, North Africa, and Spain, this
   did not happen until 1229–30.
100 Ashtor, *Les métaux précieux*, pp. 32–3. Archival sources from Venice
   and Genoa, for example, show that in the late twelfth century, silver
   bars were being exported east; Abulafia, 'Maometto e Carlomagno',
   p. 233.
101 Spufford, *Money*, p. 175. On *miliarenses*, see Baldassarri, 'Miliarenses
   and Silver Grossi'.
102 Miskimin, 'Gresham's Law', p. 155.
103 This could be one of the reasons for the possible delay in the minting
   of gold in western Europe; Watson, 'Back', p. 14.
104 Miskimin, 'Gresham's Law', p. 156. The author further argues that
   since gold was basically replacing silver in the European monetary
   system due to its scarcity, gold coins were not 'prestige coins' but a
   'coinage of last resort'. Yet, he does not seem to consider the political
   implications of minting gold, which will be illustrated below.
105 Spufford, *Money*, p. 169.
106 Ashtor, *Les métaux précieux*, p. 27; Simon Barton, 'Traitors to the
   Faith? Christian Mercenaries in al-Andalus and the Maghreb, *c.*
   1100–1300', in R. Collins and A. Goodman (eds), *Medieval Spain:
   Culture, Conflict, and Coexistence. Studies in Honour of Angus
   MacKay* (Basingstoke: Palgrave Macmillan, 2002), pp. 23–45.
107 Lopez, 'Back to Gold', pp. 234–5; Watson, 'Back', p. 21*ff.*; Walker,
   'Gold Revolution', p. 32.
108 For Genoa, see Lopez, 'Back to Gold', p. 234; for Florence, see Lopez,
   'Settecento', p. 50. On the other hand, Massimo Sbarbaro argued that
   1252 was not a favourable year to strike the new gold coins due to
   the high rate of inflation; Massimo Sbarbaro, 'Circolazione di idee e
   di esperienze economiche nell'Italia del Duecento. La coniazione del
   ducato veneziano: scelta politica o economica?', in A. L. Trombetti
   Budriesi (ed.), *Cultura cittadina e documentazione. Formazione e circolazione di modelli. Bologna, 12–13 ottobre 2006* (Bologna: Clueb,
   2009), pp. 59–72 (at p. 71). This reinforces the central role played by
   political factors.
109 Spufford, *Handbook*, pp. l–liii.
110 Watson, 'Back', pp. 22–4; Miskimin, 'Money', p. 85.

111 Lopez, 'Back to Gold', p. 234

112 Further details are provided in Chapter 2.

113 Cesare Imperiale di Sant'Angelo, *Codice Diplomatico della Repubblica di Genova dal DCCCCLVIII al MCLXIII*, vol. 1 (Rome: Tipografia del Senato, 1936), p. 254, no. 202.

114 *MEC* 12, pp. 255 and 258.

115 Gustave L. Schlumberger, *Numismatique de l'Orient latin* (Paris: Ernest Leroux, 1878), pp. 275–6; Stahl, 'Coinage and Money', p. 203.

116 Erica Salvatori, *Boni amici et vicini: le relazioni tra Pisa e le città della Francia meridionale dall'XI alla fine del XIII secolo* (Pisa: Edizioni ETS, 2002), p. 114.

117 Concioni, 'Le coniazioni', p. 71.

118 Bompaire and Bernard, 'Le retour', p. 1393. It also seems that counterfeit Saracen bezants were minted in the West to be exported to the Levant; Watson, 'Back', p. 14.

119 Goldthwaite, *Renaissance Florence*, p. 23. The key works on which this section is based also include *Storia* VI; Louis Green, 'Florence', in D. Abulafia (ed.), *The New Cambridge Medieval History Vol. 5: c. 1198–c. 1300* (Cambridge: Cambridge University Press, 1999), pp. 479–96; William R. Day Jr., *The Early Development of the Florentine Economy, c. 1100–1275* (PhD dissertation, London School of Economics, 2000); William R. Day Jr., 'Population Growth and Productivity: Rural–Urban Migration and the Expansion of the Manufacturing Sector in Thirteenth-Century Florence', in B. Blondé, E. Vanhaute, and M. Galand (eds), *Labour and Labour Markets between Town and Countryside (Middle Ages–19th Century)* (Turnhout: Brepols, 2001), pp. 82–110; William R. Day Jr., 'Economy', in Z. Baranski and L. Pertile (eds), *Dante in Context* (Cambridge: Cambridge University Press, 2015), pp. 30–46; Enrico Faini, *Firenze nell'età romanica (1000–1211). L'espansione urbana, lo sviluppo istituzionale, il rapporto con il territorio* (Florence: L. S. Olschki, 2010); Faini, 'Prima del fiorino'; Tognetti, 'Il Mezzogiorno'.

120 Tognetti, 'Il Mezzogiorno', p. 149; Karen Rose Mathews, Silvia Orvietani Bush, and Stefano Bruni (eds), *A Companion to Medieval Pisa* (Leiden and Boston: Brill, 2022).

121 Goldthwaite, *Renaissance Florence*, pp. 19–20.

122 Tognetti, 'Il Mezzogiorno', p. 149; Goldthwaite, *Renaissance Florence*, pp. 20–1. On the relations between Tuscan merchant bankers and the popes, see Chapter 4.

123 A precise analysis of this significant demographic growth appears in William R. Day Jr., 'The Population of Florence before the Black

Death: Survey and Synthesis', *JMH* 28 (2002), 93–129. See also Franek Sznura, *L'espansione urbana di Firenze nel Dugento* (Florence: La Nuova Italia, 1975).

124 Enrico Faini studied the effects of this phenomenon in Faini, *Firenze*. Elio Conti hypothesised that it was generated by the hardening of the policy of rural lordship within the Florentine *contado*; Elio Conti, *La formazione della struttura agraria moderna nel contado fiorentino. I: Le campagne nell'età precomunale* (Rome: Istituto Storico Italiano per il Medio Evo, 1965).

125 Johan Plesner, *L'emigrazione dalla campagna alla città libera di Firenze nel XIII secolo* (Monte Oriolo: F. Papafava, 1979).

126 Day, 'Population Growth', pp. 89–91; Faini, *Firenze*, p. 163.

127 Day, 'Population Growth', p. 105; Goldthwaite, *Renaissance Florence*, p. 269, Faini, *Firenze*, pp. 118–25.

128 Faini, *Firenze*, pp. 122–4.

129 Alma Poloni, 'Firenze prima di Firenze: Poloni legge Faini', *Storica* 51 (2011), 121–37 (at p. 123). George Dameron argues that due to the silence of the sources, any attempt to anticipate the development of the textile industry before the last quarter of the twelfth century would result in 'mere conjecture'; George Dameron, Review of *Firenze nell'età romanica (1000–1211). L'espansione urbana, lo sviluppo istituzionale, il rapporto con il territorio* by Enrico Faini, *Speculum*, 88:1 (2013), 288–9.

130 *Documenti*, p. 365, no. 3.

131 *Storia* VI, pp. 136–7; Day, 'Population Growth', p. 95, note 28.

132 Pietro Santini, *Studi sull'antica costituzione del comune di Firenze: la città e le classi sociali in Firenze nel periodo che precede il primo popolo* (Rome: Multigrafica, 1972), pp. 64–7; Green, 'Florence', p. 483.

133 *Documenti*, p. 376, no. 12; Day, 'Population Growth', p. 95, note 28.

134 For the earliest reference to the *Arte di Por Santa Maria*, see *Documenti*, p. 190, no. 66; for the *Arte del Cambio*, see Green, 'Florence', p. 483.

135 More details on these treaties can be found in Ignazio Del Punta, *Guerrieri, Crociati, Mercanti. I Toscani in Levante in età pieno-medievale (secoli XI–XIII)* (Spoleto: Fondazione centro italiano di studi sull'alto Medioevo, 2010), pp. 148–9 and note 378.

136 *Documenti*, p. 5, no. 4.

137 Del Punta, *Guerrieri*, pp. 149–50; Faini, *Firenze*, pp. 118–24; David Abulafia, 'Crocuses and Crusaders: San Gimignano, Pisa and the Kingdom of Jerusalem', in B. Z. Kedar, H. E. Mayer, and R. C. Smail (eds), *Outremer: Studies in the History of the Crusading Kingdom of Jerusalem Presented to Joshua Prawer* (Jerusalem: Yad Izhak Ben-Zvi

Institute, 1982), pp. 227–43, reprinted in David Abulafia, *Italy, Sicily and the Mediterranean 1100–1400* (London: Variorum, 1987), chapter 14 (at p. 234*ff*.).

138 Del Punta, *Guerrieri*, pp. 151–7; Day, 'Population Growth', pp. 99–100.

139 Day, 'Population Growth', p. 100, note 39.

140 *Documenti*, p. 190, no. 66. On the Florentine fur trade, see also *Storia* VI, pp. 482–3.

141 Hidetoshi Hoshino, *L'arte della lana in Firenze nel Basso Medioevo: il commercio della lana e il mercato dei panni fiorentini nei secoli XIII–XV* (Florence: L. S. Olschki, 1980), p. 66.

142 *Ibid.*, p. 97.

143 *Storia* VI, p. 141.

144 Raimondo Morozzo della Rocca and Attilio Lombardo, *Documenti del commercio veneziano nei secoli XI–XIII*, 2 vols (Rome: Regio Istituto Storico Italiano per il Medio Evo, 1940), vol. I, p. 212, no. 215. I will return to this in Chapter 2.

145 *Storia* I, p. 1177; Abulafia, *Two Italies*, p. 261.

146 Further details can be found in Adolf Schaube, *Storia del commercio dei popoli latini del Mediterraneo sino alla fine delle Crociate* (Turin: Unione tipografico-editrice torinese, 1915). A few of these cases will be discussed in the next chapter.

147 Goldthwaite, *Renaissance Florence*, p. 31.

148 Giuliano Pinto, *Il libro del biadaiolo: carestie e annona a Firenze dalla metà del '200 al 1348* (Florence: L. S. Olschki, 1978), p. 73.

149 Day, *The Early Development*, p. 43.

150 The *Ruga Florentinorum* may have originated in Messina in the context of the existing grain trade between Florence and the Sicilian city in 1193, but documentary sources are silent in this regard.

151 Day, 'Population Growth', p. 101.

152 Edwin S. Hunt, *The Medieval Super-companies* (Cambridge: Cambridge University Press, 1994), p. 48. Hunt based his work on Abulafia, 'Southern Italy'.

153 William R. Day Jr., Chiara Peroni, and Franca M. Vanni, 'Firenze (Toscana)', in L. Travaini (ed.), *Le zecche italiane fino all'Unità* (Rome: Istituto Poligrafico e Zecca dello Stato, 2011), pp. 667–702.

154 The mint of Lucca only interrupted its production between the reigns of Louis the Pious (814–40) and Hugh of Provence (926–47); Baldassarri, *Le monete di Lucca*, pp. 45–6.

155 Monica Baldassarri, 'Zecche e monete nella Toscana bassomedievale tra passate e recenti ricerche', in M. Baldassarri (ed.), *Massa di*

Maremma e la Toscana nel basso Medioevo: zecche, monete ed econo-mia (Florence: All'Insegna del Giglio, 2019); pp. 19–36. For further details on the coins issued by these mints and their chronology, see the Appendix. The mint of Montieri, which will be discussed in the next chapter, was just another location for the mint of Volterra in the thirteenth century, as was Cortona for Arezzo in the same period. On Volterra and Arezzo, see Magdi A. M. Nassar, *Le monete di Volterra. Vol. II: Il Medioevo e l'Età Moderna* (Pavia: Edizioni Numismatica Varesi, 2021); Magdi A. M. Nassar, *Le monete di Arezzo* (Leipzig: NumismaticaMente, 2018).

156 For a general overview of the history of each of these mints, see Lucia Travaini (ed.), *Le zecche italiane fino all'Unità* (Rome: Istituto Poligrafico e Zecca dello Stato, 2011), although some entries (especially 'Arezzo') have now been superseded by more recent studies.

157 Faini, 'Prima del fiorino', p. 90.

158 Day, 'Before the *Libro della Zecca* I', p. 459.

159 Lopez, 'Settecento', p. 167.

160 Marco Tangheroni, *Commercio e navigazione nel medioevo* (Rome: Laterza, 1996), p. 338; Baldassarri, *Zecca*, p. 115.

161 The following analysis mainly draws from *Storia* II, chapters 5 and 6; Daniela De Rosa, *Alle origini della Repubblica fiorentina: dai con-soli al 'primo popolo' (1172–1260)* (Florence: Arnaud, 1995); Green, 'Florence'; Silvia Diacciati, *Popolani e magnati: società e politica nella Firenze del Duecento* (Spoleto: Fondazione centro italiano di studi sull'alto Medioevo, 2010).

162 Green, 'Florence', p. 480; De Rosa, *Origini*, p. 43. According to Enrico Faini, the murder in 1216 of Buondelmonte dei Buondelmonti, which, as per Villani, would initiate the internal clash between the Guelph and Ghibelline parties, was instead the result of the existing rivalry between aristocratic families for the control of the city; Enrico Faini, 'Il convito del 1216. La vendetta all'origine del fazionalismo fiorentino', *Annali di Storia di Firenze* 1 (2006), 9–36.

163 *Storia* II, pp. 108–11.

164 Green, 'Florence', p. 481; for a correct understanding of the two par-ties, see Duccio Balestracci, *La battaglia di Montaperti* (Bari: Laterza, 2017).

165 *Storia* II, pp. 441–2 and 460–5. Their discontent was also due to Frederick's heavy-handed rule and the contemporary overexploi-tation of the financial resources of Florence to sustain the costs of Frederick II's military campaign against the Italian communes; De Rosa, *Origini*, p. 138.

166 *Storia* II, pp. 503–9; De Rosa, *Origini*, p. 139.

167 The end of this period coincided with the election of Rudolph of Habsburg as *Rex Romanorum* on 29 September 1273; Michael Toch, 'Welfs, Hohenstaufen and Habsburgs', in D. Abulafia (ed.), *The New Cambridge Medieval History Vol. 5: c. 1198–c. 1300* (Cambridge: Cambridge University Press, 1999), pp. 375–404.

168 '*ad faciendum guerram vivam ad sanguinem et ad ignem Pisanis et hominibus districtus ipsorum per mare et per terram*' (Author's translation: 'in order to make a living war thorough blood and fire to the Pisans and the people of their district by sea and by land'); Sabina Dellacasa (ed.), *I libri iurium della Repubblica di Genova, Vol. I/4* (Genoa: Società Ligure di Storia Patria, 1998), p. 360, no. 763.

169 Despite this being a new experience, members of the *Popolo* appear in the sources as early as 1244–5; De Rosa, *Origini*, p. 140.

170 For a clear and detailed account see Diacciati, *Popolani*, pp. 105–208, especially p. 169*ff*. On the relationship between the new *Popolo* and the old nobility, see Peter Coss, *The Aristocracy in England and Tuscany* (Oxford: Oxford University Press, 2020).

171 Diacciati, *Popolani*, pp. 183–92; De Rosa, *Origini*, p. 139.

172 *Storia* II, pp. 295–6.

173 Lopez, 'Back to Gold', p. 237; Walker, 'Gold Revolution', p. 51.

174 *MEC* 14, pp. 172–7; Kowalski, 'Die Augustalen'.

175 Among prominent studies on Bartolus' thought, see Julius Kirshner, 'Civitas Sibi Faciat Civem: Bartolus of Sassoferrato's Doctrine on the Making of a Citizen', *Speculum* 48:4 (Oct. 1973), 694–713; Magnus Ryan, 'Bartolus of Sassoferrato and Free Cities', *Transaction of the Royal Historical Society* 10 (2000), 65–89.

176 For a possible explanation of the lack of success of the Genoese and Lucchese gold coins compared to the florin, see Lopez, 'Settecento', pp. 168–98 (for Genoa); Blomquist, 'The Second Issuance', pp. 320–2 (for Lucca).

2

The florin and the merchants

The Florentine merchants' role in the florin's origins has always seemed clear. According to the fourteenth-century chronicler Giovanni Villani, the merchants asked the commune to introduce the new coin in 1252 and secured the necessary supply of gold for its minting. Villani's account has found a broad consensus among historians, and his assessment still underpins our current understanding of the florin, traditionally presented as money associated with the mercantile class of Florence.[1] Although convincing at first glance, Villani remains silent on several aspects, ranging from the actual provision of the gold, its origins, and its transportation to Florence to the practical ways in which members of the Florentine mercantile class helped their city introduce the new gold coin and turned it into an international currency.

In recent decades, much has been written on the merchants of Florence and their activities in the late Middle Ages. Throughout the thirteenth century, they were active not only in long-distance trade but also as money lenders and financial agents for rulers and clergymen.[2] It remains to be seen, however, to what extent these merchants, with their activities in and knowledge of economic and monetary policy, were instrumental in the minting and diffusing the florin.

While we know that two mint-masters – one belonging to the *Arte di Calimala* and the other to the *Arte del Cambio* – were elected approximately every six months or semester (thus twice a year) to oversee all phases of minting from the arrival of the precious metals at the Florentine mint to the issue of the finished gold, silver, and billon coins, we still lack a complete picture of their participation in the various stages of the early life of the florin, from the forming of the project of a gold coin, via the provision of gold, to its early circulation.[3]

Through the study of the Florentine mercantile class, its network, and its movements, this chapter argues that the city of Florence was able to turn the project of a new gold coin into practice primarily thanks to the multifaceted contribution of its merchants. Crucially, this was not so much due to the merchants asking for the florin (as Villani wrote) as the merchants making its production possible through their familiarity with gold and its supply and their *know-how* and *capacity* to (i) run the Florentine mint and strike innovative coins, (ii) control actual monetary production of Florence, (iii) administer the monetary policy of the Florentine government, (iv) provide a network for the early circulation of the florin, and (v) decide on the iconography of the coinage. By linking the scattered records of Florentine merchant bankers and their business in Italy, Europe, and the Mediterranean between the late twelfth and the first half of the thirteenth century, this chapter provides an in-depth understanding of the dynamics that turned the florin into the emblem of the commercial and financial activities of the Florentine mercantile class – one which also functioned as a political actor at the time of the *Primo Popolo*.

The chapter opens with a brief analysis of the chronicles of Paolino Pieri and Giovanni Villani, discusses their reliability as historical sources for the early life of the florin, and clarifies the objectives of the analysis. It then deals with the gold supply of the city of Florence and the contribution of the Florentine mercantile class. In so doing, it investigates the familiarity of the Florentines with the yellow metal while taking into account several potential routes and markets for gold supply. After this, it outlines the primary skills and practical knowledge of the Florentine merchants, including their numeracy and understanding of the monetary market and its needs, as well as their ability to run a mint. As illustrated in the last section of this chapter, the introduction of the florin and its early diffusion would not have been possible without the crucial *capacity* of these merchants, by which I mean their authority as political actors to decide the monetary policy of the city of Florence, and likely the iconography of the florin, while providing networks for its early diffusion.

The florin in the chronicles of Paolino Pieri
and Giovanni Villani

Written in the first and third decades of the fourteenth century, respectively, and thus roughly seventy years after the florin was introduced, the chronicles of Paolino Pieri (*c.* 1270–*c.* 1340) and Giovanni Villani (1275/80–1348) form the earliest narrative evidence of the origin of the Florentine gold coin.[4] Little is known about Paolino Pieri and his life, but he was likely born in Florence around the 1270s. He started to write his chronicle, which stretches from 1080 to 1305, in 1302.[5] With regard to the birth of the florin, he offers only a meagre account of that event:

> On 1 January 1252, Mr Filippo degli Ugoni of Parma of Lombardy was appointed Podesta [...] During this time, the Florentines minted the gold florin, which had never been issued before, except for petty and silver coins [the latter] worth 12 deniers each. It was then that the gold florin worth 20 shillings began to circulate, and hardly anyone wanted it.[6]

Pieri's narration lacks any practical detail regarding the historical or political context of the time or how the city of Florence decided to strike the florin. He simply relates that the florin was minted in 1252 under the *Podestà*-ship of Filippo degli Ugoni of Brescia, erroneously ascribed to the city of Parma. Nothing is said about the agents who promoted its minting or the provenance of the precious metal.[7] In contrast, the Florentine merchant, diplomat, and chronicler Giovanni Villani offers additional, but still limited, information:

> The host of the Florentines having returned and being at rest after the victories aforesaid, the city grew much in power, wealth, and authority and was at peace: therefore, the merchants of Florence, to honour the commune, arranged with the commune and the people for gold coins to be minted in Florence; and they promised to furnish the gold, whereas before only silver coins had been minted worth 12 *denari* each. And then began the good gold coins, 24 carats fine, which were called gold florins, and each was worth 20 solidi; and this was in the time of the said Mr Filippo degli Ugoni of Brescia, in the month of November, the year of Christ 1252. The said florins weighed eight to the ounce; on one side was the figure of the lily, and on the other was St John.[8]

Born in Florence between 1275 and 1280, the young Villani worked as a travelling merchant and banker in association with the Florentine companies of Peruzzi and Buonaccorsi until his early thirties. In 1308, he established himself in his native city, where he took an active role in public life, first as one of the two masters of the local mint in December 1316 (and again in November 1327) and later as one of the city priors, i.e., the highest office in Florence, appointed at the end of the same year (and again in 1321–22 and 1328).[9] His *Nuova Cronica* is a long account of the history of Florence, running from the creation of the Tower of Babel to the mid-fourteenth century. In the fifty-third chapter of its seventh book, Villani sets out a clear timeframe for the first minting of the florin, which he says occurred in November 1252.[10] He contextualises the event in a series of favourable circumstances, such as new levels of wealth and prosperity and a stronger political dominance of Florence resulting from contemporary military successes. Villani also emphasises the agency of the merchants, both as instigators and gold suppliers, thus establishing a strong link between the new coin and the Florentine mercantile class of which he was a distinguished member.

However, the very nature of Villani's work and the quality of the information provided warn against relying too much on his text as a historical source. Of course, chronicles normally set selected events in an interpretative context, excluding those episodes not relevant to the purposes of the narration.[11] Chronicles are creations of their authors, based on a communitarian background and sometimes filled with 'novella-type anecdotes' or personal comments on the period.[12] According to Peter Spufford, both Villani and Pieri might have written what they wanted to have occurred in 1252, not what actually happened.[13]

A recent study by Duccio Balestracci seems to support Spufford's claim. When analysing the Florentine military ventures of the 1250s, Balestracci noted important disparities between the accounts provided by Villani and the anonymous author of a fourteenth-century Sienese chronicle.[14] In his work, Villani claims that the years 1251–52 were a period rich in military successes for the city of Florence. At that time, the Florentine army prevailed over the Pisans and the Sienese on several occasions, including at the battles of Pontedera and Montaione. For his part, the anonymous author from Siena tells us exactly the opposite by relaying that the Florentines were heavily defeated on both occasions.

Regardless of which of the two accounts is true, the conflicting views of their authors, both writing about the same historical events and in the same years, prove that caution must be exercised when drawing information from chronicles. Other factors, such as political propaganda, may have taken precedence over facts, which may also be true of the history of the florin and its birth. Obviously, neither Giovanni Villani nor Paolino Pieri was an eyewitness to the striking of the gold coin or its early diffusion. They wrote their chronicles when the florin was already a fully established international currency. For events before their time, they admit they drew on earlier writings, which have since been lost.[15] The lack of official records from the Florentine commune does not help solve the problem. Moreover, as underlined by Sergio Tognetti, Villani's narrative only becomes more accurate after 1266, when Charles of Anjou appears in his chronicle. This was a consequence of Villani's proximity to the historical events narrated or perhaps the result of a feeling, shared by his fellow citizens and the ruling class of merchants and bankers to which he belonged, that a new Florence was being created.[16] This casts further doubts on Villani's accuracy, especially for events prior to 1266, which, of course, include the origin of the florin. All these elements and the lack of clear economic and financial figures (as discussed in Chapter 1) call into question the year 1252 as the starting point for the introduction of the florin. To date, the earliest reliable written sources confirming that Florentine gold florins were being minted and in circulation are those illustrated at the opening of this book, namely the records relating to Parma, Lucca, and Florence dated to the years 1258–59.

Villani's reconstruction also lacks clarity regarding several other important elements: for instance, he does not seem to differentiate between merchants of different sorts and different trading interests. He does not tell us through what channels they provided gold to the mint or the main activities that allowed them to collect the yellow metal. Were they merely suppliers of gold, or did they act in different roles in the early life of the florin? If so, what roles and what involvement – if any – did they have in the minting of the coin and its early circulation? Why did Florentine merchants promote the florin? These are crucial questions that still need to be adequately addressed.

Peter Spufford argued that the florin was introduced in the interests of the clothiers of the *Arte della Lana*, who used to subcontract imported raw wool to master weavers, fullers, stretchers, and so on to be processed in the Florentine countryside. A gold florin – Spufford claimed – 'was a useful unit to pay for the weaving of a single roll of cloth', as many of these subcontractors would be paid by the piece. Owing to this alleged role of the florin in the urban economy of Florence, Spufford went so far as to state that the coin was 'originally designed for internal use in the Florentine state, not for international purposes'.[17] Yet, there is no documentary evidence that provides a clear picture of the Florentine woollen industry and its costs in the mid-thirteenth century.[18] Further, Spufford's thesis does not consider two important aspects: first, throughout the second half of the thirteenth century, the value of the florin was very unstable in the local market, as its price rose continuously, shifting from Florentine s. 20 in 1252 to s. 25 in 1260, s. 29 in 1271, and s. 40 in 1294.[19] Even if the alleged ratio of one gold florin for one single roll of cloth existed, those changes would make it difficult to believe that such a ratio was maintained over time and became the primary cause of the florin's wider circulation and success. Second, gold had little practical use in day-to-day activities or within the local market, its price being so much higher than any of the practical necessities of life. In other words, the gold florin would be an inadequate means of payment for any purchase in Florence, which was normally carried out with local petty coinage. The histogram in Figure 2.1 shows how frequently gold florins, both as actual coins or money of account, occur within the *Diplomatico* collection of the State Archive of Florence, consisting of all the records and notarial acts involving the private business of Florentines, and Tuscans in general, for the period 1252–94. The documentation available for these years is particularly rich (*c.* 10,600 documents), although we cannot say the same for those sources mentioning gold florins.[20]

As illustrated, references to gold florins appear first in the mid-1260s and then almost disappear until they become more regular and increase consistently from the late 1270s, in line with an increasing overall number of records available per year.[21] Prior to this, only a very small number of documents mention gold florins, and those few do not explicitly refer to Florentine textile production and its local market. The earliest reliable reference in this

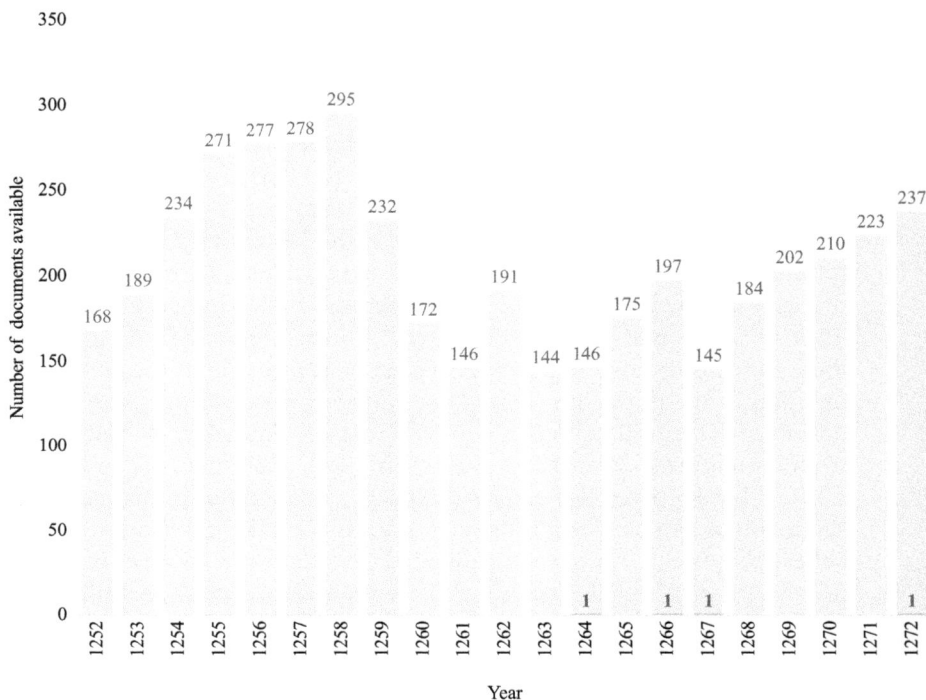

Figure 2.1 Gold florins in the *Diplomatico* collection of the State Archives of Florence, 1252–94 (10,582 parchments consulted). The light-grey bars indicate the number of documents available per year, the dark-grey bars specify the quantity of sources mentioning gold florins per year. Dates have been left as they are written in the originals.

collection, for example, mentions a loan of one florin 'of good and pure gold and of the right weight of Florence' (*'boni et puri auri et recte pondus florentino'*) and s. 31 of *floreni parvi* that a certain Ricordo Cardinale received from Ugolino Buoni with the promise to repay him within the next six months.[22] The lack of detail prevents us from knowing how that sum was spent.

Indeed, data in Figure 2.1 cannot be taken at face value as direct evidence of the increased use of florins from 1279 onwards. Many other factors, such as the incidental survival or disappearance of

354   357
336   336   347 344
329

293   285   292   291
280   275 281   274
264 271 263

226

206

184 178

	4	2	1	4	2	6	12	13	6	9	11	18	15	19	13	14	17	26	21	24	28
	1273	1274	1275	1276	1277	1278	1279	1280	1281	1282	1283	1284	1285	1286	1287	1288	1289	1290	1291	1292	1293	1294

Year

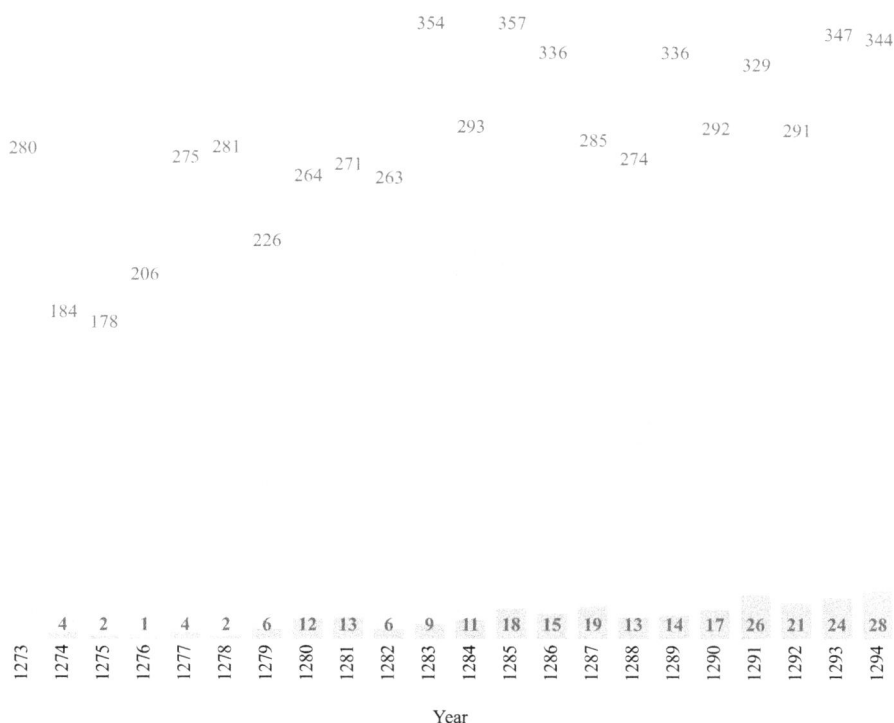

the written sources or the history of the collection, could have affected the total number of records available today. Thus, the question remains as to what extent this data can be considered representative of the circulation of the florin (or its absence) in those years.

In this regard, it is noteworthy that Pieri, contrary to Spufford's hypothesis, recorded that the Florentines were initially reluctant to adopt the florin for their own local business.[23] To some extent, Pieri was right: as this chapter will show, after its minting, the florin was mainly used, and therefore requested, outside Florence, and this almost at once. This means one must look beyond the Florentine city walls and focus on the Florentine merchants' activities to evaluate the mercantile class's contribution to the florin's birth and early life, starting with the contemporary gold supply.

Florentine merchants and gold supply:
a Euro-Mediterranean story

The minting of coins in the Middle Ages depended on the supply of precious metal brought to the mint, whether in bullion, goldware, silverware, or old coins. If the authority running the mint controlled its own mines, it was relatively easy to provide a constant supply and turn the metal into coins. Otherwise, the mint had to rely on imported metal, normally provided by private individuals, usually merchant bankers, but also goldsmiths and moneychangers. No metal would flow to any mint unless an acceptable mint price was offered for it. This corresponded to the number of new coins returned to the 'customers', which was normally lower than the number of coins actually struck. Part of what was withheld was sent as profit or fee to the authority controlling the mint and was known as *seigniorage*; the rest was called *brassage* and was used to cover the costs of coining.[24]

Tuscany had always been an important mining region since the Etruscan period, and gold was among the minerals present in the mining district known as Colline Metallifere, stretching from Campiglia (Livorno) to Massa Marittima (Grosseto). Yet, since its volume was not significant enough to guarantee profitable extraction and thus a constant supply, gold was never mined there.[25] In addition, the thirteenth-century Florentine commune does not seem to have had direct control over this area, the jurisdiction of which was traditionally disputed between the bishops of Volterra and the city of Siena.[26] Thus, Florence and its mint were obliged to base the production of the florin on imported gold.

Unfortunately, the lack of mint registers for the relevant years does not permit us to study the policy and incentives employed to attract the merchants and their reserves of precious metal to the Florentine mint in the thirteenth century.[27] Perhaps more surprisingly, virtually no gold appears in contemporary archaeological findings and written evidence from Florence. To date, only one gold coin hoard of five Fatimid dinars, dating between 972 and 1073, has been discovered in Piazza della Signoria, in the heart of the city.[28] The uniqueness of this find and its early chronology do not allow us to draw any substantial conclusions regarding the extent to which gold circulated in the city before the 1250s.[29] The same applies to the archival documentation of Florence between the late twelfth and first half of the thirteenth centuries, except for a single piece of evidence illustrated below. However, gold was clearly present in northern and central Italy and was recorded in the notarial registers of Pisa, Lucca, and Siena, the other major Tuscan cities of the time.[30] Whether and in what quantities gold was circulating in Florence and, specifically, how the Florentine merchants came into possession of this metal is not yet clear. If, as Villani wrote, they took care of the provision of gold for the local mint, they must have obtained it from somewhere.

The following analysis aims to describe the dynamics of this supply and the possible routes gold took to reach Florence. The paucity of written sources and the above-mentioned Florentine practice of posing as 'pseudo-Pisans' in the Mediterranean ports to escape the customs duties levied on non-privileged Latin merchants make our investigation more difficult. Yet, the merchants of Florence are not impossible to identify. Although poor in quantitative terms, from a qualitative perspective, the following archival sources suggest that Florentines were dealing with gold and gold coins well before the mid-thirteenth century via both commercial and financial activities and were thus collecting the precious metal.

The earliest reference to a Florentine dealing with gold in the form of foreign gold coins dates back to the second half of the twelfth century and concerns the Mediterranean business of the previously mentioned Ugolino the Florentine.[31] In October 1169, Ugolino appeared in Armiro, a port city north of Tsimova (Areopoli), on the north-west coast of the peninsula of Mani (Peloponnese), contracting a particular form of sea loan known as a *cambium maritimum* with the Venetian Giovanni Sergi. This consisted of an exchange transaction between a stationary partner (*socius stans*) and a travelling agent (*tractator*) that would trade overseas. The former would lend a given amount of capital to the latter, who would normally repay an agent of the stationary partner in another port and often in a different currency from the one he had initially received – typically what was circulating at that destination. This contract, which relied on a network of representatives in foreign cities, would normally apply to a one-way trip.[32]

Acting as travelling partner, Ugolino received from Giovanni the sum of five gold Byzantine *perperi* of the new weight ('*perpero auri paleos kenurgios pesantes*') before sailing on the ship of a certain Pietro Scivamendigo to trade along the maritime route to Constantinople. Ugolino promised to return the sum of six gold *perperi* of the old weight ('*perperos auri veteres pesantes sex*'), thus a different currency, to Martino Sergi, Giovanni's brother and his agent, within fifteen days of his arrival.[33] The difference between the two amounts presumably represented the interest for the creditor.

As this first source suggests, it was by means of long-distance trade that Ugolino could access a gold-standard area like the Mediterranean region and deal with gold, here in the form of foreign gold coins. The *cambium maritimum* gave him the opportunity to trade in the Mediterranean by exploiting a foreign port and dispose of ready cash to conduct his business in the Byzantine market. Since gold *perperi* represented the standard gold currency of the Byzantine world at that time, it is no surprise that the loan was contracted in that currency. It is also worth noting that these kinds of transactions occurred as early as the 1160s, a period for which we know very little about the trade relations of the city of Florence. Yet, whether such contracts were already a common practice among the Florentines trading overseas in those early years is, although likely, impossible to establish conclusively.[34] The few details we have about Ugolino do not even permit us to assess whether he contributed via his activities to either the economic development of Florence or the circulation of gold and gold coins in the Florentine territory. However, further documentary evidence from the late twelfth century provides new details in this regard.

On 26 February 1180, Pietro Zoppo of the village of San Donato in Poggio, in the vicinity of Florence, donated all his late father's estate, i.e., lands and other immovable properties, to Silimanno, priest of the rural church (*pieve*) of San Pietro in Poggio for the sake of his (Pietro's) soul ('*pro amore Dei et remedio anime sue*'). These donations, offered by laymen to religious institutions, were quite common at the time: usually enacted on their deathbeds, the donors believed that a gesture of this kind would deliver them from their sinful attachment to material existence and help them embrace the spiritual life. To validate the donation, it was customary that the recipient paid a token fee to the donor, typically money or an article of clothing, which was called *launechild* in the Lombardic Law of the time.[35] In this case, Pietro received some leather from

Silimanno, which is expressly said to be worth '*quatuor bisantes*' or four bezants.[36]

As seen, the term 'bezant' originally meant the Byzantine gold *solidi* or *nomismata*, replaced in 1092 by the *hyperpyra* or *perperi* of Emperor Alexius I Komnenos. According to Marc Bompaire, however, in the medieval documentation, 'bezant' could also refer to gold coins more generally, including Arabic coins such as Almoravid gold dinars (*morabitinos*) and their Christian imitations, Almohad *doble* and gold dinars (*massamutini*), as well as Saracen bezants of the Kingdom of Jerusalem and Syria when specified.[37] Bezants could also stand for an extensively used unit of account at the (theoretical) value of the canonical dinar, which was popular among the Europeans, especially in the Levant and the Maghreb.[38]

The fact that bezants appear here in a random donation taking place in a village of the Florentine countryside as a unit of value for some leather is illuminating. Generally, the standard money of account for contracts redacted in Florence and its *contado* between 1171 and 1181 was the *denari* of Lucca and Pisa, and from the middle of 1181 onwards, it was the Pisan coinage alone.[39] Yet, the use of *bisantes*, preferred here to these other monies of account, suggests that there might have been people accustomed to reckoning in such foreign currency on a very local level. How widespread this practice was and whether it reflects a significant circulation of foreign gold coins in the Florentine territory cannot be proved on the basis of such a circumstantial piece of evidence, especially as almost nothing is known about the people involved in the affair.[40] Yet the idea that these coins were exchanged locally is tantalising.

Further cases of Florentines dealing with gold and gold coins are documented in the first half of the thirteenth century. The fragments of the oldest book of account available today, belonging to a Florentine company of merchant bankers operating at the trade fair of San Procolo near Bologna in 1211, show that Florentines also dealt with gold through banking and financial activities.[41] From the last decade of the twelfth century, Bologna was an important market for traders from all over northern and central Italy.[42] From the year 1196 on, two urban fairs took place on the river Reno, the major one being the fair of San Procolo in May. According to the surviving ledger, several merchants of Florence conducted their business there. Specifically, many of the eighty-one Florentines recorded were members of the same families that would lead the economy and politics of Florence in the following decades, including Tornaquinci, Cavalcanti, Albizzi, Giugni, and Bencivenni.[43] Among them, Buoninsegna Falconi and Alberto son of Ubertino are also noteworthy. This is what the fragments tell us about them:

> On the same day Buoninsegna [Falconi] is due to give s. 12 for one massamutino.

> ... Alberto son of Ubertino is due to give us s. 22 d. 4 for two massamutini.[44]

Buoninsegna and Alberto were two debtors expected to return the total amount of three gold *massamutini*, another name for the Almohad gold dinars in circulation in Christian Europe, as noted. Yet, virtually nothing is said about the purposes of these two loans. We know that in 1225, Buoninsegna became a member of the *Arte della Seta*, the Silk Guild of Florence, together with his son Arnolfo.[45] His involvement in the fairs of San Procolo could be related to that kind of business or to the cloth trade more generally. This is also suggested by another entry, where Buoninsegna was due to pay £2 s. 19 to the Florentine company on behalf of Tornaquinci, who reimbursed him with his cloth (*'k'ei pagò nei panni suoi'*).[46] The fact that in this specific case, Buoninsegna accepted a payment made in cloth from Tornaquinci and that he paid the Florentine company in turn with the money that the latter was due to give provides further evidence for his involvement in the contemporary textile trade. One could also speculate that the loan of one gold *massamutino* was related to this very sort of business.

Other foreign coins also appear in this source. For example, Banzara del Garbo was due to give £15 of 'new' *provisini* that had been loaned to Bartolo the spice seller, Apollonio Tribaldi was due to return s. 35 d. 6 of *deniers tournois*, and Attigliante exchanged £3 for English 'sterling' pennies and other coins.[47] Robert Davidsohn has considered the mention of these currencies and specifically of the *provisini*, originally the silver deniers of the counts of Champagne struck at the mint of Provins, as clear proof of the participation of the merchants of Florence at the Champagne Fairs, although he relied on a single piece of evidence for this argument.[48] However, further documentation confirms that it was precisely in these years that the Florentines began to import cloth from the Fairs (1215), and their presence intensified towards the middle of the thirteenth century, along with the scale of their commercial affairs and financial transactions.[49]

This growing involvement in the major commercial centres of northern Europe would have benefitted Florence and its gold supply. Gold was among the precious metals circulating at the Fairs, and its import and export are documented by detailed lists of custom duties from the thirteenth and early fourteenth centuries, also known as *tarifs de tonlieux*.[50] In 1265, gold coins such as Sicilian taris and *augustales* or *paiola* gold were exchanged there too.[51] Uncoined gold could also be employed as a means of payment in loans and financial transactions. In 1222, for example, certain merchants of Bologna were expected to receive at Provins the sum of 35 marks in gold rods 'of the weight of Cologne' as reimbursement for a loan to Engelbert of Berg, archbishop of Cologne (1185/6–1225).[52] Two years before, the same archbishop was in debt to Giovanni and Gherardo of Florence, who had lent him 120 marks.[53] Under threat of excommunication by Pope Honorius III (1216–27), Engelbert eventually returned the sum to the two Florentines, although the details of his repayment are unknown. As the transaction with the merchants of Bologna suggests, it is possible that Giovanni and Gherardo were paid in gold rods too.

At any rate, despite the lack of direct proof, the large body of indirect evidence attesting to the clear involvement of Florentine merchants at the Champagne Fairs suggests that by exploiting that market, not only did the Florentines contribute to the economic development of their city but also they acquired gold and imported it to Florence, possibly in exchange for spices and other luxuries from southern Europe and the Mediterranean.[54] The Fairs also promoted the Florentine gold supply by providing the necessary raw materials, such as wool or unfinished cloth, which were processed in Florence before being traded in the Mediterranean basin. The following episode suggests a close relationship between the Florentine cloth trade and the yellow metal in that region.

In a trial between two merchants that occurred in San Gimignano in 1224, Saraceno Grugnoli claimed back the sum of one gold bezant from a certain Gradalone for a loan that the former had given to Dando, Gradalone's son, when they were both in Acre.[55] Dando was a former crusader who fought at Damietta in the Fifth Crusade but found refuge in Acre after the crusaders' defeat. Once there, he ran out of money and began to beg in return for clothes, wandering half-naked in the streets of the city. To help him, Saraceno borrowed the sum of two and a half gold bezants (*'mei mutuaretis mihi II bisanzios et dimidium'*) from the merchants Bonincontro Bonincontri and Ristoro of San Gimignano and bought him a tunic or *'gonnella'* from the cloth shop (*apoteca*) of Rainerio the Florentine. Despite his efforts to avoid paying, Gradalone was sentenced to return the sum of one gold bezant to Saraceno for his son's debt.

The small quantities of cloth and gold recorded here and the sparse details regarding Rainerio's activities do not provide anything like a comprehensive picture of the actual scale of the Florentine cloth trade in that region or the gold supply that might have originated from that business.[56] Moreover, if we rely on just this source, it is impossible to say what kind of cloth and in what proportion the Florentines were trading in the East, thus allowing them to acquire gold with the related profit. The cloth could have been either northern European high-quality coloured textiles or cheaper varieties of Florentine cloths, which constituted a significant component of the long-distance and 'luxury' trade of the time.[57]

Nevertheless, this is an interesting document, as it shows that the Florentine presence in the Mediterranean region became increasingly organised in the early decades of the thirteenth century. Specifically, the merchants of Florence were not only conducting their business as 'pseudo-Pisans', exploiting the port of Pisa and its sea routes.[58] They also formed part of the community of Tuscan merchants from inland cities that resided with their goods in Pisan *fondacos*.[59] There, the Florentines submitted to the Pisan consul in charge so that they could enjoy the tax privileges and trade benefits (i.e., freedom from customs duties) normally granted to Pisan merchants in foreign trading centres. For the city of Pisa, the 'collaboration' with non-Pisans favoured the injection of new capital and expertise from specialist traders into its own business. For the city of Florence, the institutionalisation of its trade in Pisan *fondacos* provided its merchants with invaluable access to the Mediterranean, regulated and structured commerce, and cross-cultural interactions with the major trading centres overseas. In turn, this facilitated their economic affairs and eventually promoted the import of gold.[60] The extensive network of *fondacos* that Pisa had built since the mid-twelfth century – if not before – encompassing key centres such as Valencia and Denia (1150), Alexandria and Cairo (1154), Tunis (1157), Seville (1167), Tyre and Jaffa (1187), Béjaïa (late twelfth century), Messina (1232), Tripoli (1234), and Naples (1243), vividly illustrates the growing opportunities for the Florentines to engage with the Mediterranean gold trade while residing in those *fondacos*.

Further written evidence shows that, like Rainerio, other Florentines were running their business in the Mediterranean region. On 26 October 1225, Fiesco of Florence stipulated in Genoa a *commenda* contract with Aldana, widow of Bucuccio de Fossato, and Bonadonna, wife of Biagio Castagna, to trade in Tunis. Similar to the *cambium maritimum* mentioned above, the *commenda* consisted of a formal agreement between a stationary partner or investor (*commendator*) and a travelling agent (*tractator*) to trade overseas. The stationary partner would entrust the capital to the travelling agent, who would take it with him and trade abroad. At the end of the contract, the travelling agent would return to the city of departure and divide the profits with the investor. In the standard or 'unilateral' *commenda*, where the capital was supplied by the stationary partner only, that partner would receive three-quarters of the profit and would bear the risks of the loss of capital; the remaining one-quarter went to the travelling agent.[61] This was also the case of the Florentine Fiesco (travelling agent), who received from Aldana and Bonadonna (stationary partners) £25 and £11 s. 14 d. 8, respectively, to purchase products in Tunis, although nothing is said about the goods involved.[62] Tunis was also the commercial destination of a new mercantile company between the Florentine Lazario son of Bonagiunta Botto, Bonagiunta son of Rustichello Pistore de Laborante, Meliore son of Osilioto, and Bartolomeo Martini Arcolai of Lucca, which was created in Genoa on 21 June 1233.[63] In both cases, we cannot exclude that gold was among the goods traded: Tunis was one of the major port cities of the northern African coast that received Sudanese gold before it was shipped northwards to southern Europe.[64] The fact that the Florentines were trading there, possibly residing in the Pisan *fondaco*, could indicate that large quantities of gold for the future minting of the florin were coming from Tunis too. No wonder Villani set his anecdote on the early diffusion of the florin in that very city. This is what he wrote:

> The said new florins having begun to circulate through the world, they were carried to Tunis in Barbary; and being brought before the king of Tunis, who was a worthy and wise lord, they pleased him much, and he caused them to be tried; and finding them to be of fine gold, he much commended them, and having caused his interpreters to interpret the imprint and legend on the florin, he found that it said: St John the Baptist, and on the side of the lily, Florence. [...] He asked if there were among them [the Pisans] anyone from Florence, and there was found there a merchant from Oltrarno, by name Pera Balducci, discreet and wise. The king asked him of the state and condition of Florence, whom the Pisans called their Arabs [to denigrate them]; He [Pera] answered wisely, showing the power and magnificence of Florence, and how Pisa in comparison was neither in power nor in inhabitants the half of Florence, and that they had no golden money, and that the florin was the fruit of many victories gained by the Florentines over them.[65]

Despite Pera's disparaging comments with their strong political connotations, the city of Pisa and its port continued to play a crucial role in the provision of gold for Florence. On Friday, 18 September 1243, the Florentine Brocardo son of Ricovero acknowledged that he owed Maffeo d'Afflitto of Scala (near Amalfi) the sum of £465 in *denari* of Lucca or Pisa for 100 ounces of gold of the weight of Naples, which he promised to pay in a week in the city of Pisa. Maffeo was to give these gold ounces to either Brocardo, his heirs, or whoever would be indicated by Brocardo, within a month of his arrival in Naples. It was specified that each ounce was worth £4 s. 13, giving the indicated price of £465. As a pledge, Maffeo promised Brocardo he would give him everything he bought with the aforesaid money (or for a similar amount), plus extra money out of his own pocket equal to the fourth part of the sum received. The risks of the venture to Naples (shipwrecks, pirate attacks, and so on) were to be borne by Brocardo himself. Additionally, mutual guarantees were established: if Brocardo did not pay that money, he would be fined £10 in *denari* of Lucca or Pisa. The guarantor who would then pay for any other reason on his behalf was a certain Accetate, son of the late Stefano.[66] Instead, if Maffeo did not collect the said sum in gold and did not give it to Brocardo, or he refused to perform the pledge as established, he would pay £10 in *denari* of Lucca or Pisa. Magister Rocchisciano was appointed as his guarantor for any other payment for whatever reason. The act was signed in the tower of Passavante, where the notary Ser Ciabatto operated in the years 1227–61.[67]

At first glance, it is hard to say whether this document refers to the actual purchase of uncoined gold that the Florentine Brocardo supposedly bought from Maffeo. This is mainly due to the double meaning of the term 'ounces' in the Kingdom of Sicily. There, it could represent either a unit of weight for medieval goods, especially metals, or a unit of account in the local monetary system of ounces/taris/grains (o.t.gr.).[68] In the latter case, this source would be another example of a sea loan or *cambium maritimum*, in which the interest was possibly concealed within the value specified for each ounce or hidden in the penalties.

This vagueness of the term 'ounces' could apply to another document concerning the economic activities of another Florentine, a certain Soldano son of Guidone, operating in southern Italy. On 30 August 1238, in the city of Brindisi, Soldano paid 51½ gold ounces to Enrico Brodaiolo, a citizen of Lucca who had lent that sum to a certain Bartolomeo.[69] In this case, however, the fact that the source refers to a debt previously contracted by Enrico indicates that here, the term 'ounces' was used as a unit of account to express the sum due without any specification of the actual payment.[70] But for Brocardo and his business, there is evidence that raw gold was effectively being exchanged. The participation of a member of the d'Afflitto family is the first and most significant aspect to point in that direction.

The d'Afflitto were a rich and powerful Amalfitan family originally from the Pontone district of Scala (Amalfi Coast), who were prominent in the thirteenth-century economy and politics of the Kingdom of Sicily.[71] They were not simply merchants or bankers, as the source seems to suggest. Already under the Hohenstaufen, but mainly during the reign of King Charles I, several members of the family were either acting as royal officials involved in the minting of money, tax farming, and public administration or had prestigious ecclesiastical careers as bishops.[72] As regards minting in particular, we know that in 1266, Angelo and Costanzo d'Afflitto were the first mint-masters directly appointed by Charles to strike his new gold *reale*, half-*reale*, and taris in the cities of Barletta and Brindisi, respectively. Costanzo was appointed again at the mint of Brindisi in 1270, which was then administered by Orso in 1274, Bartolomeo in 1275, and Bernardo and Tommaso in 1280, all members of the d'Afflitto family. Orso was also the mint-master at Messina in 1278, where Stefano d'Afflitto had worked two years earlier as assayer, testing the fineness of the alloy of each parcel of bullion brought to the mint and of each new coin produced.[73] The importance of so many members of the d'Afflitto family in minting operations under Charles of Anjou, probably also due to their longstanding expertise in the market for precious metals, which formed the practical knowledge of a medieval mint-master, makes it very likely that Brocardo actually purchased raw gold from Maffeo d'Afflitto.

Further convincing evidence comes to light if we take a closer look at the writing style of the notary Ciabatto. Two elements in particular stand out: the first concerns the use of specific expressions in the guarantees established between Brocardo and Maffeo. Ciabatto employed terms such as '*et quod aurum*', '*pro predicto auro*', or '*pretium auri*' to refer to the object of the commercial transaction, i.e., gold, instead of '*pecunia*' or '*pecunia mutuate*', literally 'money' or 'money lent', which are usually more frequent in his loan contracts.[74]

The second and more compelling element relates to the specification regarding the monetary value of each ounce of gold, which is introduced by the Latin expression '*ad rationem*'. Ciabatto makes use of this construct in other acts within the same notarial register. On 2 March 1243, Bonviso of the late Banagiunta and Aldobrandino of the late Arrigo Martini were to pay a total amount of £97 s. 10 of *denari parvi* of Lucca to Uguiccione of the late Lanfranco Maghiario, for the purchase of 1½ *centenarium* or 150 pounds of wheat. In this case, too, Ciabatto adopted the formula '*ad rationem*' to indicate the price of each *centenarium*, which he said was worth £65 at that time.[75] The same applies to two other large purchases of wheat that took place later that year: the first involving the same actors but occurring on 24 April, when the *centenarium* was worth £61, and the second between a certain Lutterio and the same Uguiccione on 29 April.[76]

The employment of the construct '*ad rationem*' in all these examples is not coincidental: when analysed together, they show that Ciabatto made use of this formula when large purchases of products typically sold by weight were recorded in his register. But this is the same expression that also appears in the transaction between Brocardo and Maffeo, as noted. On this basis, and following Ciabatto's writing style, it is therefore safe to assume that those 100 'ounces' of the weight of Naples did not correspond to units of account in the local monetary system of the Kingdom of Sicily but rather to units of weight in connection with the considerable amount of uncoined gold that was sold and purchased on that occasion. This makes this document one of the rarest attestations – if not the first – of a gold purchase made by a Florentine, Brocardo, in one of the most important Tuscan cities of the time, Lucca, less than ten years before the minting of the gold florin. Unfortunately, the lack of further detail prevents us from knowing exactly how and where the metal was used. Yet, this is also an interesting source for the relationships it describes. While further corroborating the centrality of Pisa and its port for the Florentine business in the Mediterranean, it also highlights the key role of the Kingdom of Sicily in the contemporary gold supply.

As seen, Messina might have hosted a Florentine settlement as early as the final decades of the twelfth century (1187), cloth from Florence was already circulating there (1237), and Florentine moneychangers were active in the Italian south (1238). The opening of a Florentine *fondaco* at Naples in 1243 – the same year as the source discussed above – further emphasises the increased importance of the merchant bankers of Florence in the southern Italian commerce and of the Kingdom of Sicily for the economic development of the Tuscan city. From those territories, gold could reach Tuscany and possibly Florence via the port of Pisa, along with other goods, such as wheat, to support the demographic expansion of the Florentine city. Given the existence of this link between Florence, Pisa, and the Kingdom of Sicily, one can also speculate that, when Emperor Frederick II died in 1250 and the production of gold *augustales* in his name decreased or even stopped, it probably became more convenient to sell some of the gold in the kingdom to foreign merchants, including the Florentines. This is quite possible, especially considering that, with their *fondaco*, the Florentines were a constant presence in the kingdom by the early 1240s.

By the mid-thirteenth century, however, another port city in northern Italy played an important role in the provision of gold for the city of Florence: Genoa. A final piece of evidence seems to confirm that it was also from there that the merchant bankers of Florence could have obtained – or at least attempted to obtain – the necessary gold for the production of the florin. On 13 September 1251, Genoa and Florence signed a five-year agreement. Florentine merchants were given, among other things, full right to travel by sea or inland throughout the Genoese territory under the protection of the commune of Genoa.[77] This treaty, a consequence of the contemporary clash with the mutual rival Pisa, is presented as a series of arrangements ranging from customs duties to trade routes. One of these states that:

> As regards the money that the Florentines will buy in Genoa and its district for the purpose of trade – except that one (i.e., money) in exchange for gold, silver, money, or bullion – and that one (i.e., money) that they will transport by sea and will bring to Portovenere, they (the Florentines) will have to pay 8 *denari* of Genoa per *libra*, except that the Florentines could not export bullion from Genoa.[78]

This is a typical bullionist provision that Genoa included in the agreement to regulate the export of precious metals from its territory. According to the provision, the Florentines could export only minted gold, not *bolçonalie* and *boçonagiam*, two synonyms of 'bullion'. Their meaning is clearly defined in the famous mercantile notebook of the Florentine Francesco Balducci Pegolotti (1290–1347):

> *Buglione* or *bolzonaglia* means gold and silver plates or rods, or fragments of silver jars, or gold and silver coins no longer in circulation; and this is what *buglione* means, thus a broken thing to discard or melt; and *bolzonaglia* is used to refer to petty coins not in circulation in any place, where they are melted or discarded.[79]

The fact that the commune of Genoa needed to insert such a protectionist provision, specifically aimed at prohibiting the Florentines from taking possession of its raw gold, along with other precious metals, is interesting in two respects: not only does it suggest that episodes of this practice were quite common at the time, but it also seems to imply that, perhaps because of the frequency and economic damage those exports were causing, it was high time to put an end to them. In other words, the Genoese wanted to safeguard their gold reserves for the imminent striking of the *genovino* and prevent their yellow metal from disappearing to its future competitors' minting. This makes the hypothesis of a mutual agreement between Genoa and Florence to mint gold coins even more unlikely, especially considering that no documentary evidence in support of this view survives.[80] That said, the measure adopted by the Genoese commune constitutes a final but indirect piece of evidence for the contemporary gold supply of the city of Florence and perhaps the most significant, as it dates to only a year before the introduction of the gold florin.

Know-how: recording, accounting, mining, and minting

Once the precious metal was collected, the city of Florence also needed technical expertise and the opportunity to turn that metal into an innovative and competitive currency on the money market. No one outside the mercantile class could have accomplished this task as efficiently. Unlike other social groups, the merchant bankers had the essential *know-how* and *capacity* to help Florence introduce its new gold coin. This section deals with the main features of that *know-how*; *capacity* is discussed in the next.

In the Middle Ages, the profits of a mint depended, among other things, on the numeracy of the officials in charge and on their ability to measure the weight and the fineness of the metal entering the mint, make the maximum profit from its processing, and run the bookkeeping efficiently.[81] Numbers, accounts, technological skills, and experience with money and metals formed the expertise of a medieval mint-master. Yet, these were also the skills that merchants needed to be efficient in the market. It comes as no surprise, therefore, that mints were often entrusted to the management of merchant bankers in the late Middle Ages.[82] This was certainly true for Florence and its mercantile class.

Florentine merchants would read, write, and study grammar, i.e., the rudiments of Latin, from age five to seven. When they were ten or eleven, they would attend an abacus school or *scuola d'abaco*, an elementary commercial school where they learned the basics of arithmetic and acquired information regarding the contemporary monetary system, loans, interests, and other techniques crucial for their future career in the business world.[83] More advanced skills, like accounting and foreign exchange operations, were not taught at school. Those would be learned on the job once school was over and the students started their apprenticeship at the age of thirteen or fourteen, usually in a branch office of a mercantile company, either a cloth shop or a bank office away from Florence. In their twenties, they could decide to either become branch managers or go into business themselves. Hence, it was during their teenage years that they would familiarise themselves with all the complexities of long-distance trade, such as trading commodities of different values, managing various monetary and measure systems, dealing with the myriad of coins in circulation, operating international monetary exchange, and above all, keeping accounts of commercial and financial transactions. The Florentines were particularly good at this.

The fragments of the 1211 account book previously discussed are a clear example of the level of financial sophistication that an ordinary company of Florence had already attained in accounting at that early stage. They show a complex set of methods for settling debts, either by off-sets between two clients or with the use of negotiable instruments, the origins of which could date back to the late twelfth century.[84] Moreover, as already noted, participation in long-distance trade would give those merchants the necessary knowledge and information about the quality of the different metals in circulation, and the dynamics of the contemporary metal market, especially considering that as early as 1200, the Florentines were already active in such a trade. For instance, on 21 November of that year, Martino of Florence acquired 160 'pieces' of steel (*'cent. LX açaris de numero set non de peso'*) in twenty-one bags from the Lucchese merchant Guglielmo Doloto in the city of Genoa.[85]

Further documentary records show that the Florentines were also involved in activities such as mining and minting well before the opening of the mint in Florence and the introduction of the florin. In 1214, the bishop of Volterra, Pagano Pannocchieschi (1212–39), farmed out the running of the mint and mines of Montieri to the Florentine mercantile company of Raniero Remitti, Cambio Giugni, and Gundo and Remitto Ruggeri.[86] Once established, the company began to expand, raising the number of its members and enhancing its reputation. Four years later, on 9 June 1218, the judges Gerardo di Rinaldo da Prata and Usimbardo da Picchena put an end to a dispute between the bishop and several members of the company, addressed as '*domini montis et monete de Monterio*', or 'lords of the mount and the mint of Montieri'. Pagano was ordered to return to them, over the next three years, the sum of £12,000 of old *denari* of Pisa for all the money he and his predecessor and uncle, Bishop Ildebrando Pannocchieschi, had borrowed and never paid back.[87] To this end, two-thirds of all the revenues coming from the mines and the mint of Montieri, as well as from Pagano's office, had to be allocated to the Florentine company; the full amount was returned on 7 July 1221.[88]

Similarly, on 4 November 1243, at the siege of Viterbo, Emperor Frederick II, who was in need of money to fund his military campaign in northern Italy, granted the mint and the mines of Montieri to another Florentine merchant, a certain Bentivegna d'Ugolino, at the price of £11,000 of *denari* of Pisa for the duration of two years. Bentivegna, who also received imperial revenues from the villages of San Miniato, Fucecchio, and Val di Nievole, was ordered to mint silver *miliarenses* following the example of the ones produced in Pisa at that time ('*ad modum et formam que in Sicha Pisarum servatur*').[89]

It is hard to say exactly how long those Florentines remained in charge of the mint or whether any coin was ever produced under their administration. Yet, these are interesting cases showing that, within the Florentine merchant class, there were already people with the proper skills and expertise to run a mint, almost twenty years before Florence started minting its own money. It cannot be ruled out that this early involvement in mining and minting worked as a training period for Florentine merchants in view of a new domestic monetary production.[90]

Given all these aspects, ranging from a profound knowledge of and excellent skills with numbers, measures, coins, exchange rates, and accounts of all kinds to proven expertise in mining and minting, it is no wonder that the Florentine government tended to appoint its mint-masters from two of the seven major guilds or *Arti Maggiori* of the city, namely the *Arte di Calimala* and the *Arte del Cambio*, as noted. In this respect, one could also argue that the late opening of the mint around the mid-1230s did not represent a disadvantage for Florence but rather an advantage for innovation, pushing minting further. The longer exposure of those merchant bankers to the economic and financial world would allow them to gain more knowledge about the monetary issues and needs of the time, including the debasement of silver coins and the lack of a solid gold currency, and to understand the complications that could arise when producing innovative coins. This may also explain why, when they started minting money in their own city, the Florentines did not initially strike *denari*, namely petty coins for local circulation, but rather silver *grossi* and gold florins for larger and more important transactions.[91]

Unfortunately, the names of only a few mint-masters survive in the existing documentation up to the year 1303, when the entries in the mint register or *Libro della Zecca* become clearer and more accurate. The first mint-master for gold on record was Lamberto dell'Antella in 1252.[92] Lamberto was a merchant registered in the *Arte di Calimala* in 1242. In 1253, one year after the alleged introduction of the florin, he was lending money to two Florentines in Genoa where, by the 1260s, he was well established with his *fondaco* to trade in cloth.[93] In the decades following the minting of the florin, he held political offices in Florence, such as Ghibelline councillor in 1260 and city prior representing the Calimala guild in 1283 and 1285.[94] He was thus not merely a businessman but a politician too. Similar involvement in the politics of the city of Florence also characterised the lives of the few other mint-masters documented, such as Guido Cambi Falconieri and Tedicio Mannelli in 1280 (semester I), and Coppo Giuseppi and Ticio Manovelli in 1286 (semester I).[95]

The Falconieri were a family of merchants enrolled in the *Arte di Calimala* from 1235. Guido Cambi Falconieri was twice appointed its consul in 1278 and 1281, while in 1278, he was also one of the advisors or *consiglieri* of the commune.[96] Coppo Giuseppi corresponded with Coppo di Giuseppe Caniginiani, whose participation in the commune's politics seems more significant than Guido's. The Canigiani family appeared in the *Arte di Calimala* from 1237 and was particularly active in trade and banking activities. Yet, before and after his experience at the mint, Coppo held prominent positions in the city government. He became prior five times between 1282 and 1295, as well as *sindacus* for the Guelph party in 1285, consul of the *Arte di Calimala* in 1289, and *camerarius* of the commune in 1290.[97] As for Tedicio Mannelli and Ticio Manovelli, these two names may refer to the same person, namely Tedice di Manovello, who was prior of the commune five times and a member of the *Arte del Cambio*, for which he was also consul.[98]

If, as noted, the decision to rely on merchants for the administration of the local mint was a habit common to many other Italian and European cities in general, in the case of Florence, the participation of the mint-masters in the politics of the commune represented a crucial aspect, telling us much about the *capacity* of Florentine merchants to promote the minting of the florin and its early diffusion, as will be explained in the following and final section.

Capacity: politics and networks

The fact that merchants oversaw the Florentine mint would in itself be sufficient to explain their *capacity*, by which I mean the authority and power to introduce the florin and put it into circulation. Yet, the mint-masters were simply the executors of monetary policies that were normally discussed and decided by the local governments. This is particularly true for the majority of mints in the late Middle Ages when, following the experience of the communes, many cities introduced the practice of farming out the local mint to a group of entrepreneurs, usually coming from outside the local area.[99] Florentines, for example, achieved great success as mint-masters throughout Europe in the years following the minting of the florin.[100] Yet, Florence itself was an exception to this practice.

The Florentine mint was one of the few medieval mints that was always and entirely administered by the local authority and not contracted to foreign merchants.[101] The local government decided the city's monetary policy and pursued its plans by directly administering the mint and recruiting its official from within the city. As previously seen, the florin was the result of the choice of the *Primo Popolo* and thus an expression of Florence's new political condition. Yet, the *Popolo* was also responsible for an important change in internal politics. A large number of its members were, in fact, merchants, bankers, and entrepreneurs from the guilds of *Calimala*, *Por Santa Maria*, *Cambio*, and *della Lana*. Up to that point, none of them had played leading roles in the Florentine political scene.[102] The majority of the people forming the ruling group of the city council of elders or *Anziani* were also newcomers to the public life of Florence.[103] While not formalised, there might have been a tendency to exclude members of the old aristocracy.[104]

Under these circumstances, if the merchants were running the mint that produced the gold florin, and the mint was under the direct authority of the *Primo Popolo*, which in turn was formed by the new members of the mercantile society (including the mint-masters), then it is safe to argue that in these very years, the mint, both as physical building and public institution, represented an asset of economic and political power in the hands of the Florentine mercantile class. From this perspective, the florin acquires a new dimension: not only did it function as an expression of the city's autonomy and new identity, governed by the *Primo Popolo*, but also as a vehicle for the self-representation of the ruling mercantile class.[105] Several elements related to both its iconography and materiality support this view.

Traditionally acknowledged as the patron saint of the city, St John the Baptist was also the protector of the *Arte di Calimala*.[106] According to Giovanni Villani, from the mid-twelfth century, that guild was responsible for the upkeep of the Baptistry of Saint John, the spiritual and symbolic centre of medieval Florence. More precisely, Villani wrote that in 1150, its consuls financed the construction of the lantern on the top of the sacred building.[107] This assertion, which anticipates the first appearance of the *Calimala* guild in the surviving documentation of Florence (i.e., 1182) by several decades, is difficult to prove. Documentary evidence from 1216, however, mentions an agreement between the local ecclesiastical authority and the *Calimala* guild that, from then on, the guild would run the Baptistry workshop known as Opera di San Giovanni.[108] The relationship between the saint and the guild, as well as its chronology, are quite significant. They offer a different perspective from which to reconsider the choice to depict first the bust and then the standing and blessing figure of the Baptist on the earliest Florentine coins ever produced, the silver *grosso* (*c.* 1236) and the gold florin, respectively. This may even have occurred at the suggestion of the members of the *Calimala* guild, who were running both the mint and the local government in the mid-thirteenth century.

As for the lily, whose origins as a symbol of Florence seem to date back to the eleventh century, its bond with the ruling mercantile elite harks back to the episode of the expulsion of the Ghibellines, who conspired against the new commune in 1251. Following this event, both the *Popolo* and the Guelphs decided to change the old symbol of the city, namely a white lily on a red field, which was also used by the emperor's supporters, to adopt a red lily on a white field, which still forms the modern coat of arms of Florence.[109]

The unique fineness of the florin and its vernacular name *fiorino* may also be expressions of the ideology of the *Primo Popolo*. Scholars have shown how the myth of ancient Rome and its greatness was a central and recurrent theme in the imagery of contemporary Florentine society.[110] In the earliest available civic chronicles, namely the anonymous *Chronica de Origine Civitatis Florentiae*, probably composed around 1228, and the *Gesta Florentinorum* written by Senzanome no later than 1245, Florence was presented as a new Rome, just as Dante would do in his *Convivio* roughly eighty years later.[111] Once in power, the *Primo Popolo* built its new identity around the same myth.

The now famous and still extant dedication inscription that the ruling group affixed to the west wall of the *Palazzo del Popolo* in 1255 not only explicitly compares Florence to Rome but also calls it a worthy heir destined to renew its ancient glory.[112] With this in mind, and considering that 24 carats were also the standard fineness of the Roman *aureus*, the gold coin of ancient Rome *par excellence*, the florin thus appears as an ideological carrier of the Florentine mercantile elite, i.e., a new gold *aureus* for a new Rome. This is also supported by the choice of translating *florenus*, the Latin name for the gold florin and Florentine coins more generally, with the vernacular *fiorino*.

In a study on the construction of Florentine identity in the first half of the thirteenth century, Enrico Faini pointed out that *florenus* bears a remarkable resemblance to *Florinus*, the Roman consul and eponymous hero that, according to the aforesaid civic chronicles, was killed in the battle against Fiesole, and on the site of whose death Florence was built. Faini also recognised that, despite the different spelling in Latin, both terms were later rendered in the vernacular with the same noun *fiorino*. Evidence of such a practice can be found, albeit years later, in Villani's chronicle, one of the first vernacular texts to narrate both the mythical origins of Florence and the birth of the gold florin. *Fiorino* is the name adopted in the text to indicate both the hero – but with a capital initial – and the coin.[113] Despite the clear overlap, however, Faini was hesitant to establish a direct link between the myth and the coin.[114] Yet, the very use of the same vernacular term for both Latin names seems to corroborate this connection.

Indeed, from a purely linguistic point of view, the Latin long vowel /ē/ in *florenus* should have been retained in the passage to the Tuscan dialect, so the result would have been *fioreno* instead of *fiorino*.[115] The fact that this phonetic rule was not observed might suggest that historical, cultural, and political reasons, not necessarily linguistic, could have influenced the transition from *florenus* to *fiorino*, or in other words, its 'vernacularization', a phenomenon 'antagonistic to the humanist movement and its philological approach to texts'.[116] Thus, the desire of the *Primo Popolo* to preserve, celebrate, and perpetuate through Florentine coinage the memory of Florence's mythical origins and its greatness as a new Rome, while building the emerging identity and reinforcing the political leadership of the new ruling group, could be a valid argument. The diffusion of the vernacular term *fiorini* for Florentine gold florins as early as the 1260s, that is, just a few years after their first minting and during the rule of the *Popolo*, would also support this view.[117]

Against this background, we can therefore read the images on the florin on two different levels. Beyond the mercantile class, these would represent the symbols of the city of Florence, especially the lily. An analysis of the vocabulary used in the sources mentioning gold florins in the *Diplomatico* collection of the State Archives of Florence, for instance, shows that notaries used to refer to the lily when describing the gold coins; none of them mention the Baptist. Recurrent expressions were '*florenos de auro ad gilium ad rectum pondus et conium florentinum*' ('florins of gold with a lily and of the right Florentine weight and dies') or '*florenos aureos boni et puri et expendibilis cum lilio*' ('good, pure and expendable gold florins with a lily'). It is likely that in the hustle and bustle of daily business, it was much easier for people to refer to the lily to denote Florentine florins, probably also because it was a more recognisable and less complex image compared to that of the patron saint.

Yet within the ruling mercantile class, particularly among the *Calimala* guild members, those images would appear as clear expressions of group identity and ideology, symbols of self-representation. As an economic and political instrument in the hands of the *Popolo*, it is not surprising that the earliest documented references to gold florins appear in payments directly involving the mercantile elite in power, as in the cases of Gherardo dei Denti da Correggio (1258) and Manfred (1259).

This is part of the final aspect of the *capacity* of the merchants of Florence: their ability to create networks of circulation for the florin within their economic and political circles. In 1259, for example, the Florentine merchants Conterio and Burgense paid an unspecified amount of '*denariis aureis de Thoscana*', namely gold coins of Tuscany, thus including florins and *grossi d'oro* of Lucca – the only gold coins minted in that region at that time – for a load of barley moving from Genoa to Pisa.[118] Florins were also circulating at the Champagne Fairs and in Alexandria before the 1270s as a result of Florentine commercial activity there. However, if the use of gold florins in long-distance trade is well-known among scholars, its diffusion in political circles remains unclear. This aspect will be explored in the following chapters.

As a final remark, it is interesting to note the rapid diffusion of the florin in the very earliest years following its introduction (i.e., 1258–59), which is symptomatic of the almost immediate but growing success of this currency and of the Florentine monetary standards in general. When, in 1259, the commune of Perugia commissioned two Lucchese merchants to open a mint, they were instructed to strike gold, silver, and billon coins to the standards of the Florentine florin, the Sienese *grossi*, and the *denari* of Siena, respectively. The very fact that the florin already represented a benchmark for potential gold coins only seven years after its reported minting is a clear indication of its contemporary reputation. And there is more. In January 1260, the commune of Perugia ordered a committee of consuls of the local guilds of merchants and moneychangers to ratify the contract with the two Lucchesi. Most of the previous conditions were approved, except for the minting of the new silver *grossi*: those had to be minted to the standard of the *grossi* of Florence and no longer to that of the *grossi* of Siena. In other words, Perugia's new gold and silver coins were based on

Florentine models.[119] This change did not entail any major variation in terms of metal content for the new *grossi* of Perugia. Instead,
this disposition was dictated primarily by the growing contemporary importance of the city of Florence, its politics, and economics,
and thus of the gold florin, its natural extension.

Conclusions

This chapter set out to provide a more rounded picture of the contribution of the Florentine mercantile class to the introduction of
the florin. As illustrated, the new gold coin was not solely the result
of a request by the merchants to the city government, as narrated
by Giovanni Villani. Besides being too distant in time and written
for propaganda purposes, his chronicle provides only a truncated
and rather simplistic image of the birth of the florin. Not a word
is spent on crucial aspects in the process of making the new coin,
including the provision of gold and the routes taken by the yellow
metal to reach Florence, where it was accumulated and eventually
minted. In the absence of solid archaeological evidence and consistent quantitative data, however, the qualitative analysis of scattered
sources documenting the commercial and financial activities of the
Florentines from the second half of the twelfth century onwards
has shed new light on aspects hitherto only partially addressed in
the literature.

The gold for striking the florin came, in the first instance, from
the long-distance trade that extended from the Champagne Fairs,
where precious metals were being exchanged, to the territories of
North Africa and the Middle East. The Florentines ensured a growing presence in both destinations of this commercial axis. In particular, in the Mediterranean, not only did they trade under the
Pisan flag of convenience to avoid customs duties, but they also
began to reside in Pisan *fondacos* located in the major port cities of the region, where they could have better access to the gold
market. Although poor in number, the documented cases have
shown on more than one occasion, the close connection between
the yellow metal – even if only in the form of Arabic coins – and
the Florentine cloth trade. However, the episodes of archbishop
Engelbert and those of the *commenda* contracts and the merchant

company agreement concluded in Genoa suggest that the financial operations carried out by its merchant bankers offered the city of Florence another source of gold.

The obvious limitations of these written sources make it impossible to establish the volumes of gold collected in one way or another. It is also difficult, and perhaps unnecessary, to try to explain such a lack of information regarding the gold trade. A number of factors may have caused it. For instance, secrecy was a predominant feature of the work in the mint. In various contexts over the centuries, mint-masters had to promise under oath to strike good coins without revealing any information about their activities to the outside world. In return, the issuing authority granted them a whole series of fiscal and military exemptions. Thus, as a kind of protective measure for the mint's work and profit, what happened inside its walls had to stay there.[120] It is fascinating – and somewhat naïve – to think that the same applied to the economic transactions of merchants involved in the gold trade, who avoided writing about it to protect their sources and income. That said, the usual suspects are most likely to blame, particularly the poor preservation of medieval sources and the loss of archival documentation through the centuries.

Once collected, gold took several different routes to reach Florence. The Lucchese document of 1243, one of the rarest if not the first attested purchase of gold involving a Florentine, emphasises the importance of maritime routes and, more specifically, of the sea trade with Naples and the Kingdom of Sicily for the provision of the precious metal. It also offers a snapshot of the kind of economic and social network around which that trade orbited. From the southern Italian city, the yellow metal was brought to Pisa by sea, and from there, it could reach Lucca, Florence, or any other destination either by land or going up the river Arno.[121] Like Naples and Pisa, however, another port city of the time, Genoa, played a part in the Florentine gold supply, and probably a significant one if, a year before the minting of its *genovino*, the Ligurian city decided to introduce a protectionist measure to prevent the depletion of its resources of precious metals.

In Florence, it was when the need for a new gold coin met the numerical and accounting skills of the members of the urban mercantile society, together with their deep familiarity and knowledge of currencies, measures, and markets, and time-tested expertise in mining and minting, that the idea of the florin was first conceived and then realised with the imported metal. The right moment for its introduction, however, came when the Florentine merchants also acquired political power and authority within the urban walls and became responsible for the city government at the time of the *Primo Popolo*.

Against this background, therefore, the florin represented a 'merchant currency' in all respects, that is, the end product of the financial activities of the mercantile elite and a manifestation of its political autonomy and identity through its chosen iconography – and perhaps its name. Nevertheless, it was not only thanks to Florence and its merchants that the florin achieved such a rapid and long-lasting success.

Notes

1 Extensive literature on this topic can be found in the Introduction. For Villani's account, see below.
2 See, for instance, Goldthwaite, *Renaissance Florence*, pp. 23–34. Further bibliography is provided in Chapter 1.
3 The start dates of those six-month mandates could change, as could their duration; Alexander Carson Simpson, 'The Mint Officials of the Florentine Florin', *American Numismatic Society Museum Notes* 5 (1952), 113–55 (at pp. 123 and 127 *ff.*). On the functioning of the Florentine mint in the Middle Ages, see *Bernocchi* III and, more recently, Day, Peroni, and Vanni, 'Firenze (Toscana)', pp. 668–81.
4 Paolino Pieri, *Croniche della città di Firenze*, ed. C. Coluccia (Rome: Pensa Multimidia, 2013); Villani, *Nuova Cronica*, vol. 1.
5 For a full account, see Pieri, *Croniche*, pp. viii–xx.
6 '*Nel MCCLII in kalen gennaio fu fatto Podestà messer Filippo degli Ugoni da Parma di Lombardia* [...] *In questo tempo fecero gli fiorentini battere il fiorino dell'oro, che in prima non erano may essuti, né altra moneta se non piccioli et d'ariento, che valea l'uno danari XII. Allora fu dato corso al fiorino dell'oro soldi XX et non era quasi chi 'l volesse*'; Pieri, *Croniche*, pp. 30–1. Author's translation.
7 This rather peculiar reference to the unpopularity of the florin is discussed below.
8 Villani, *Nuova Cronica*, vol. 1, p. 345. Author's translation, based on Philip H. Wicksteed (ed.), *Villani's Chronicle: Being Selections from*

the First Nine Books of the *Chroniche Fiorentine of Giovanni Villani*, trans. R. E. Selfe (London: Archibald Constable & Co., 1906), online at www.elfinspell.com/VillaniBk6b.html#sect53, accessed 20 September 2024.

9 On Villani's appointment as 'master' of the mint, see *Bernocchi* III, pp. 22–3 and 43. For a full and up-to-date account of all the public offices Villani held from 1316 to 1343 (forty identified to date), see Gabriella Albanese, Bruno Figliuolo, and Paolo Pontari, 'Dei notai, cartolai e mercanti attorno al *Liber Dantis* di Giovanni Villani e del modo di leggere i documenti antichi', *Studi danteschi* 84 (2019), 285–385 (at pp. 309–16). On Villani's life, see also Marino Zabbia, 'Villani, Giovanni', in *Dizionario Biografico degli Italiani*, vol. 99 (Rome: Istituto della Enciclopedia Italiana, 2020), pp. 333–8, online at www.treccani.it/enciclopedia/giovanni-villani_%28Diziona rio-Biografico%29/, accessed 24 September 2024. On the Florentine Priorate, see Piero Gualtieri, *Il comune di Firenze tra Due e Trecento. Partecipazione politica e assetto istituzionale* (Florence: L. S. Olschki, 2009), pp. 173–204.

10 The Florentine chronicler Baldassarri Bonaiuti (1336–85), who was a near contemporary to Giovanni Villani, wrote instead that the minting of the gold florin took place in September; Niccolò Rodolico (ed.), *Cronaca Fiorentina di Marchionne di Coppo Stefani* (Città di Castello: S. Lapi, 1903), p. 41.

11 See, for example, Louis Green, *Chronicle into History: An Essay on the Interpretation of History in Florentine Fourteenth-Century Chronicles* (Cambridge: Cambridge University Press, 1972).

12 John K. Hyde, 'Some Uses of Literacy in Venice and Florence in the Thirteenth and Fourteenth Centuries', *Transactions of the Royal Historical Society* 29 (1979), 109–28 (at p. 124). It was not until the first half of the fifteenth century that the city of Florence had an official chancellor-chronicler in the person of Leonardo Bruni (*c.* 1370–1444).

13 Spufford, 'The First Century', p. 423.

14 Balestracci, *Montaperti*, pp. 47–8.

15 Spufford, 'The First Century', p. 422.

16 Tognetti, 'Il Mezzogiorno', p. 153. It must be acknowledged that the data Villani recorded for the city of Florence in the fourteenth century have proved to be more reliable; Day, 'The Population of Florence'.

17 Spufford, 'The Provision', pp. 234–5.

18 This is due to the severe lack of commercial records for the period under investigation; Hoshino, *L'arte della lana*.

19 Goldthwaite and Mandich, *Studi*, p. 111.

20 There may be slight differences between the numbers of documents available per year shown in the graph and those that can be calculated at www.archiviodigitale.icar.beniculturali.it/it/1/home. The data were gathered by analysing digitised parchments of the *Diplomatico* collection prior to the revamp of the online platform in 2020. Since the update, online consultation has become less intuitive and more cumbersome and time-consuming. Moreover, much of the previously accessible information, including the parchment ID codes frequently referred by scholars, has been discarded or not yet uploaded online.

21 The earliest *Consulte* of the Commune of Florence available to us, i.e., the minutes of all the meetings of the various city councils, where references to gold florins are frequent, also date from 1280 onwards, thus in the final years of the 'early life' of the florin as reconstructed in this monograph; Alessandro Gherardi, *Le consulte della Repubblica fiorentina dall'anno MCCLXXX al MCCXCVIII*, 2 vols (Florence: G. C. Sansoni, 1898). The detailed analysis of these and other sources will be the subject of a paper I am preparing with the provisional title 'The Gold Florin in the Age of Dante: Beyond the Macroeconomic Paradigm'.

22 ASF, Diplomatico, Firenze, S.ma Annunziata (serviti), 1267 Dicembre 21, online at www.archiviodigitale.icar.beniculturali.it/it/185/ricerca/detail/68658, accessed 20 September 2024. The two documents mentioning gold florins recorded for the years 1264 and 1266, as shown in Figure 2.1, are seventeenth-century forgeries and were therefore excluded from the analysis; Andrea Bocchi, 'L'avventura di un filologo. Le carte dei Cicci di Fucecchio', in V. Formentin (ed.), *Letteratura e Filologia. Voci da un Seminario* (Padua: Cleup, 2023), pp. 11–78.

23 Pieri, *Croniche*, pp. 30–1.

24 Bolton, *Money*, pp. 68–9; Arthur J. Rolnick, Francois R. Velde, and Warren E. Weber, 'The Debasement Puzzle: An Essay on Medieval Monetary History', *Quarterly Review* (Fall 1997), 8–20 (at p. 9).

25 The percentage of gold was no more than 1 per cent of all the minerals extracted from those mines, and the majority was silver, iron, lead, and copper; Guido Pratellesi, *Studio giacimentologico delle mineralizzazioni argentifere della zona di Massa Marittima – Montieri (Grosseto)* (Unpublished dissertation, Università degli Studi di Firenze, 1984); Marco Benvenuti *et al.*, 'Studying the Colline Metallifere Mining Area in Tuscany: An Interdisciplinary Approach', *IES Yearbook* (2014), 261–87.

26 Jacopo Paganelli, *Dives episcopus. La signoria dei vescovi di Volterra nel Duecento* (Rome: Viella, 2021).

27 Mint operations are better documented for the fourteenth century; *Bernocchi* III, pp. 33–52.
28 Michele Asolati, 'Nota preliminare sul gruzzolo di dinar fatimidi rinvenuto in Piazza della Signoria a Firenze (1987–88)', in *Simposio Simone Assemani sulla monetazione islamica. Padova, II Congresso Internazionale di Numismatica e Storia Monetale. Padova 17 maggio 2003, Musei Civici agli Eremitani-Museo Bottacin (Biblioteca)* (Padua: Esedra, 2005), pp. 127–35.
29 XRF analysis to understand where the gold of the florins was mined has proved unfeasible; Monica Baldassarri *et al.*, 'X-Ray Fluorescence Analysis'. Although gold was being used for painting in thirteenth-century Florence prior to the minting of the florin, it was not needed in large quantities; Lucia Travaini, 'Monete, battiloro e pittori. L'uso dell'oro nella pittura murale e i dati della cappella degli Scrovegni. Coins, Gold-beaters and Painters. How Gold Was Used in Wall Paintings: Some Examples from the Scrovegni Chapel', *Bollettino d'Arte* (2005), 145–52.
30 For Siena and Pisa, see Baldassarri, *Zecca*; for Lucca, see Concioni, 'Le coniazioni'.
31 See Chapter 1.
32 Roberto S. Lopez and Irving W. Raymond, *Medieval Trade in the Mediterranean World: Illustrative Documents* (New York: Columbia University Press, 1995), p. 157; Raymond de Roover, 'The Cambium Maritimum Contract according to the Genoese Notarial Records of the Twelfth Centuries', *Explorations in Economic History* 7:1 (1969), 15–33.
33 '*In nomine Domini nostri Ihesu Christi. Anno Domini millesimo centesimo sexagesimo nono, mense octubris, indicione tercia, Armiro. Manifestum facio ego quidem Ugolinus Florentinus de confinio Sancte Marie Matris Domini, quia recepi cum meis heredibus de te Iohanne Serzy de confinio Sancti Apollinaris et tuis heredibus, perperos auri paleos keniurgos pensantes quinque quos ad presens mecum portare debeo de hinc in Constantinopoli cum nave in qua nauclerus vadit Petrus Scivamendigo* [...] *et tunc infra quindecim postquam in Constantinopoli intravero debeam per me vel per meum missum dare et deliberare Marino Serzy fratri tuo ut suo misso in Constantinopoli perperos auri veteres pensantes sex*' (Author's translation: 'In the name of our Lord Jesus Christ. A.D. 1169, October, 3rd indiction, in Armiro. I, the Florentine Ugolino of the parish of Santa Maria Mater Domini, declare to have received together with my heirs, the sum of five Byzantine gold *perperi* of the new weight from Giovanni Sergi of the parish of Sant'Apollinare and his heirs that, from this day, I will

carry with me to Constantinople, on the ship of Pietro Scivamendigo [...] and within fifteen days from my arrival in Constantinople, one of my agent or I will return the sum of six gold *perperi* of the old weight to Martino Sergi, your brother and agent in Constantinople'); Morozzo della Rocca and Lombardo, *Documenti*, vol. I, p. 212, no. 215.

34 Business partnerships between merchants from minor cities and merchants of the great maritime Italian republics formed the first way in which the former found themselves regarded as the latter; David Abulafia, 'The Levant Trade of the Minor Cities in the Thirteenth and Fourteenth Centuries: Strengths and Weaknesses', *Asian and African Studies* 22 (1988), 183–202; reprinted in David Abulafia, *Commerce and Conquest in the Mediterranean, 1100–1500* (London: Variorum, 1993), chapter 11 (at p. 187).

35 Friedrich K. von Savigny, *The History of the Roman Law during the Middle Ages, Vol. I* (Edinburgh: A. Black, 1829), p. 137; Paolo Grossi, *L'ordine giuridico medievale* (Bari: Laterza, 2003).

36 '*Qua propter recepi ego ad te plebano pellem unam valens quatuor bisantes*' (Author's translation: 'For which I received from you, priest, a piece of leather worth four bezants'); ASF, Diplomatico, Passignano, S. Michele (badia, vallambrosani), 1179 Febbraio 26, online at www.archiviodigitale.icar.beniculturali.it/it/185/ricerca/detail/87871, accessed 20 September 2024.

37 Bompaire, 'Le Mythe'.

38 Spufford, *Handbook*, p. 294.

39 Day, 'Before the *Libro della Zecca* I', p. 448.

40 Silimanno appears in other transactions implying some sort of political role in the local context, but not involving gold. I am grateful to Enrico Faini for this information.

41 Pietro Santini, 'Frammenti di un libro di banchieri fiorentini scritto in volgare nel 1211', *Giornale storico della letteratura italiana* 10:28/29 (1887), 161–77; Geoffrey Lee, 'The Oldest European Account Book: A Florentine Bank Ledger of 1211', *Nottingham Mediaeval Studies* 1:16 (1972), 28–60; Geoffrey Lee, 'The Florentine Bank Ledger Fragments of 1211: Some New Insights', *Journal of Accounting Research* 11:1 (1973), 47–61.

42 Trade between Bologna and Florence flourished extensively in the first decades of the thirteenth century, as also attested by three commercial treaties signed between the two cities in 1203, 1216, and 1220; *Storia* VI, p. 846*ff.*

43 *Storia* I, p. 848.

44 '*Item die dare Buonessegnia soldi XII per u massamutino* [...] *Alberto f. Ubertini no die dare soldi XXII e denari IIII per due massamutini*'; Ernesto Monaci (ed.), *Crestomazia italiana dei primi secoli* (Città di Castello: S. Lapi, 1912), pp. 20 and 27, respectively. Author's translation.

45 Santini, 'Frammenti', p. 162.

46 Monaci, *Crestomazia*, p. 20.

47 '*Banzara del Garbo no di dare libre XV provesini nuovi ke demmo a Bartolo ispeziale*' and '*Item* [Apollonio Tribaldi] *die dare soldi XXXV e ÷ per urromeo* [sic], *ke i ne demmo tornesi*' (Author's translation: 'Barzara del Garbo has to give us £15 of new *provisini* that we gave to Bartolo the spice seller' and 'Also [Apollonio Tribaldi] is due to return s. 35 d. 6 for *urromeo* [sic], which we gave him in *deniers tournois*'); Monaci, *Crestomazia*, p. 21; '*Attigliante ci à ddato libre III ke deve avere i ssterlino e altro cambio*' (Author's translation: 'Attigliante gave us £3 for sterling and other change'); Monaci, *Crestomazia*, p. 28.

48 *Storia* I, p. 1181 and note 1.

49 Schaube, *Storia*, pp. 435–6.

50 Louis F. Bourquelot, *Études sur les foires de Champagne* (Paris: Imprimerie Imperiale, 1865), p. 300. Further details on this type of sources can be found in Georges Despy, *Les tarifs de tonlieux* (Turnhout: Brepols, 1976).

51 Cesare Paoli and Enea Piccolomini (eds), *Lettere volgari del secolo XIII scritte da senesi* (Bologna: G. Romagnoli, 1871), p. 57.

52 Schaube, *Storia*, p. 420.

53 Richard Knipping (ed.), *Die Regesten der Erzbischöfe von Köln im Mittelalter III, 1205–1304* (Düsseldorf: Droste, 1985), nos 279–80.

54 The lack of direct evidence is also due to the nature of commerce at the Fairs, which was primarily based on credit: the majority of the surviving documents record loans in the form of exchanges to be repaid at the Fairs, and only once in a while do they specify that payments had to be made in gold or silver coins and not in credits; Richard D. Face, 'Techniques of Business in the Trade Between the Fairs of Champagne and the South of Europe in the Twelfth and Thirteenth Centuries', *EHR* New ser. 10:3 (1958), 427–38 (at p. 437).

55 The episode is narrated in detail in Abulafia, 'Crocuses', p. 228*ff.*, and Del Punta, *Guerrieri*, p. 200*ff.*

56 Yet, the presence in Acre of Florentine merchants engaged in the cloth trade 'is echoed' in other documents of the same series; Abulafia, 'Crocuses', p. 229.

57 Patrick Chorley, 'The Cloth Exports of Flanders and Northern France during the Thirteenth Century: A Luxury Trade?', *EHR* New ser. 40:3 (1987), 349–79 (at p. 349). A cape or cloak made in Florence, for example, appeared in a bequest written in Palermo in 1237; Ugo Monneret de Villard, 'La tessitura palermitana sotto i Normanni e i suoi rapporti con l'arte bizantina', *Miscellanea Giovanni Mercati III* (Vatican City: Biblioteca Apostolica Vaticana, 1946), pp. 464–89 (at p. 484).

58 The original treaty of 1171 was renewed in 1215, but this time regulating only the resolution of debts between the inhabitants of the two cities; *Documenti*, p. 175, no. 61; p. 177, no. 62.

59 Abulafia, 'Crocuses', pp. 227–43; Del Punta, *Guerrieri*, p. 200*ff.*

60 Olivia Constable, *Housing the Stranger in the Mediterranean World: Lodging, Trade, and Travel in Late Antiquity and the Middle Ages* (Cambridge: Cambridge University Press, 2003), p. 110.

61 John H. Pryor, 'The Origins of the Commenda', *Speculum* 52:1 (1977), 5–37.

62 Hilmar C. Krueger and Robert L. Reynolds (eds), *Lanfranco 1202–1206, Vol. II* (Genoa: Società Ligure di Storia Patria, 1951), p. 306, nos 1656–7.

63 Ferretto, *Codice Diplomatico*, p. 6.

64 Spufford, *Money*, p. 164.

65 Villani, *Nuova Cronica*, vol. 1, pp. 346–7. Author's translation but drawing on Wicksteed, *Villani's Chronicle*.

66 Possibly a member of the Accettanti family; Maria Elisa Soldani, 'Da Accettanti a Setantí: il processo di integrazione di una famiglia lucchese nella società barcellonese del Quattrocento', in C. Iannella (ed.), *Per Marco Tangheroni. Studi su Pisa e sul Mediterraneo medievale offerti dai suoi ultimi allievi* (Pisa: Edizioni ETS, 2005), pp. 209–33.

67 '*Brocardus florentinus quondam Ricoveri confessus fuit se debitorem esse et dare debere Maffeo de Flicto de Scala quondam Mauri libras CCCCLXV denariorum lucensium vel pisanorum parvorum pro pretio centum unciarum auri ad pondus Neapoli ad rationem quattuor libras et soldos XIII per unciam et quos denarios promisit ei dare et convenit hinc per totam proximam die jovis in civitate pisana. Et quod aurum dictus Maffeus promisit et convenit dicto Brocardo dare ei vel suis heredibus aut cui praeceperit a die qua fuerit Neapoli ad unum mensem. Et pro predicto auro sic dando ut dictum est dictus Mafeus dare debet et promisit dicto Brocardo loco pignoris totum avere quod conperabitur de dictis denariis vel similibus et tantum plus de alio suo avere quantum est quarta pars dicte pecunie. Et hoc debet ire ad risicum et fortunam Brocardi*

maris et gentis usque Neapolim. Item pactum et conventum fuit inter eos quod si dictus Broccardus non daret eidem Maffei suprascriptos denarios ut dictum est supra promittit dare ei libras X denariorum lucensium vel pisanorum. Et pro predictis denariis solvere debet fideiubsit pro eo Accetatem quondam Stefani et pagator est in precibus Broccardi in omnem causam. Et si dictus Mafeus non reciperet suprascriptum pretium auri et non daret vel non faceret de predicto pignore et quantum plus ut dictum est supra promisit dare Brocardo libras X denarios pisanos vel lucenses. Et supra predictis denariis libras X solvendis fideiubsit pro eodem Magistro Rocchisiano et pagator est item in precibus Mafei in omnem causam. Et sic facere et attendere ut dictum est supra per omnia. Intersese pro et contra obligando sese et suos heredes et bona sua omnia presentia et futura iure pignoris et ypothece ad penam dupli et illius potestatis seu dominii sub quo pro tempore fuerit. Actum Luce in turre Passavantis coram Galdo et Magistro Ivano MCCXLIII XIIII Kalendas Octubris indictione secunda Ciabattus iudex et notarius hec scripsi'; ASDLu, Archivio Capitolare, Libro Segnato, LL no. 17, fo. 87r. Graziano Concioni only refers to this document in a footnote in Concioni, 'Le coniazioni', p. 57, note 60.

68 For further details on this system of account, see p. xvi.

69 ASPi, Diplomatico, Primaziale, 1238, 30 Agosto; briefly mentioned in Robert Davidsohn, *Forschungen zur Geschichte von Florenz III* (Berlin: Ernst Siegfried Mittler und Sohn, 1901), p. 7, no. 22. The parchment is partially ruined.

70 Yet, it is very likely that the debt was paid in gold coins since the transaction took place in the Kingdom of Sicily, where gold formed the monetary standard, as noted.

71 Jill Caskey, *Art and Patronage in the Medieval Mediterranean: Merchant Culture in the Region of Amalfi* (Cambridge: Cambridge University Press, 2004).

72 Costantino and Matteo d'Afflitto were appointed bishops of Scala from 1207 to 1226 and 1227 to 1244, respectively; Norbert Kamp, *Kirche und Monarchie im Staufischen Königreich Sizilien, I: Prosopographische Grundlegung: Bistümer und Bischöfe des Königreichs 1194–1266, Teil I: Abruzzen und Kampanien* (Munich: Fink, 1973), pp. 416–20.

73 Alfredo M. Santoro, *Circolazione monetaria ed economica a Salerno nei secoli XIII e XIV* (Florence: All'Insegna del Giglio, 2011), pp. 29–30.

74 Andreas Meyer, 'Organisierter Bettel und andere Finanzgeschäfte des Hospitals von Altopascio im 13. Jahrhundert', *Pariser Historische*

Studien 57 (2007), 55–105, especially p. 86 no. 16; p. 89 no. 21; p. 91 no. 23; p. 94 no. 28; p. 96 nos 31–2.

75 ASDLu, Archivio Capitolare, Libro Segnato, LL no. 17, fo. 17r.

76 *Ibid.*, fos 30v.–31r.

77 Dellacasa, *I libri iurium*, p. 206, no. 727; Gino Arias, *I trattati commerciali della Repubblica fiorentina, vol. 1: secolo XIII* (Florence: Successori Le Monnier, 1901), pp. 52–4.

78 'De pecunia vero quam Fiorentini comperabunt in Ianua vel districtu mercandi causa, excepto cambio auri vel argenti vel monetarum seu bolçonalie, et de illa quam supra mare detulerint et versus Portumvenerem portabunt debent solvere pro pedagio Portusveneris denarios octo ianuinorum per libram, salvo quod de Ianua non possint Fiorentini trahere boçonagiam'; Dellacasa, *I libri iurium*, p. 207, no. 727. Author's translation.

79 'Buglione o bolzonaglia vuol dire oro e argento in piastre o in verghe o in vasellamenta rotte d'argento, o in moneta d'oro e d'argento non correnti ne' luoghi; e questo si intende buglione siccome cosa rotta per disfare o per fondere; e la bolzonaglia si è tanto a dire monete piccole non corsibole in quegli luoghi ove sono per fondere o per disfare', Allan Evans (ed.) *Francesco Balducci Pegolotti. La Pratica della Mercatura* (Cambridge, MA: The Mediaeval Academy of America, 1936), p. 17ff. Author's translation.

80 Spufford, *Money*, p. 177.

81 Lucia Travaini, 'Le zecche italiane', in L. Travaini (ed.), *Le zecche italiane fino all'Unità* (Rome: Istituto Poligrafico e Zecca dello Stato, 2011), pp. 31–126.

82 See the cases of Bologna and Perugia in Giuliano Milani, 'Monete, cambiatori e popolo. Un tentativo di riforma monetaria bolognese nel 1264', *Annali dell'Istituto Italiano di Numismatica* 57 (2011), 131–56, and Angelo Finetti, *La zecca e le monete di Perugia nel medioevo e nel rinascimento* (Perugia: Volumnia, 1997), respectively.

83 Richard A. Goldthwaite, 'Schools and Teachers of Commercial Arithmetic in Renaissance Florence', *Journal of European Economic History* 1:2 (1972), 418–33; Elisabetta Ulivi, 'Masters, Questions and Challenges in the Abacus Schools', *Archive for History of Exact Sciences* 69 (2015), 651–70; Jens Høyrup, 'Mathematics Education in the European Middle Ages', in A. Karp and G. Schubring (eds), *Handbook on the History of Mathematics Education* (New York: Springer, 2014), pp. 109–24.

84 Lee, 'The Florentine Bank', p. 57.

85 M. V. Hall-Cole, H. C. Krueger, R. G. Reinert, and R. L. Reynolds (eds), *Giovanni di Guiberto (1200–1211)*, vol. 1 (Genoa: Deputazione di Storia Patria, 1939), p. 20, no. 43.

86 Enrico Fiumi, *Volterra e San Gimignano nel medioevo*, ed. G. Pinto (Siena: Grafica Pistolesi, 1983), pp. 264–7.

87 Alessandro Lisini, 'Le monete e le zecche di Volterra, Montieri, Berignone e Casole', *RIN* 22 (1909), 266–7; Fedor Schneider (ed.), *Regestum Volaterranum: Regesten der Urkunden von Volterra (778–1303)* (Rome: E. Loescher & Co., 1907), pp. 128–9, no. 363.

88 It is interesting to note that the bishop had to return extra sums for some cloths, a horse, and a silver bowl that the Florentines had bought for him; Fiumi, *Volterra*, pp. 265 and 267.

89 Lisini, 'Le monete', pp. 269–70; Fiumi, *Volterra*, p. 269.

90 William R. Day Jr., 'Fiorentini e altri italiani appaltatori di zecche straniere, 1200–1600: un progetto di ricerca', *Annali di Storia di Firenze* 5 (2010), 9–29 (at p. 19).

91 Silver *denari* only appear from 1255–56; Day, 'Before the *Libro della Zecca* I', p. 468.

92 Salvo Dini, the notary instructed in 1317 to assemble details regarding the mint personnel and its output for the compilation of the mint registers, wrote that he had obtained this information from oral sources instead of written records; *Bernocchi* I, p. xxiii. This further emphasises the lack of certainty regarding the year 1252 as a major date for the minting of the florin.

93 Ferretto, *Codice Diplomatico*, p. 60, no. 1; Clare M. Baggott, *Business, Politics and Family Ties. Three Case Studies: The Cerchi, dell'Antella and Portinari of Florence 1260–1360* (PhD dissertation, University of Keele, 1985), p. 119.

94 On the political activities of Lamberto and the dell'Antella family in the second half of the thirteenth century, see Baggott, *Business*, pp. 119–21; Jacobi, 'Reconsidering', p. 149.

95 We also have the names of the mint-masters for the year 1300: Ricco di Lapo Arrighi and Vanni Colti for semester I, and Geri Cardinale and Senuccio Albizzi del Bene for semester II; *Bernocchi* I, p. xxiii; Day, 'Before the *Libro della Zecca* I', p. 445.

96 On the Falconieri family, see Michele Luzzati, 'Falconieri', in *Dizionario Biografico degli Italiani*, vol. 44 (Rome: Istituto della Enciclopedia Italiana, 1994), pp. 369–71, online at www.treccani.it/enciclopedia/falconieri_(Dizionario-Biografico), accessed 20 September 2024.

97 Diacciati, *Popolani*, pp. 118–19.

98 *Ibid.*, p. 169, note 289.

99 Travaini, 'Le zecche italiane', p. 84.

100 Florentines obtained the right to mint at Cuneo in 1258 and were running mints at Perugia in 1266, Trento and Bologna in 1269, Tirolo and Merano in 1272, Naples in 1278, Udine in 1300, and

in Bohemia and Hungary in the early fourteenth century; Day, 'Fiorentini', p. 19.

101 Day, 'Before the *Libro della Zecca* I', p. 442.

102 Diacciati, *Popolani*, especially at pp. 37–43.

103 This was also true for other offices, as in the case of the treasurer Migliorato di Domenico; Elisabetta Gigli, 'Operatori economici fiorentini a cavallo del primo popolo: intorno alla "societas filiorum Falconerii"', in L. Gatto and P. Supino Martini (eds), *Studi sulla società e le culture del Medioevo per Girolamo Arnaldi*, 2 vols (Florence: All'Insegna del Giglio, 2002), vol. 1, pp. 229–43.

104 Diacciati, *Popolani*, p. 149.

105 It is worth noting that the *Popolo* regime was an experience common to many cities of northern and central Italy during the thirteenth century, including Genoa, Lucca, Pisa, and Siena. Only in Florence was there this close, almost symbiotic relationship between the *Popolo* and the gold coin. In Genoa and Lucca, the first *Popolo* governments date to 1257 and the early 1260s, respectively, thus a few years after the introduction of their gold coins. Pisa and Siena experienced *Popolo* regimes too, which also initiated monetary reforms, but neither of them minted gold coins during the thirteenth century.

106 Anna Benvenuti, 'Il sovramondo delle arti fiorentine. Tra i santi delle corporazioni', in *Arti fiorentine. La grande storia dell'artigianato, I – Il Medioevo* (Florence: Giunti 1998), pp. 103–28.

107 Villani, *Nuova Cronica*, vol. 1, p. 90.

108 Lorenzo Fabbri, 'Calimala e l'Opera di San Giovanni: il governo del Battistero di Firenze fra autorità ecclesiastica e potere civile', in F. Guerrieri (ed.), *Battistero di San Giovanni. Conoscenza, Diagnostica, Conservazione. Atti del Convegno Internazionale Firenze, 24–25 Novembre 2014* (Florence: Mandragora, 2017), pp. 73–85 (at p. 75 and note 30). See also *Storia* VI, pp. 272–5.

109 Alessandro Savorelli, 'Giglio di Firenze', in M. M. Donato and D. Parenti (eds), *Dal Giglio al David. Arte civica a Firenze fra medioevo e rinascimento* (Florence and Milan: Giunti, 2013), p. 141. The episode is narrated in Villani, *Nuova Cronica*, vol. 1, p. 335 and in Dante Alighieri, *La Divina Commedia*, 3 vols, ed. Anna Maria Chiavacci Leonardi (Milan: Mondadori, 2005), vol. 3: Paradiso, canto XVI, lines 151–4.

110 Nicolai Rubinstein, 'The Beginnings of Political Thought in Florence', *Journal of the Warburg and Courtauld Institutes* 5 (1942), 198–227; Francesco Salvestrini, 'Giovanni Villani and the Aetiological Myth of Tuscan Cities', in E. Kooper (ed.), *The Medieval Chronicle II. Proceedings of the 2nd International Conference on the Medieval*

Chronicle, Driebergen/Utrecht 16–21 July 1999 (Amsterdam and New York: Rodopi, 2002), pp. 199–211; Diacciati, *Popolani*, pp. 183–92; Enrico Faini, 'I notai e la costruzione dell'identità fiorentina entro il 1260: prime indagini', in G. Pinto, L. Tanzini, and S. Tognetti (eds), *Notariorum itinera. Notai toscani del basso medioevo tra routine, mobilità e specializzazione* (Florence: L. S. Olschki, 2018), pp. 15–25.

111 Riccardo Chellini (ed.), *Chronica de Origine Civitatis Florentiae* (Rome: Palazzo Borromini, 2009) (especially at pp. 113–32 for the proposed dating); Otto Hartwig, *Quellen und Forschungen zur ältestern Geschichte der Stadt Florenz* (Marburg: N. G. Elwert'sche Verlasbuch Haundlung, 1875), pp. iii–xv and 1–34. Dante refers to Florence as '*la bellissima e famosissima figlia di Roma*' (Author's translation: 'Rome's most beautiful and famous daughter'); Dante Alighieri, *Convivio*, ed. Giorgio Inglese (Milan: Biblioteca Universale Rizzoli, 1999), p. 50 (I, ch. 3, par. 4).

112 J. Mac Cracken, 'The Dedication Inscription of the Palazzo del Podestà Dating from the Period of the First Democracy (1250–1260) Probably Composed by Brunetto Latini', *Rivista d'Arte* 30 (1955), 183–205; Diacciati, *Popolani*, p. 188.

113 Villani, *Nuova Cronica*, vol. 1, pp. 55–62 and 345–7, respectively.

114 Faini, 'Notai', pp. 21–2.

115 Gherard Rohlfs, *Grammatica storica della lingua italiana e dei suoi dialetti. Fonetica* (Turin: Einaudi, 1966), p. 70. I am grateful to Giuseppina Orobello for this information.

116 Alison Cornish, *Vernacular Translation in Dante's Italy: Illiterate Literature* (Cambridge: Cambridge University Press, 2011), p. 8.

117 Paoli and Piccolomini, *Lettere volgari*, p. 57. The full reference will be discussed in detail in the next chapter.

118 Giorgio Falco and Geo Pistarino (eds), *Il cartulario di Giovanni di Giona di Portovenere (sec. XIII)* (Turin: Istituto grafico Bertello, 1955), p. 34.

119 Despite all the preparations, the production of 'gold florins' in Perugia did not work out; Finetti, *La zecca e le monete*, pp. 23–8.

120 Lucia Travaini, 'Sacra Moneta: Mints and Divinity: Purity, Miracles and Power', in Burström and Ingvardson (eds), *Divina Moneta*, pp. 174–89 (at pp. 177–8).

121 Francesco Salvestrini, 'Tra "civiltà" e "natura". La presenza del fiume nei contesti urbani, il caso toscano fra Medioevo e prima Età Moderna', in D. Canzian and R. Simonetti (eds), *Acque e territorio nel Veneto medievale* (Rome: Viella, 2012), pp. 133–46.

3

The florin and the Crown

The round-shaped image that opens this chapter is not that of a coin, not even one of those gold dinars known as *morabetini* or *massamutini*, despite the Arabic inscriptions. It instead depicts 'The Circle of the Sphere' in the Pseudo-Aristotelian treatise known as the *Secretum Secretorum*, or *The Book of the Secret of Secrets* (see Figure 3.1).[1] Likely composed in Arabic in the tenth century and translated into Latin in the twelfth so it could circulate in Europe, this work enjoyed extraordinary success and diffusion

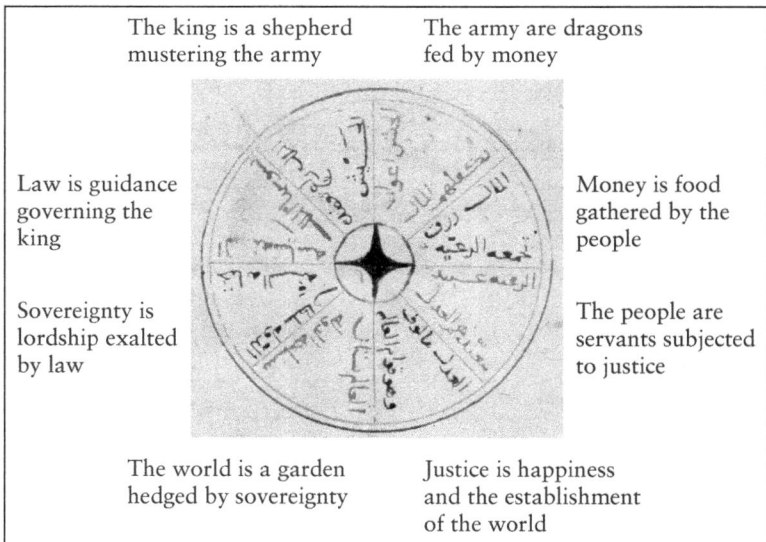

Figure 3.1 The 'Circle of the Sphere' in the *Secretum secretorum.*

from about the 1140s through to the end of the Middle Ages and was copied far more than any of the writings of the real Aristotle.[2] It belongs to the literary genre of 'mirrors for princes' (or *specula principum*) – manuals intended to instruct medieval rulers about their duties, virtues, and conduct as political leaders and moral exemplars and about the philosophical and theological meaning of their office.[3] The *Secretum Secretorum* consists of a long letter allegedly from Aristotle to his pupil, Alexander the Great, covering an encyclopaedic range of topics, including statecraft, politics, and moral advice, serving as a guide for practical government. The circle in the figure here appears in a fourteenth-century Arabic version of the *Secretum* and was intended to summarise the main gist of the treatise.[4] Its eight segments refer to the core elements forming the structure of a centralised political authority, linked together by a causal relationship, i.e., 'there is no king without an army' and so on. Two in particular concern money, which, like food, was accumulated by the people and used to feed the armies, thus becoming an essential component to secure the government of a medieval ruler and on the availability of which his activities would depend.

The interdependence between money, rulers, and armies was also emphasised around the same time in the *Dialogus de Scaccario* (or *Dialogue of the Exchequer*), written in 1177–79 by Richard Fitz Nigel, treasurer of King Henry II of England. This is what the author says in its preface:

> We are, of course, aware that kingdoms are governed and laws maintained primarily by prudence, fortitude, temperance and justice, and the other virtues ... But there are occasions on which sound and wise schemes take effect earlier through the agency of money ... Money is no less indispensable in peace than in war. In war it is lavished on fortifying castles, paying soldiers' wages and innumerable other expenses, determined by the character of the persons paid, for the defence of the realm; in peace, though arms are laid down, noble churches are built by devout princes, Christ is fed and clothed in the persons of the poor, and by practising the other works of mercy mammon is distributed.[5]

These two examples introduce the general topics of this chapter: the role of the gold florin of Florence in what we might call, slightly anachronistically, 'public finance', especially the financing of war in thirteenth-century kingdoms, and the contribution of medieval rulers to the early diffusion of the coin. As previously seen, many developments took place within the so-called 'Commercial Revolution', but not all of them were directly related to the methods of doing business or to the increasing scale of long-distance trade. The transition to an economy in which money became the measure of all things generated a 'revolution in attitudes towards money' at every level of medieval society.[6] For governments, this monetary invasion led to a significant transformation of the ways in which they conducted their politics. In times of peace, for example, the greater availability of money among farmers and urban dwellers enabled rulers to impose direct taxation, thus creating new systems of public finance based on money that were crucial for the maintenance of their kingdoms. In times of war, money allowed them to engage in protracted military campaigns, recruit mercenary troops, pay for more sophisticated equipment, build fortresses, and so on.[7] Money became such a fundamental medium of power projection for late medieval governments that 'monetization and bureaucratisation grew up together'.[8]

Nevertheless, given the crucial role of money in the world of public finance, the extent to which this milieu and its agents, including kings, princes, etc., contributed to the diffusion of the Florentine gold florin in the early decades after its minting remains unclear. In a study on the monetary circulation of Sicily and southern Italy between the eleventh and fifteenth centuries, for instance, Lucia Travaini found written evidence of gold florins collected through taxes in the Kingdom of Sicily in 1280.[9] Yet, a systematic analysis of the role that a 'foreign' gold coin like the florin, i.e., one not minted in the local mints, would have had in the public finances of the kingdom is still lacking in today's scholarship.

Such an omission is surprising for two reasons: first, monetary historians have repeatedly stressed that gold coins were primarily used not only in long-distance trade but also in governmental dealings.[10] However, they do not clarify in which specific types of transactions those coins were employed, how their supply and demand worked, or how their circulation operated in that milieu. Second, as has been noted, gold florins appeared in the public finances of the Florentine commune quite early, around the years 1258–59.

On this premise, this chapter analyses the role played by the Florentine florin in the milieu of public finances in the first decades of its minting. Specifically, I argue that a major stimulus for the florin's early spread came from its involvement in the financial system and military spending of medieval rulers. The case study here, therefore, is not the Florentine commune and its public finances but the Kingdom of Sicily in the reign of King Charles I. This choice is due to the exceptional number of fiscal documents that survive for that kingdom, as well as to the historical importance of Sicily and southern Italy for the political and economic growth of Florence in the second half of the thirteenth century.[11] Further, it allows us to shed light on one of the main topics of a relatively recent debate among medieval monetary historians, namely the role of foreign currencies in the monetary circulation of foreign kingdoms.[12] Although this was a common phenomenon in the Middle Ages, the case of the Kingdom of Sicily is particularly interesting, as the kingdom already had a full set of domestic gold coins, including gold taris, *augustales*, *reali*, and later *carlini*, together with their fractions.[13]

The study of the circulation of the florin in those territories and the use that the Angevin ruler made of it reveals that by the late 1270s, Florentine florins were broadly circulating in all the dominions of the Angevin Kingdom, being not only collected through direct/indirect taxation (i.e., *subventio generalis*/tax on export of grain) on par with local gold currencies but also paid by order of the king to those mercenaries or royal officials active both within the kingdom and in the Mediterranean dominions of the Angevin Crown. Gold florins were also used to cover the expenditure of the royal court. This additional but complementary facet of the multiform circulation of the florin in the second half of the thirteenth century provides new insights into the early life of this currency. As will be illustrated, the important role of the Florentine coin in the military spending of the kingdom, which had its roots in the military expedition of Charles of Anjou in the early 1260s, was the effect of the demand for florins coming directly from mercenary troops.[14] In this context, the florin will be reconsidered both as an economic tool and a political instrument that contributed to the achievement of the king's political plans by securing the necessary military support of the mercenaries. The analysis will also show how the florin opened up new opportunities for the merchants of

Florence in the political arena of the time and how they became an asset for foreign rulers and their 'public finances'.

The Sicilian affair

Following the death of Emperor Frederick II in 1250, the Kingdom of Sicily was in turmoil.[15] The crown of Sicily was inherited first by his son Conrad (1250–54) and later by Conradin (1254–68). In 1252, Pope Innocent IV (1243–54) seized the opportunity to engage in negotiations with foreign rulers to garner their support for the conquest of the kingdom and assert papal authority. He sent his emissary, the apostolic notary Alberto da Parma, to seek alliances both with Richard, earl of Cornwall and brother of Henry III, king of England, and Charles of Anjou, brother of Louis IX, king of France. The new ally would receive the kingdom as a fief from the pope, who would exercise direct control of the religious sphere. Negotiations continued until June 1253, when both princes declined the offer. Compelled to seek an alternative, Innocent identified Edmund, son of King Henry III, as a new candidate to enact his plan. These negotiations also ended in failure.

In August 1258, Manfred, the illegitimate son of Frederick II, proclaimed himself the new king of Sicily, becoming a serious threat to the papacy due to his support of the Ghibelline faction in northern and central Italy. In 1259, Siena broke with Rome and swore allegiance to Manfred.[16] This was regarded as a rebellion by the Holy See since the city and its merchant bankers had been providing financial services to the papal Curia from at least the 1220s. On 18 November 1260, Pope Alexander IV excommunicated Siena and all the supporters of Manfred in Tuscany, but without any real effect.[17]

The situation began to change with his successor, the French Pope Urban IV (1261–64), who organised a proper counteroffensive. In January 1262, he reiterated Alexander IV's excommunication of Siena and ordered the debtors of the Sienese merchant bankers not to pay their debts. This disposition generated a huge loss for many Sienese companies active in England, Germany, and France.[18] In order to salvage their affairs, a small group of merchant bankers, mainly members of the Bonsignori, Tolomei, and Salimbene families, left the city in December 1262 and sought refuge in the fortress of Radicofani (southeast of Siena), where they remained on good terms with the papacy.[19] In 1263, it was the turn of the merchants of Florence, now ruled by the Ghibelline faction: they were ordered to stop trading in the Kingdom of Sicily and to leave the territory under threat of confiscation of all their goods. Acceptance of this papal order was widespread among the Florentines.[20]

In the same year, the pope made an initial agreement with Louis IX of France for a military campaign that would place the crown of the kingdom on the head of Charles of Anjou.[21] The final compromise, however, was made only under the pontificate of Clement IV (1265–68). As a 'champion of the Church', Charles would protect the papacy from any abuse, promising not to lay any claim to any territory in northern and central Italy and to respect the jurisdiction of the pope in ecclesiastical matters within the kingdom. Further, he would not claim imperial rights, he would provide the papal territories with 300 knights and a certain number of ships, and he would make a one-off payment of 50,000 marks sterling, plus the annual census of 8,000 gold ounces, to the Apostolic Chamber.

However, money represented 'a source of conflict' between the popes and the French prince from the very beginning.[22] The papacy wrongly believed that Charles would rely on his resources in Provence and on the financial sources of the French monarchy to sustain the costs of his military campaign. Yet, the Angevin ruler was short of troops and cash when he embarked on the initiative. Pope Urban IV was forced to proclaim a new crusade in 1264 and establish a special three-year tithe on the French clergy in Provence and France to cover the costs of Charles' expedition. The Holy See relied heavily on the Sienese company of the Bonsignori for the collection of the sums. However, due to the high costs of the French army, the slowness in the money transfers, and the excommunications imposed on Siena, Pope Clement IV asked King Louis IX to cover part of the costs with funds from the French Crown. On his refusal, the pope had to turn to the Guelph merchant bankers of Tuscany, and especially of Florence, who had recently sworn loyalty to Rome.[23] It was therefore in the name of a Guelph system of alliances, also known as 'Guelphism', that the Florentines could establish a direct link with the papacy and the Angevin dynasty, winning for themselves those positions which hitherto had been prerogatives, among the Tuscans, of the merchant bankers of Siena.[24] Overall, it has been estimated that the Angevin prince received more than 350,000 *livres tournois* from the Tuscan companies, although the high costs of the venture forced the pope to mortgage several Roman churches and pawn part of the goods of his chapel to raise even more funds.[25] All those efforts were rewarded first on 26 February 1266 when Charles of Anjou killed Manfred in the battle of Benevento and became King of Sicily (1265–85), and then again on 23 August 1268, with the defeat of Conradin in the battle of Tagliacozzo (see Map 2).

The victory of Charles of Anjou constituted a watershed moment for the economic development of Florence in the second half of the thirteenth century. In recognition of the several war-loans granted to the ruler, the Florentines obtained direct access to the kingdom, safe-conducts, and fiscal benefits. This enhanced their commercial presence in the Angevin territories and laid the foundation for their dominance in the trade and politics of southern Italy by the turn of the century.[26] At this early stage, however, the merchant bankers of Florence were far from a dominant market position that would, for instance, allow them to explicitly demand the use of gold florins in their business. They still had to overcome competition from other more established Tuscan companies, in particular those of Siena, Lucca, and Pistoia, as long as these remained loyal Guelphs.[27] The implications of the Angevin conquest of the Kingdom of Sicily for the early diffusion of the florin therefore remain unclear, especially considering that those war-loans were usually recorded in *livres tournois*, a French money of account.[28] Other documentary evidence from the period, however, suggests that Florentine gold florins were indeed part of the vast transfer of funds from France to Italy to finance the Angevin venture.

In a letter of 29 November 1265, the Sienese merchant banker Andrea de Tolomei informed the members of his company in Siena that, at the Cold Fair of Troyes (starting on 2 November), Florentine florins were being exchanged for s. 7 d. 9 of *deniers provinois* each, and no longer for s. 8 d. 1 as at the previous fair of St. Ayoul of Provins (starting on 14 September).[29] He specified that this was an old exchange rate in use at the time of the '*crocieria*', meaning 'crusade' in the Italian vernacular, namely the one launched by Pope Urban IV in 1264.[30] On this basis, one might expect that the conquest of the kingdom coincided with the creation of a new

Map 2 The Kingdom of Sicily under King Charles of Anjou (1266–85) – including the main localities mentioned in the chapter.

market for the florin in Sicily and southern Italy, which would also have benefited from the particular – but not exclusive – treatment that Florentine merchants received from the Angevin Crown. The appearance of exchange rates for florins immediately after the

Angevin conquest points in that direction.[31] In any case, by the end of the 1270s, thousands of gold florins were flowing in and out of Naples, as is also documented by one of the oldest Tuscan books of account in our possession today, namely the cash register of a Sienese merchant company that was particularly active in the cloth market in the years 1277–82.[32]

Before analysing the circulation of the florin in the Kingdom of Sicily, its pattern, and dynamics, it is worth illustrating the primary sources of this study: the registers of the Angevin chancery in the reign of King Charles I.

The first mention of the existence of royal archives of the Kingdom of Sicily under Charles dates to 1269, specifically 9 September, when the king sent his officials to Melfi, Canosa, and Lucera to collect certain registers or *quaterni* kept there.[33] Under Charles II (1285–1309), all the documentation produced in the years of the Angevin domination was gathered first in Naples, but part of this material was subsequently moved to other places. Over the centuries, the original archives of the Angevin Kingdom suffered several losses due to natural disasters or the outbreak of wars. In September 1943, the German army set fire to the building hosting the Angevin archives, causing their near total destruction. Under the direction of Riccardo Filangieri, Neapolitan archivists managed to reconstruct part of the lost records. Since 1950, when the first volume was printed, to the present time, fifty volumes have been published under the title *I Registri della Cancelleria Angioina*, and of these, the first twenty-seven deal with the reign of Charles of Anjou.[34]

Written evidence for the first years of Charles's reign is quite sparse, with only thirty-nine records for the period from 16 July 1265 to 1 April 1266. This might reflect the instability and political turmoil of the time, with the chancery still in the process of creation and the Angevin Crown engaged in several military campaigns, including the war against Conradin and the Siege of Lucera (1268–69).[35] Following the appointment of Geoffroy de Beaumont as royal chancellor in 1268, the chancery received greater discipline and new regulations: for example, acts began to be recorded in proper volumes or *quaterni*, indicating whether they were produced by the chancery or by the royal *Camera*, which dealt with the wealth and finance of the Crown. The period from 1274 to 1280 is well documented by a whole range of acts concerning the political, administrative, military, and financial business of the Kingdom of Sicily. The complete series of records related to the activity of the royal treasury for the years 1277–78 is crucial for the following analysis. Although relatively late in Charles's reign, they provide clear evidence of the involvement of the Florentine gold florin in those territories, and its use appears to be multiform.

The gold florin in the tax system of the Kingdom of Sicily as seen from the *apodixe* (detailed receipts), late 1260s–85

An interesting type of documentation that demonstrates the extent to which Florentine gold florins were well-established within the kingdom is the one appearing in the registers under the name of *apodixa* (pl. *apodixe*). The exact nature of this source is illustrated in the *Statutum Thesauriorum Castri Salvatoris ad Mare*, the charter of the royal treasuries introduced in 1277 for the opening of the new royal treasury at Castel dell'Ovo in Naples.[36] Among the dispositions regulating the office, it is clarified that treasuries had to release a sort of receipt or '*apodixa*' for any deposit of money they received. The *apodixa* had to be written according to specific guidelines: it had to indicate which currencies were actually paid, whether Sicilian taris, *augustales*, florins, or any other denomination, their quantity, and the reasons for that income.[37] Then, the *apodixa* had to be signed and sealed by all three officiating treasurers, who gave a copy of this text or *antapoca* to the depositor, which confirmed they had received the exact quantity as it appeared in the *apodixa*. Each payment to the treasury and the related *apodixa*, together with a detailed account of the expenditure of the treasury, had to be recorded in two different volumes or *quaterni*, one in Latin and one in French, and sent to the Crown at the end of each month for auditing.[38] Regulations or *capitula* issued by the king in 1272 and sent to his justiciars, i.e., the representatives of the Crown within the provinces or justiciarates, show that the *apodixe* were also used by these royal officials to note any transfer of money that occurred throughout their time in office.[39]

All these elements leave no doubt about the importance of this documentation for the purposes of our enquiry. As seen in previous sections, currency in medieval documents is very often used only as money of account. Yet, in the *apodixe*, actual coins were recorded. This is fundamental evidence to understand the currencies used in payments within the royal administration of the Kingdom of Sicily under the Angevins. The bulk of *apodixe* belongs to the period 1277–78, for which there is a whole series of fiscal sources from September 1277 to August 1278.[40] Nevertheless, fragments of *apodixe* dating back to the late 1260s confirm that Florentine florins were already being collected by the officials of the kingdom through local taxation and deposited in the royal *Camera*. On 10 July and 3 August 1269, respectively, the officers of Bartolomeo of Sorrento, the administrator for the province of Abruzzo, paid 100 gold florins to Nicola Buccelli and another undefined quantity of florins but worth 11 ounces of gold – likely 55 gold florins given the exchange rate of five florins to the ounce – to Pietro Farinelli, both representing the royal *Camera*.[41] An additional deposit of 100 gold florins from the same province occurred in February 1270.[42]

Unfortunately, in these specific cases, it is not possible to know what generated the collection and the deposit of those florins in the coffers of the Angevin treasury. It is interesting to note, however, that Florentine florins were already being recorded alongside other local gold coins, which normally exceeded the number of florins paid at this early stage of the coin's life. In the case of Nicola Buccelli, for instance, the 100 gold florins he received were worth only 20 gold ounces out of a total of 198; the remaining 178 ounces were paid in gold *augustales*. As appears in the written sources of this period, the name *augustalis* was the expression most commonly used for the new gold coin introduced by King Charles I in November 1266, officially called a '*regalis*' or '*reale*', according to the minting ordinance. This was produced at Messina, Barletta, and later Brindisi, with the same weight (5.31 g), fineness (20½ carats), and nominal value (worth 7½ taris, i.e., one-quarter of an ounce) as the Hohenstaufen gold coin, which was subsequently banned from circulation.[43] The decision to keep the same features was mainly dictated by Charles' monetary policy of retaining the existing monetary system, with his new gold coin intended to fit perfectly within it without introducing major structural changes.[44] A similar attitude characterised Charles' political approach to the existing kingdom, as he innovated as little as possible at first, maintaining the previous political structure and building upon the Hohenstaufen legacy.[45]

The same feature, with florins in smaller quantities compared to other local gold coins, especially *reali/augustales*, can also be detected in other early *apodixe*, and it could be suggested that the florin had not yet won the competition in the monetary market in the early period of its spread. Nevertheless, new elements come to light when considering Table 3.1 that lists the *apodixe* for the period September 1276–February 1277, which concern payments made by royal officials to the Angevin *Camera*.

The first striking element is the number of gold florins recorded, which far outweighs the quantities in the earlier examples. This is even more interesting because these sources are all concentrated in only six months. Given the exchange rate of five gold florins to the gold ounce, thousands of gold florins were filling the coffers of the *Regno* in a very short period of time, and this suggests an enhanced presence of the Florentine gold coin in Sicily and southern Italy by that date. The second important aspect is related to the nature of this income. It is expressly reported that many of these gold florins had been collected by the *subventio generalis* or general subvention. Under the Angevins, this was a direct tax collected on an annual basis and related to the movable goods and revenues of all laymen, excluding the clergy and the very poor.[46] The total amount of the general subvention to be exacted from the kingdom was usually fixed by the Crown, while the *Camera* assigned to each justiciar the amount to be paid by his province. Local *taxatores* would apportion it among the many fiscal subdivisions of each justiciarate, while the so-called *collectores* would proceed with the collection. All the money was finally transferred to a local *executor*, who would send the collected amount to the royal *Camera*. Owing to the lack of documentation for the actual collection of this tax, there is no way of knowing whether gold florins were actually paid at the local level or whether they were obtained through exchange transactions once the sum was gathered. However, these *apodixe* at least show that gold florins were actually deposited in the royal *Camera*. And this abundance of florins collected through the subvention acquires even more importance when we consider that, taking all the sources of income of the kingdom (i.e., indirect taxes, *Adoa*, ship money,

Table 3.1 *Apodixe* for the period September 1276 to February 1277

No.	Date	Depositor(s)	Money	Reason(s)
1[a]	26 Sep. 1276	Guglielmo Buccelli, royal official	4,800 *reali/augustales* 1,000 gold florins o. 983 gold taris	–
2[b]	20 Oct. 1276	Gautier de Sommereuse, administrator for the province of Terra di Lavoro	2,000 gold florins	*Subventio generalis*
3[c]	22 Oct. 1276	Guillaume de Aubervilliers, administrator for the province of Abruzzo	44 *reali/augustales* 1,445 gold florins	*Subventio generalis* and personal revenues
4[d]	2 Nov. 1276	Russo Caffaro of Trani, official for the distribution of the new deniers in Abruzzo	1,500 gold florins	Revenues from the distribution of the new deniers
5[e]	3 Nov. 1276	Federico de Afflicto of Naples, official for the distribution of the new deniers in Principato and Terra Beneventana	80 *reali/augustales* 1,295 gold florins o. 21 gold taris	Revenues from the distribution of the new deniers
6[f]	13 Dec. 1276	Herbert d'Orleans, administrator for Principato and Terra Beneventana	104 *reali/augustales* 2,370 gold florins	*Subventio generalis*
7[g]	17 Feb. 1277	Magister Guglielmo Buccelli, *locumtenens thesaurorum*	o. 1,595 *reali/augustales* o. 1,405 gold florins	–

[a] *RCA* XVII, p. 125, no. 320.
[b] *RCA* XVII, p. 125, no. 321.
[c] *RCA* XVII, p. 126, no. 323.
[d] *RCA* XVII, p. 127, no. 326.
[e] *RCA* XVII, p. 127, no. 327.
[f] *RCA* XVII, p. 128, no. 328.
[g] *RCA* XVII, p. 129, no. 331.

road guard money, etc.) together, the *subventio generalis* provided
c. 40 per cent of the total income every year.[47]

Nevertheless, Florentine gold florins were also being collected
through indirect taxation, such as the export tax on cereals known
as '*ius exiture*'. In an *apodixa* of 21 June 1277, Nicola Frezza of
Ravello and Sergio Pinto of Naples, both *magistri procuratores et
portulani* of Apulia and Abruzzo, paid a lump sum of 5,000 gold
florins to the royal *Camera*.[48] This was a down payment for all the
latter's claims on grain customs due in those ports ('*de pecunia exi-
tatione seu exhoneratione frumenti*') and other fees related to their
office.[49] According to William A. Percy Jr., between January and
August 1277, the *ius exiture* on wheat within the kingdom ranged
between 25 and 30 gold ounces per 100 *salmae* of grain.[50] If these
calculations are correct, and recalling that five florins were worth
one gold ounce, that payment would potentially correspond to the
revenues for a maximum of 4,000 to 3,333 *salmae* of grain.[51] This
is just a small quota compared, for example, to the 40,000 *salmae*
from Sicily that the Crown authorised for export on 16 January
1277, an amount which was later raised to 60,000 on 12 August.[52]
However, we are not dealing with Sicily here, but with exports
from some unspecified ports in Apulia and Abruzzo over an unclear
period. The fact that this transaction seems to relate to tax farming
suggests that the actual revenues would be substantially higher, and
so would the number of florins collected.

Unfortunately, the lack of further documentation does not allow
for a clearer assessment of the volume of Florentine florins involved
in the contemporary grain trade of the kingdom. Given the several wheat export contracts between the Angevin Crown and the
commune of Florence in 1276, however, large numbers of florins may have circulated from the north to the south of the Italian
peninsula as a result of this commerce.[53] On 2 August, for example, 800 *salmae* worth 240 gold ounces (at a rate of 30 ounces
per 100 *salmae*) were paid by the Florentine *podestà* and the city
council, and imported via Pisa by certain merchants of Florence
operating as *nuntii* or representatives of the commune for the sus-
tenance of the urban population.[54] The same operation occurred
on 21 September for 300, 600, and another 600 *salmae* of grain
worth 450 gold ounces in total.[55] Since two of the leading institutions of the Florentine government were directly involved in these

purchases, and considering that gold florins were being spent to buy grain for the Angevin royal household, as illustrated below, florins could have been paid on these occasions too. Furthermore, since the years 1275–77 coincided with a period of significant grain shortages in Tuscany, part of northern Italy, and Provence, one can expect that Florence and its merchants would have made grain purchases involving gold florins at that time.[56] Nevertheless, in contrast with what argued by Robert Davidsohn, the generic term 'gold ounces' denoting the sums of money paid in those sources, with no reference to gold florins, prevents a clear evaluation of the effective contribution of the grain trade to the early diffusion of the Florentine coin.

Overall, the documentation analysed so far clearly illustrates that florins were deeply embedded in the finances of the reign of Charles I, and specifically, the higher volume recorded in the second half of the 1270s suggests an entirely new role of the coin in the Angevin territory, being employed on the same scale as the local gold currencies. This begs the crucial question as to how all those gold florins were being spent. A first answer lies in the words of King Charles himself: with regard to the *subventio generalis*, he claimed that its collection was vital 'for the defence of the Kingdom against possible invaders', and more specifically, 'to pay the wages of our mercenary soldiers'.[57] With this in mind, the following section analyses royal expenditures carried out in gold florins by the Angevin Crown, with a particular focus on military spending.

Florentine gold florins for military personnel and court expenses

The earliest evidence of gold florins paid to mercenary soldiers fighting for the Angevin Crown dates to 13 July 1273. On that occasion, Charles I sent an amount of 4,000 gold florins to the commune of Piacenza to be distributed among the Angevin troops in the defence of the city.[58] However, the wording of this document raises doubts about the nature of these florins, namely whether they were actual coins or rather money of account. Later records show nonetheless that Florentine gold florins were often paid by the Angevin Crown to the military personnel of the kingdom.

On 6 March 1278, the troops serving Pierre d'Angicourt and Jean de Toul at the fortress of Lucera (Foggia) complained about the delay in payments for their military services. Charles ordered the justiciar of the province of Capitanata to cover all the costs and pay their salaries expressly in gold florins.[59] Similarly, on 3 April 1278, Guglielmo de Malassisia and his twenty mercenaries claimed a salary for three months of service defending the northern borders of the province of Terra di Lavoro. On this occasion, too, gold florins were disbursed on the direct order of the king.[60] This preference for gold florins also characterised the payments for troops fighting in regions outside the territories of Sicily and southern Italy but still under Angevin dominion.

Within the Italian peninsula, for example, 600 gold ounces of Florentine florins were given to mercenary soldiers stationed in Rome on 2 April 1278.[61] A few weeks later, on 25 June, Charles decided to repay the Sienese merchant bankers Bernardino Bonaventura, Giacomo Ranieri, and their partners for a loan of 100 gold ounces, which was also designed to pay mercenary troops in Rome. Charles expressly ordered his *camerarii* or treasurers to use gold florins first, then *reali/augustales*, and finally '*or menu*', literally 'small gold', perhaps uncoined gold in little pieces, in case florins and *reali/augustales* were not enough.[62] The same number of ounces, but entirely in gold florins, was also paid to Teodisco di Cuneo for his army in Siena on 3 June 1282.[63]

Outside Italy, florins were sent to troops in defence of Charles' Mediterranean dominions.[64] After the defeat of Manfred in 1266, the northern coastline of Albania and the island of Corfu fell under Angevin rule. Between 1279 and 1283, Charles managed to gain control over the entire Albanian shoreline.[65] On 1 July 1280, the justiciar of the Terra d'Otranto was ordered to collect o. 300 t. 6 of gold florins and send them to Drivo de Vallibus, who was responsible for the Castle of Valona, for the payment of the mercenaries and the repair of a pit there. Four trusted men carried this and other sums on a ship from Brindisi, who delivered the money to Hugh 'the Red' of Sully, vicar-general of the Kingdom of Albania, before being redistributed.[66]

In an account register of 1278, it appears that from March to May, the Angevin Crown paid the sum of o. 2,542 t. 12 of gold florins, o. 895 t. 7 gr. 10 of gold *reali/augustales*, o. 723 t. 12 of

Sicilian taris, and a few other silver coins for the services of certain troops, including those in the Principality of Achaia.[67] This was one of the vassal states of the Latin Empire formed in the aftermath of the Fourth Crusade (1204), which became a formal Angevin possession with the Treaty of Viterbo of 1267.[68]

Further documentary evidence related to another Mediterranean domain of the Angevin Crown, namely the Kingdom of Jerusalem, shows that florins were also in use there in the late 1270s.[69] On 29 January 1278, for example, Charles ordered his treasuries in Naples to pay Guillaume de la Mestrie, a delegate of the Master of the Hospital of the Order of Saint John in Acre, the sum of 450 ounces of gold florins that were borrowed by Roger of San Severino and Eudes Poilechien, respectively *bailo* (bailiff) and *siniscalco* (seneschal) of the Kingdom of Jerusalem, from the Master of that order in Acre.[70]

Overall, these sources leave no doubt about the role of the Florentine coin in payments for the wages of mercenary troops. The fact that gold florins were expressly used at the king's request is probably the most crucial element to take into consideration. By that time, the Kingdom of Sicily had its own gold coins, as noted. Also, minting coins in the medieval period involved a variety of costs for the royal mint, ranging from the wages of the workers to the price of the materials and equipment.[71] Yet, Charles explicitly opted for a foreign gold coin like the Florentine florin as a means of payment for military spending instead of any of the domestic gold coins at his disposal, and this applied in all his dominions. The cases of Valona, Achaia, and Acre, in particular, provide crucial details about the contemporary diffusion of the Florentine currency: they show that gold florins were circulating widely in the Mediterranean basin, not just via the long-distance trade of the time but rather as a result of the military and foreign policy of the Angevin king, who provided an additional and important stimulus for the spread of the florin. Before discussing the reasons behind this choice, it is worth pointing out that Florentine florins were also being used for other expenses within the kingdom involving the Angevin Crown and its court.

On 10 March 1278, Charles ordered his treasurers to pay 5,000 gold florins to his chamberlains, Jean de Torchevache and Martin de Dourdan, to cover the costs of the royal household and purchase

grain for his entourage.[72] This document, which further corroborates the link between the florin and the grain trade, as already
noted, is only one of several such cases documented in the registers.
Another sum of gold florins was granted, for example, just a few
weeks later on 20 April. On this occasion, the chamberlains received
o. 790 t. 14 of florins in exchange for an equal amount of Sicilian
gold taris, the metal from which was to be used for the minting of
a new coin known as the *carlino*. In this case, too, Charles specified
that those florins had to be used for the wages of knights, valets,
and servants at his court.[73]

Further evidence appears in the previously discussed account
register of 1278.[74] From March to May, the services of various
household officials, including the baker (*panectarie*), the librar-
ian (*stacionarie*), the master cook (*coquina*), the clerk of the stable (*marestalle*), the fruiterer (*fructuarie*), and the clerk for the
ovens (*fornarie*), were reckoned at *c.* 1,365 ounces (o. 1,364 t. 4
gr. 19). Almost half of that amount was paid in gold florins (o. 672
t. 24) and the remainder in gold *reali*/*augustales* (o. 571 t. 7 gr. 10),
Sicilian taris (o. 41 t. 13), silver *gros tournois* (o. 73 t. 7 gr. 16), and
a few petty coins. Florentine florins also played a significant role
in the payment of the salaries and grain for other members of the
royal entourage, such as clerics, doctors, and valets: out of *c.* 585
ounces (o. 584 t. 22 gr. 19), o. 395 t. 6 were gold florins, and the
remaining payments were split between gold *reali*/*augustales*, silver
gros tournois, and *grossi* of Venice. Gold florins were also a common means of payment for the salaries of the staff of the Angevin
chancery, such as scribes, notaries, and judges.[75]

By the end of the 1270s, therefore, the florin had such a strong
presence in the economy of the Angevin Crown that not only
did it act as a common means of payment for military expenditure and for the financing of the royal court, but it also trickled
down into the local economy of the kingdom through the channel
of royal expenditure. This is what the episode of the construction
of the abbey of Santa Maria della Vittoria in Scurcola Marsicana
(Abruzzo) between 1274 and 1284 seems to suggest. This abbey
was built to celebrate the victory of Charles against Conradin, the
last hope of the Hohenstaufen dynasty in southern Italy, in the battle of Tagliacozzo. It was the Crown that covered all the building
costs and entrusted royal officials or *expensores* to administer the

sums of money provided by the royal *Camera*.[76] On that occasion, it seems that it was mainly gold florins and gold *carlini* that the royal treasurers sent on behalf of the Angevin Crown to cover any expenses.[77] In November 1278, for example, Charles asked the royal treasurers to send the abbot Bartolomeo o. 24 t. 12 explicitly in gold florins for the rent and clothes of twenty workers.[78] Indeed, due to their high price compared to the requirements of the local market, gold florins would have had little practical use in such a restricted and local context. A possible explanation for such a use could be found in the direct involvement of the Angevin monarchy, which might have been so well accustomed to the presence of the florin by then that turned it into a habitual means of payment, present in all the stages of the monetary circulation of the kingdom.

Pull or push?

The previous analysis has clearly proved that not only did the florin succeed in establishing itself as a foreign currency used domestically within the kingdom of Charles of Anjou, but also that it was often preferred to the local gold coins, especially in military and royal expenditure. This begs a series of important questions: how can one explain this prominent role of the florin? Why did the Angevin monarchy rely so heavily on this coin? What were the mutual benefits for the monarchy and the florin? And was the Crown 'pushing' the florin or 'being pulled' by its contemporary success?

It is hard to prove whether the significant role of the Florentine gold coin depended on the contemporary scarcity of gold coins produced by the local mints. On 4 June 1278, Charles sent new instructions to the minters in Naples for an accurate design of the images on the two sides of his new gold *carlino*. He ordered them to speed up production and strike the new money in a 'convenient and abundant' quantity to cover imminent costs for his troops, military outposts, and other expenditures.[79] Charles' eagerness to have a decent quantity of the new gold coin at his disposal in a short period of time might hint at the contemporary inadequacy of the existing stock of local gold currencies. Unfortunately, in the absence of mint accounts, which would make it possible to evaluate the levels of the mint's production, the suggested scarcity remains mere speculation. However, if we turn our attention away from the monetary production of the Angevin Kingdom and investigate the contemporary demand for florins, a possible answer to our questions comes once again from the military context of the time.

On 30 March 1278, Charles asked his French treasurer Guillaume Boucel to take 6,500 ounces of gold florins out of the treasury in Naples and escort the money to his royal residence in Capua to pay the wages of his mercenaries for three months' service.[80] On 3 April, after discovering that only 2,800 gold ounces of florins were actually stored at the royal treasury, the king instructed his treasurers to find a moneychanger in Naples to collect the missing amount. They were ordered to exchange all domestic currencies at their disposal for gold florins of Florence and at the best price available. For that to happen, they did not have to inform the moneychangers that the Crown or the court would be the beneficiaries of the money. Only in the event that gold florins were not enough were the treasurers to also accept the local gold *augustales*, i.e., Charles's *reali*.[81]

This source corroborates the notion that war and military expenditure promoted the diffusion of the florin, mainly as a means of payment for the services of mercenaries, as noted above. Yet, it also appears to indicate that the need or demand for florins might have originated with the mercenaries themselves. Specifically, the fact that, upon discovering the temporary lack of florins in his treasury, Charles neither abandoned his request nor turned to other gold coins but instead expressly sent his officials to Naples to exchange his domestic money for a foreign currency suggests there was a strong pressure from the soldiers to be paid specifically in Florentine florins, which would have prevailed over the other gold coins then in circulation. This is probably why Charles seems unwilling to ask his officials to use domestic gold coins to remedy the issue; he was afraid of the rejection by his mercenary troops. Moreover, Charles' concern about possible exploitation by the merchants in Naples, who might raise interest rates or drive up costs if they knew the Crown was involved in the affair, indicates that the king had a certain degree of familiarity with this sort of transaction. This becomes even clearer on 12 April 1282, when Charles ordered his treasurers to pay o. 564 for the wages of certain mercenaries in Rome and invited them to borrow the necessary gold florins from certain merchant bankers or 'some of our friends' (*ab aliquibus nostris amicis*), as they were expressly called.[82]

Both the evident need for florins by the Angevin Crown and the fact that Charles ordered his treasurers to turn to merchants to satisfy his request provide clear examples of the role of the florin as a pivot point between economic and political spheres. The florin represented the instrument that allowed the merchants, and especially the Florentines as makers of the coin, to project political power through financial power onto the Angevin ruler. And it is also likely that the same ruler had to resort to the merchants' financial operations on several other occasions in the same years, especially considering that by 1278, the payment of royal mercenaries in Florentine gold florins had become 'customary', as emphasised by this further evidence.[83]

On that same day (30 March 1278), Charles instructed the justiciar of Capitanata on the payment of the salary of certain squires. He ordered the justiciar to give them the monthly amount of two ounces of gold so that they would be properly equipped and protected. With regard to the money, he specified that the salaries had to be paid in gold florins, as usual, but the way the order was formulated is the most interesting aspect here. Charles stressed that those squires had to be paid 'in the custom of the royal mercenaries (*more Regiorum Stipendiariorum*), that is, in gold florins, five to an ounce'.[84] In other words, paying mercenary troops in gold florins represented a standard practice for the Angevin Crown at that time. The fact that the king referred to this act as a long-established habit suggests that its origins date back in time, and possibly to the days of the '*crocieria*' mentioned above, i.e., the military expedition of Charles in southern Italy, when the Florentines were already lending money to the king.[85] Over the years, more and more florins were paid by the Angevin Crown to meet the growing demand coming from the troops to the point that this act became common practice by the late 1270s.

It is hard to establish how much a florin was worth in the soldiers' hands. For example, archers and crossbowmen could afford to buy one of those long shields or *pavisia* used to cover their entire body on the battlefield for less than a florin, worth t. 6 in the local monetary system. Their prices ranged between t. 2 gr. 10 for small *pavisia* used in hand-to-hand combat and t. 5 for the largest ones.[86]

It has also been estimated that the average individual consumption of grain per year corresponded to one *salma* (*c.* 275 litres.)[87] Based on the figures previously provided – i.e., 25–30 gold ounces per 100 *salmae* – a single soldier would have needed between t. 7 gr. 10 and t. 9 to afford such a quantity of grain, thus slightly more than a florin per year. Unfortunately, the lack of a consistent series of prices covering several years and relating to other goods and basic necessities does not allow for a clearer picture. Nor can we be certain that the few prices at our disposal were not affected and altered by additional charges, such as customs duties or other fees. They could also vary widely from place to place and from one year to the next, owing to speculation or contemporary economic conditions.

However, new details come to light if we look at the salaries of different occupations in Table 3.2. Although speculative, as it is based on fragmentary evidence, the table informs us of the costs of living in the Kingdom of Sicily at the time of King Charles I. It shows how significant the purchasing power of one single florin was in the local market, especially considering that its value in the domestic monetary system (gr. 120) far exceeded the smallest wage per day recorded in the table, namely gr. 6 for unskilled workers over the summer period (1 April–30 September).[88]

Yet, how can we explain such an interest in florins among mercenaries? For soldiers, being paid in florins would have had a twofold advantage. On the one hand, the Florentine florin was the most valuable gold coin among the several denominations in circulation – the only one made of pure gold (24 carats). Since money was an important part of their reimbursement, mercenaries must have been well aware of the distinctiveness of that currency.[89] Thus, due to their gold content, it is not surprising that florins were the most requested coins among the troops, who preferred them over other baser gold coins. This preference even became a condition in mercenary recruitment contracts of the late thirteenth century, as also attested by a *condotta* agreement stipulated on 13 May 1294 between the commune of Bologna and the four commanders of a mercenary band of 100 cavalrymen hired by the city for twelve months.[90] On the other hand, mercenaries also demanded florins because of the high mobility of their military activity. Since they had to travel and fight in many different territories, each with its own monetary system, those troops might have wanted to be paid with a

Table 3.2 Salaries of different professions in the Kingdom of Sicily under King Charles I

Occupation		Daily salary	Monthly salary	Notes
Royal treasury				
Royal treasurers[a]		t. 4	o. 4[b]	The amount includes expenses for 4 horses and 1 squire (*scuterius*). Extra o. 5/year for clothing
Notaries[c]	for French records	–	o. 1 t. 15	Extra o. 5/year for clothing
	for Latin records	–	o. 2 t. 11 gr. 5	Extra o. 5/year for clothing
Papal officials				
Papal inquisitor[d]		t. 4	–	The amount includes expenses for a friar, a notary and his family, and horses
Castles				
Provisor castrorum[e]		t. 3	–	–
Castellan[f]	if knight (*miles*)	t. 1	–	with lands
		t. 2	–	(no lands)
	if squire	gr. 10	–	with lands
		t. 1	–	(no lands)

Occupation		Daily salary	Monthly salary	Notes
Army[g]				
French knight (*miles Gallicus*)	with 4 horses and 1 squire	–	o. 4	–
	with 3 horses and no squire	–	o. 3	
French squire (*scuterius Gallicus*)	with 2 horses	–	o. 2	–
	with 1 horse	–	o. 1	
Latin mercenary knights		–	o. 1 t. 15	–
Saracen archers	mounted	–	t. 19 gr. 10	–
	on foot	–	t. 9 gr. 15	–
Crossbowmen		–	t. 2	–
Artillery builders and crossbow makers[h]		–	t. 12 to o. 1	–
Construction sites (funded by the Crown)[i]				
Executive director (*praepositus* or *credencerius*)[j]		t. 2 to t. 4	o. 2 to o. 4	
Financial director (*expensor* or *spenditore*)[k]		t. 1	o. 1	
Architects[l]	with horse	t. 1	o. 1	–
	no horse	gr. 15	t. 22 gr. 10	–
Valets (transporting money)[m]		t. 1	o. 1	

(*Continued*)

Table 3.2 (Cont.)

Occupation	Daily salary		Monthly salary		Notes
Wardens	gr. 10		–		
Skilled workers (quarrymen, stonemasons, bricklayers, blacksmiths, carpenters)	Summer gr. 15	Winter gr. 12	Summer (24 days) t. 18	Winter (24 days) t. 14 gr. 8	–
Carters (carrying straw)	–	–	gr. 150		–
Ox-carters (four oxen)	gr. 20 (up to)		o. 1 (up to)		–
Unskilled workers (labourers)	gr. 7	gr. 6	t. 8 gr. 8	t. 7 gr. 4	–

ᵃ RCA XXVI, p. 268, no. 95; Barone, 'Ratio', p. 419 (4 May 1278).

ᵇ This data has been extrapolated from other sources referring to the wages of the treasurers at the Cistercian abbeys of Santa Maria della Vittoria (Scurcola Marsicana) and Santa Maria di Realvalle (south of Pompei), who had the same salary conditions as the royal treasurers; RCA XXV, p. 161, no. 83.

ᶜ RCA XLIII, p. 183, no. 150.

ᵈ Barone, 'Ratio', p. 431 (18 February 1282).

ᵉ Ibid., p. 654 (17 April 1282). This was a royal official responsible for the provisioning of castles within a given province; for further details see Eduard Sthamer, L'amministrazione dei castelli nel Regno di Sicilia sotto Federico II e Carlo I d'Angiò (Bari: Adda, 1995).

ᶠ Barone, 'Ratio', X:IV, p. 654 (17 April 1282).

ᵍ Details in RCA X, p. 277, no. 57; Barone, 'Ratio', X:IV, p. 660 (3 June 1282). For a clear description of the Angevin army and its forces see also Enrico Cuozzo, 'Le investiture cavalleresche', in G. Musca (ed.), Le eredità normanno-sveve nell'età angioina. Persistenze e mutamenti nel Mezzogiorno (Bari: Dedalo, 2004), pp. 137–49.

ʰ RCA XXV, p. 152, no. 25; Barone, 'Ratio', p. 427 (24 March 1281).

ⁱ The following wages were the same in every construction site funded by the Crown as established by King Charles in 1278; Egidi, 'Carlo d'Angiò e l'abbazia', p. 753.

ʲ See, for example, the credencerius at Castel Nuovo (Naples) in Barone, 'Ratio', p. 427 (15 July 1279); or the cases of Pietro de Chaule and Rinaldo Villani credencerii at Santa Maria della Vittoria (Scurcola Marsicana) in Egidi, 'Carlo d'Angiò e l'abbazia', p. 742; RCA XXI, p. 78, no. 7 and p. 79, no. 10, respectively.

ᵏ On this office, and the one above, see Egidi, 'Carlo d'Angiò e l'abbazia', pp. 734–5.

ˡ RCA XXI, p. 78, no. 7.

ᵐ Egidi, 'Carlo d'Angiò e l'abbazia', p. 743.

currency that was highly fungible, broadly accepted, and thus easy to exchange for any other local coin. The florin, as it was also in circulation along the routes of long-distance trade and exchanged for local currencies throughout Italy, northwards to France, and in the Mediterranean region, was exactly what they needed.[91] Hence, it was probably also due to convenience that florins were in high demand among soldiers. Yet, they also represented a convenient means of payment for the Angevin Crown.

Since gold florins granted him the military services of mercenary troops, Charles would have had no reason to turn down the Florentine coin. In his eyes, the florin was a trusted and secure means of payment, allowing him to be competitive in the market for mobile military assets and build his army, especially considering the documented demand for florins among the soldiers. This, in turn, would help him maintain control, authority, and power over his domains while pursuing his political plans. Under these circumstances, the florin's role in Angevin military spending ultimately benefitted the currency itself. It gave the Florentine gold coin a new and previously overlooked dimension, which complemented its role as a means of payment and economic tool in the world of long-distance trade. In this context, the florin also acted as a political instrument at the disposal of the Angevin king, crucial for the implementation of his politics. One could even argue that the success of Charles's kingdom eventually depended on the availability of florins. Thus, while the demand for florins originated with the mercenary troops, as this case suggests, there is little doubt that the king endorsed this demand precisely for all the benefits outlined above. Still, was the Crown 'pushing' the florin or 'being pulled' by its success?

There is no straightforward answer to this question. The latter case, and the fact that florins were being paid by order of the king, who also adopted the Florentine coin in his foreign politics, as noted, seem to indicate that Charles was 'pushing' the florin and thus fostering its diffusion in other territories including the Mediterranean region. However, if the king had to sideline his domestic gold coins and exchange them for a foreign gold currency to assert his authority, this means that the Angevin Crown was also 'being pulled' by the florin and its contemporary success. Interestingly, Charles only expressly ordered the use of gold coins other than the florin on one occasion. This was for the payment of the annual census of 8,000 gold ounces that the king was expected to make to the Holy See as a result of the agreement for the conquest of the Kingdom of Sicily described above. On 6 April 1278, Charles instructed his treasurers to collect the given amount only in old *reali/augustales* ('*vieux augustales*') or gold in small pieces ('*or menu*') to pay the papacy.[92] Considering the contemporary importance of the florin in Angevin military and royal expenditures, on this occasion, Charles likely chose to employ old coins and un-minted gold to save Florentine florins for his own business. This episode begs one final and legitimate question: if the florin was so important for the finances of the kingdom, and considering that Charles was striking gold too, why did he not produce his own florin?

This happened in 1278, when Charles organised a new mint at Castel Capuano in Naples to produce his new gold and silver *carlini*. The king expressly ordered that the gold *carlino* have the same fineness as the florin but be valued as a *reale*, containing less gold than the Florentine coin. To that end, he appointed Francesco Formica, an experienced merchant and moneyer from Florence – probably not incidentally – as the new mint-master in charge of the entire operation.[93] It is hard to say why Charles did not make such a decision earlier in his reign. From a monetary perspective, for example, this could be dependent on several factors ranging from the availability of gold or the costs of its minting to the revenues from coining or the opportunity to acquire florins from outside the kingdom. The case study discussed above, for example, suggests that, at that time, it was more convenient for Charles to send his officials to Naples and buy gold florins from merchant bankers to meet the demand coming from the war market.[94] Yet, political and circumstantial reasons may also explain why Charles introduced his new gold *carlino* only later. The year 1278 coincided with a period of political change for the kingdom, with the transfer of the administrative centre of the Angevin monarchy from the island of Sicily to the mainland and the creation of the major royal mint in Naples. According to Arthur Sambon, this was also a measure to prevent fraud committed by merchant bankers in the exchange of domestic and foreign gold coins.[95] A complete study of all the possible economic, political, and circumstantial aspects that led to the minting of the *carlino* is, however, beyond the scope of this chapter.

What is important to stress here is that Charles' 1278 reform of the kingdom's gold coinage was ultimately triggered by the contemporary success of the Florentine florin, which was taken as a benchmark for the minting of his new gold *carlino*. In doing so, Charles also hoped to counteract the excessive power of the florin in his territories. To promote the spread of the new coinage, on 25 January 1279, the king wrote to his officials to ban from circulation all foreign coins such as gold florins, gold *doblas*, silver *gros tournois*, sterling, Venetian *grossi*, miliarenses, and *deniers tournois*, which could now only be accepted in payment of taxes, including the *subventio generalis*, but at a fixed rate or by weight. Florentine florins, in particular, had to be paid '*pro auro rupto*', literally 'as broken gold', thus at a rate of t. 5 gr. 14 and not t. 6 as before.[96] The only gold coins permitted to circulate would have been the gold taris, the *reali*, and, obviously, the new *carlini*.[97]

Nevertheless, this order had little effect since gold florins continued to function in the finances of the kingdom and continued to appear in the *Registri* as they had before. On 14 April 1283, for example, Charles, Prince of Salerno, ordered the royal treasurers to pay the total amount of 244 gold ounces to a group of French mercenary knights who had lost their horses while fighting in the Angevin army. The payment had to be in gold *carlini*, *reali/ augustales*, or florins in this specific order.[98] Thus, despite the king's initial dispositions, gold florins continued to be employed in the royal military expenditure. It seems probable that the creation of a kingdom-specific gold 'florin' went somewhat against the mercenaries' desire to have access to a 'universal' coin that could cross all boundaries.

Conclusions

A full understanding of the early success of the gold florin of Florence must take into consideration its circulation in the world of 'public finances' rather than simply analysing its role in the long-distance trade of the time. This chapter has demonstrated that the involvement of the florin in the military expenditures of medieval kingdoms was essential for its early diffusion. In particular, the relationship that the Florentine currency established with the Angevin

Crown, which began at the time of the crusade of Charles of Anjou in southern Italy, represented a crucial event in the florin's conquest of new markets.

Evidence from the surviving registers of the Angevin chancery for the period 1266 to 1285 has shown that florins circulated widely in the Kingdom of Sicily and were employed in three main areas: local taxation, as a means of payment for the wages of the military personnel, and in local affairs involving the Crown once they had trickled down into the economy. Florins also spread to other territories under Angevin rule, such as the cities of central and northern Italy (Rome, Siena, and Piacenza) and among the royal officials of the Crown's Mediterranean domains, including the Kingdom of Albania, the Principality of Achaia, and the Kingdom of Jerusalem. For the most part, florins were accepted and paid by the royal *Camera* and were often used at the direct request of the Crown, including for the expenses of the Angevin court.

Conversely, almost nothing is known about the dynamics that underpinned the spread of the florin in Piedmont, whose cities were among the first in Italy to submit to the Angevins. Beginning in 1259, and thus in the same years when Charles took possession of the kingdom that had belonged to the Hohenstaufen, more and more Piedmontese communes placed themselves more or less voluntarily under his political protection.[99] Yet, the economic and financial agreements in the surviving pacts concluded between these centres and the ruler do not mention Florentine florins either as actual coins or money of account.[100] And even if today, we have a clearer and more defined picture of the instruments and methods used by the Angevins to collect money and manage finances in the northern Italian domains, the lack of local tax registers and fiscal records makes it virtually impossible to observe whether and to what extent the diffusion of the florin in Piedmont was linked to and accompanied by the spread of Angevin power and its Guelph alliance.[101]

Nevertheless, contemporary documentation from the Kingdom of Sicily has revealed the existence of an ongoing demand for florins, especially among the mercenaries fighting for the ruler, which explains the importance held by the Florentine coin in all the dominions of the Angevin monarchy. Specifically, it was through the florin that the merchants of Florence could interact with the

Angevin ruler, who in turn needed florins to finance his political and military projects. In these circumstances, the florin acted both as an economic tool and a political instrument, granting power to the king while funding his politics. By 1278, the gold florin was being employed as a local currency, despite its original 'foreign' nature. In that year, Charles reformed the whole monetary system of his kingdom, and the florin was taken as a monetary reference for the minting of his new gold *carlino*. Although the latter was expressly produced with the same fineness as the Florentine currency, it could do nothing to curb the dominance of the florin in the monetary circulation of the Angevin territories. When Sicily and southern Italy ceased to mint domestic gold coins and entered a silver phase in the early years of the fourteenth century, therefore, it is little wonder that the only gold coins that continued to circulate and be used in those territories up to the mid-fifteenth century were imported foreign currencies, notably Florentine gold florins and Venetian gold ducats.[102]

Notes

1 For further details on this treatise see, for example, Alexander Murray, *Reason and Society in the Middle Ages* (Oxford: Oxford University Press, 1978; reprinted 2002), pp. 83–5 and 120; Mahmoud Manzalaoui, 'The Pseudo-Aristotelian "Kitāb Sirr al-Asrār". Facts and Problems', *Oriens* 23/24 (1974), 147–257. For a brief account on the figure of the Pseudo-Aristotle, see Thomas F. Glick, Steven J. Livesey, and Faith Wallis (eds), *Medieval Science, Technology, and Medicine: An Encyclopedia* (New York: Routledge, 2005), p. 424.

2 Murray, *Reason and Society*, p. 120.

3 For further details on this literary genre, see Roberto Lambertini, 'Mirrors for Princes', in H. Lagerlund (ed.), *Encyclopedia of Medieval Philosophy: Philosophy between 500 and 1500* (Dordrecht and London: Springer, 2010), pp. 791–7; Lisa Blaydes, Justin Grimmer, and Alison McQueen, 'Mirrors for Princes and Sultans: Advice on the Art of Governance in the Medieval Christian and Islamic Worlds', *The Journal of Politics* 80:4 (2018), 1150–67.

4 Cf. Murray, *Reason and Society*, plate II.

5 Charles Johnson (ed.), *Dialogus de Scaccario: The Course of the Exchequer by Richard Fitz Nigel and Constitutio Domus Regis. The*

Establishment of the Royal Household (Oxford: Clarendon Press, 1983), p. 2.

6 Spufford, *Money*, p. 245.

7 Norman Housley, 'European Warfare, *c.* 1200–1320', in M. Keen (ed.), *Medieval Warfare: A History* (Oxford: Oxford University Press, 1999), pp. 113–36 (at p. 126).

8 Kaye, *Economy and Nature*, p. 17.

9 Lucia Travaini, 'Romesinas, provesini, turonenses…: monete straniere in Italia meridionale ed in Sicilia (XI–XV secolo)', in L. Travaini (ed.), *Moneta locale, moneta straniera: Italia ed Europa, XI–XV secolo/ Local Coins, Foreign Coins: Italy and Europe 11th–15th Centuries, The Second Numismatic Symposium* (Milan: Società Numismatica Italiana, 1999), pp. 113–33 (at p. 125).

10 Lane and Mueller, *Money and Banking*, pp. 11–12.

11 Key studies here remain Georges Yver, *Le commerce et les marchands dans l'Italie méridional au XIIIe et au XIVe siècle* (Paris: Fontemoing, 1903); *Storia* VI, pp. 781–895; Abulafia, 'Southern Italy'; Petralia, 'I toscani'; Tognetti, 'Il Mezzogiorno'.

12 See Travaini, *Moneta locale, moneta straniera*.

13 For a sense of the varieties of coins issued in Sicily and southern Italy at that time, see Barrie Cook, Stefano Locatelli, Giuseppe Sarcinelli, and Lucia Travaini (eds), *The Italian Coins in the British Museum. Vol. 1: South Italy, Sicily, Sardinia* (Bari: Edizioni D'Andrea, 2020).

14 On Charles' army, see Jean Dunbabin, *Charles I of Anjou: Power, Kingship, and State-Making in Thirteenth Century Europe* (London and New York: Routledge, 2014), pp. 166–78.

15 This section draws from classical works on the Angevin conquest of the Kingdom of Sicily, such as Edouard Jordan, *Les origines de la domination angevine en Italie* (Paris: A. Picard fils, 1909); Émile G. Léonard, *Les Angevins de Naples* (Paris: Presses universitaires de France, 1954), trans. Renato Liguori, *Gli Angioini di Napoli* (Milan: Dall'Oglio, 1967); Norman Housley, *The Italian Crusades: The Papal-Angevin Alliance and the Crusades against Christian Lay Powers, 1254–1343* (Oxford: Clarendon Press, 1982); David Abulafia, *The Western Mediterranean Kingdoms 1200–1500: The Struggle for Dominion* (London: Longman, 1997); Jean Dunbabin, *Charles I of Anjou*; Jean Dunbabin, *The French in the Kingdom of Sicily, 1266–1305* (Cambridge: Cambridge University Press, 2011).

16 On this specific episode, see Sergio Raveggi, 'Siena nell'Italia dei Guelfi e dei Ghibellini', in G. Piccinni (ed.), *Fedeltà ghibellina, affari guelfi. Saggi e riletture intorno alla storia di Siena fra Duecento e Trecento*, 2 vols (Ospedaletto: Pacini editore, 2008), vol. 1, pp. 29–61 (at p. 42).

17 Duccio Balestracci, 'Quando Siena diventò guelfa. Il cambiamento di regime e l'affermazione dell'oligarchia novesca nella lettura di Giuseppe Martini', in G. Piccinni (ed.), *Fedeltà ghibellina, affari guelfi*, vol. 1, pp. 363–83 (at p. 368).

18 In this regard, see the letter that the Sienese merchant banker Andrea de Tolomei sent from the Champagne Fairs to his company in Siena on 4 September 1262 in Arrigo Castellani (ed.), *La prosa italiana delle origini*, 2 vols (Bologna: Patron, 1982), vol. 1, pp. 273–89.

19 Giuliano Milani, 'Uno snodo nella storia dell'esclusione. Urbano IV, la crociata contro Manfredi e l'avvio di nuove diseguaglianze nell'Italia bassomedievale', *Mélanges de l'École Française de Rome – Moyen Âge* 125:2 (2013), online at https://journals.openedition.org/mefrm/1278, accessed 20 September 2024.

20 *Storia* II, p. 763.

21 For details, see Liguori, *Gli Angioini*, p. 56*ff*.; Dunbabin, *Charles I of Anjou*, p. 132.

22 Quotation from Dunbabin, *Charles I of Anjou*, p. 133.

23 On the relations between the Florentines and the papacy, see Chapter 4.

24 Sergio Raveggi, 'La vittoria di Montaperti', in Piccinni (ed.), *Fedeltà ghibellina, affari guelfi*, vol. 2, pp. 447–66 (at p. 461). For the Guelphism at the core of the spread of the Florentine trade, see Hoshino, *L'arte della lana*, p. 67.

25 It seems that Charles' wife also started pawning the family jewels; Liguori, *Gli Angioini*, p. 60.

26 There are numerous examples of these concessions in Sergio Terlizzi, *Documenti delle relazioni tra Carlo d'Angiò e la Toscana (1265–1285)* (Florence: L. S. Olschki, 1950).

27 Tognetti, 'Il Mezzogiorno', p. 158; Petralia, 'I toscani', p. 298*ff*.

28 See Jordan, *Les origines*, chapters 3 and 4.

29 '*Fiorini valsero in Santaiuolo oto s. l'uno e uno d. più, per chasione dela crociera, e ora no credo que si potesero vendare più d'oto s. meno tre d.*' (Author's translation: 'Florins were worth at St. Ayoul s. 8 each and d. 1 more, because of the crusade, and now I do not think they can be sold for more than s. 8 minus d. 3'); Paoli and Piccolomini (eds), *Lettere volgari*, p. 57; Spufford, *Money*, p. 160, note 1.

30 See '*crocerìa*' at http://tlio.ovi.cnr.it/TLIO/, accessed 20 September 2024. Further evidence of its use can be found in Villani, *Nuova cronica*, vol. 1, p. 469. For Urban's appeal to the crusade, see Jessalyn Bird, Edward Peters, and James M. Powell (eds), *Crusade and Christendom: Annotated Documents in Translation from Innocent III to the Fall of Acre, 1187–1291* (Philadelphia: University of Pennsylvania Press, 2013), p. 397.

31 Spufford, *Handbook*, p. 59.
32 Guido Astuti, *Il libro dell'entrata e dell'uscita di una compagnia mercantile senese del secolo XIII (1277–1282)* (Turin: S. Lattes & C., 1934), especially pp. 110, 115, 122, 134, 144, and 257. These are the earliest documented references to actual gold florins employed in cloth trade transactions within the Angevin Kingdom of Sicily that I have been able to find.
33 On the history of the archives of the Angevin chancery, see the detailed analysis by Jole Mazzoleni in *RCA* XXXVII. On the Angevin chancery in general, see Andreas Kiesewetter, 'La Cancelleria angioina', in *L'état angevin. Pouvoir, culture et société entre XIIIᵉ et XIVᵉ siècle. Actes du colloque international organisé par l'American Academy in Rome (Rome–Naples, 7–11 novembre 1995)* (Rome: École Française de Rome, 1998), pp. 361–415.
34 *RCA* I–XXVII.
35 *RCA* XXXVII, p. 17.
36 *RCA* XIX, p. 89, no. 61; *RCA* XX, p. 52, no. 67.
37 '*Aut aurum tarenum, aut augustales, aut floreni, aut alia moneta* [...] *et quantum de unaquaque moneta et de quibus nostris proventibus, exitibus et redditibus illa moneta provenit*' (Author's translation: 'Or gold taris, or *augustales*, or florins, or any other currency [...] and the amount of each currency and from which of our proceeds, incomes and revenues that currency came'); *RCA* XIX, p. 89, no. 61.
38 For further details, see Léon Cadier, *Essai sur l'administration du royaume de Sicile sous Charles Iᵉʳ et Charles II d'Anjou* (Paris: E. Thorin, 1891); Romualdo Trifone, *La legislazione angioina: edizione critica* (Naples: L. Lubrano, 1921).
39 *RCA* VIII, pp. 268–74.
40 *RCA* XXXVII, p. 19*ff.*
41 *RCA* XLII, p. 37, no. 72, and p. 35, no. 63, respectively.
42 *RCA* XLII, p. 42, no. 92.
43 *MEC* 14, p. 198*ff.*
44 Arthur Sambon, *Sulle monete delle provincie meridionali d'Italia dal XII al XV secolo*, ed. L. Lombardi (Terlizzi: Biblionumis, 2015), p. 137; Michele Fuiano, *Carlo I d'Angiò in Italia: studi e ricerche* (Naples: Liguori, 1974), p. 266.
45 Dunbabin, *Charles I of Anjou*, p. 66.
46 For a detailed account of this taxation, see William A. Percy Jr., *The Revenues of the Kingdom of Sicily under Charles of Anjou 1266–1285 and their Relationship to the Vespers* (PhD dissertation, Princeton University, 1964), pp. 52–4; Dunbabin, *Charles I of Anjou*, pp. 57 and 102–3.

47 The percentage is calculated on the basis of data reported by Percy for the years 1267–76; Percy, *The Revenues of the Kingdom of Sicily*, p. 304.

48 These were royal officials responsible for the administration of the ports in the provinces of the kingdom. According to the source, Nicola and Sergio also held the position of *magistri salis* of Abruzzo and were thus concerned with the salt trade. Further details on these offices can be found in Cadier, *Essai sur l'administration*, p. 20*ff.*

49 *RCA* XVII, p. 142, no. 372.

50 Percy, *The Revenues of the Kingdom of Sicily*, pp. 149–50.

51 My calculations do not take into account the portion of florins that, according to the source, Niccolò and Sergio paid as part of the fees related to their office as *magistri portulani* ('*de pecunia officii procurationis ratione*'); *RCA* XVII, p. 142, no. 372. The percentage of these fees is not clear from the source.

52 Percy, *The Revenues of the Kingdom of Sicily*, p. 152.

53 On the activity of the Tuscans as 'grain exporters', see, for example, David Abulafia, 'A Tyrrhenian Triangle: Tuscany, Sicily, Tunis 1276–1300', in C. Violante (ed.), *Studi di storia economica toscana nel Medioevo e nel Rinascimento in memoria di Federigo Melis* (Pisa: Biblioteca del bollettino storico pisano, 1987), pp. 53–75; reprinted in David Abulafia, *Commerce and Conquest in the Mediterranean, 1100–1500* (London: Variorum, 1993), chapter 7.

54 Terlizzi, *Documenti*, p. 398, no. 733.

55 *Ibid.*, pp. 402–5, nos 737–9.

56 On grain shortages see Pinto, *Il libro del biadaiolo*, p. 80*ff.*

57 '*Pro defensione Regni contra invasores*' and '*pro stipendiis stipendiarium nostrorum*' (Author's translation: 'For the defence of the Kingdom against the invaders' and 'for the wages of our mercenary troops'); Percy, *The Revenues of the Kingdom of Sicily*, p. 53 and note 35.

58 '*IV milia florenorum auri... transmictemus, distribuenda inter stipendiarios nostros, ad vestre custodiam civitatis deputatos*' (Author's translation: 'We send four thousand gold florins... to be distributed among our mercenaries, deputed to the custody of your city'), *RCA* X, p. 133, no. 536.

59 '*Stipendiariis gagia eorum predicto modo solvenda exhibeas in florenis auri ad rationem V pro uncia auri una*' (Author's translation: 'You give the wages to be paid in the aforesaid manner to their mercenaries in gold florins at a ratio of five to one ounce of gold'), *RCA* XVIII, p. 286, no. 598. A report with all the expenses of that official for the period January–July 1278 confirms that gold florins were indeed paid; *RCA* XVIII, p. 322, no. 647.

60 '*Pro dictis vero omnibus gagia eorum predicto modo solvenda exhibeas in florenis aureis ad rationem de florenis auri V pro uncia auri una*' (Author's translation: 'For all that has been said you give the wages to be paid in the aforesaid manner in gold florins at a ratio of 5 gold florins to one ounce of gold'), *RCA* XVIII, p. 128, no. 259.

61 '*Pro satisfactione stipendiariorum nostrorum*' (Author's translation: 'For the compensation of our mercenaries'), *RCA* XIX, p. 147, no. 162.

62 '*Deus cenz et cet unces et dis tarins a pois general en florins d'or a la raison de V florins pour unce ou en augustaires ou en or menu se tant n'aviez de augustaires ou de florin*' (Author's translation: 'o. 207 and t. 10 of general weight in gold florins at a ratio of 5 florins to the ounce or in *reali/augustales* or in "small gold" if you do not have enough *reali/augustales* or florins'), *RCA* XX, p. 64, no. 81. On the meaning of *or menu* see www.cnrtl.fr/definition/menu, accessed 20 September 2024.

63 *RCA* XXV, p. 151, no. 17, and p. 169, no. 133.

64 For a full account of Charles' dominions see Gian Luca Borghese, *Carlo I d'Angiò e il Mediterraneo: politica, diplomazia e commercio internazionale prima dei Vespri* (Rome: École Française de Rome, 2008).

65 Charles never called himself *Rex Albaniae* (King of Albania) in official documentation, and the name *regnum Albaniae* (Kingdom of Albania) no longer appears in the Angevin registers after 1277. These were likely propaganda devices created *a posteriori* to justify the Angevin presence in those territories; Andreas Kiesewetter, 'L'acquisto e l'occupazione del litorale meridionale dell'Albania da parte di re Carlo I d'Angiò (1279–1283)', *Rassegna storica salernitana* 32:63 (2015), 27–62 (at pp. 36–7).

66 *RCA* XXII, p. 167, no. 277.

67 *RCA* XX, p. 69, no. 93.

68 On that occasion, William II Villehardouin, Prince of Achaia and vassal of the Latin Emperor Baldwin II of Constantinople, recognised King Charles as his lord and agreed to pass the Principality to him if there were no heirs from the marriage between his daughter Isabel and Philip, Charles's son. The death with no child of the latter in 1277 and the one of William II in 1278 gave Charles full control over the Greek region; Borghese, *Carlo I d'Angiò e il Mediterraneo*, chapter 3.

69 The Kingdom of Jerusalem formed part of the Angevin territories from 1277, when Charles purchased the title from Maria, Princess of Antioch; Borghese, *Carlo I d'Angiò e il Mediterraneo*, chapter 6 (at p. 186).

70 *RCA* XX, p. 31, no. 16; Xavier Hélary, 'Les rois de France et la Terre Sainte de la croisade de Tunis à la chute d'Acre', *Annuaire-Bulletin de la Société de l'histoire de France* (2005), 21–104 (at p. 67).

71 On the costs of minting in the Middle Ages, see Lane and Mueller, *Money and Banking*, p. 16*ff*.

72 '*V mile florins d'or por fere les despens et poier les grains et les gaiges de nostre Hostel*' (Author's translation: 'five thousand gold florins to pay the expenses and for the grain and the wages of our household'), *RCA* XX, p. 35, no. 23. See also Jean Dunbabin, 'The Household and Entourage of Charles I of Anjou, King of the Regno, 1266–85', *Historical Research* 77:197 (2004), 313–36 (at p. 321 and note 44).

73 *RCA* XX, p. 40, no. 39.

74 *RCA* XIX, p. 278, no. 588.

75 Kiesewetter, 'La Cancelleria angioina', p. 408*ff*.

76 Further details can be found in Pietro Egidi, 'Carlo d'Angiò e l'abbazia di S. Maria della Vittoria presso Scurcola', *Archivio Storico per le Province Napoletane* 34:2 (1909), 732–67.

77 *Ibid.*, p. 759.

78 *RCA* XXI, p. 201, no. 24.

79 '*...quod de eis in medietatem presenti mensis mutuum stipendiariis nostris fiat et successive de ipsis ea quantitas habeatur que comode et habunde sufficiat solutionibus eorundem stipendiariorum et castrorum nostrum...*' (Author's translation: '...that of them [i.e., new gold *carlini*] you make a loan to our mercenaries in the middle of the present month and successively make sure you have the same quantity that is convenient and abundant for the payments of the same mercenaries and of our outposts...'), *RCA* XIX, pp. 217–18, no. 363.

80 '*Por fere le prest a noz soudoires de trois mois*' (Author's translation: 'To make an advanced payment of wages to our soldiers/mercenaries for three months'), De Boüard I, p. 67, no. 26 (full text); *RCA* XX, p. 36, no. 27.

81 '*Challes etc. a maistre Guillaume Boucel de Paris, clerc, Ris de la Marre et Pierre Boudin d'Angers, receveurs etc. [...] que tu, maistre Guillaume, aportasses a nostre presence de la pecune de nostre tresor, laquele est gardée par vos touz, sis miles et cinc cent unces en florins pour feire le prest a nos soudoiers de trois mois [...], et come, d'icele pecune, ne soit trovée en nostre tresor presentement que deus miles et oit cent unces en florins d'or, a la raison de cinc florins de l'or pour ounce, nos voillons et vos coumandons que se la quantité defaillant pour aemplir la some desus dite ou une partie d'icele peut estre trovée a changier a Naples en florins, en bone maniere, en tel maniere que l'on ne puisse apercevoir que ce soit pour nous ne pour notre cour,*

*que vos changiez a florins de notre autre monoie, le mieus e a mendre
pris que vos pourre trover* [...] *Et se c'est chose que toute quantité
desus dite ne pouist ester aemplie en florins, nous voillons que cele
soit aemplie en augustaires.* [...] *Donée a la Tourt de Seint (Herasme)
pres de Capes, le tier jour d'avri de la sixte indicion'* (Author's translation: 'Charles etc. to master Guillaume Boucel of Paris, clerk, Riso
della Marra and Pier Boudin of Angers, collectors etc. [...] that you,
master Guillaume, would bring into our presence the money of our
Treasury, which is guarded by you all, six thousand and five hundred
ounces in gold florin to make an advanced payment of wages to our
soldiers/mercenaries for three months [...] and since of that money,
only two thousand and eight hundred ounces in gold florins can be
found at present in our Treasury, at a ratio of five gold florins per
ounce [i.e., 14,000 gold florins!], we want and order you that if the
quantity is lacking to meet the aforesaid sum, a part of it can be found
by exchange into gold florins in Naples, in a good manner, in such a
manner that one cannot perceive that those are for us and our Court,
and that you exchange our other coins for florins, at the best price
you can find [...] And if by chance the aforesaid quantity cannot be
filled with florins, we want it to be filled only with *reali/augustales*
[...] Given at the Saint Erasmus Tower near Capua, 3 April, 6th indiction'), *RCA* XX, p. 38, no. 32.

82 Nicola Barone, 'La Ratio Thesaurariorum della Cancelleria angioina',
Archivio Storico per le Province Napoletane 10:3–4 (1885), 413–34
and 653–64 (at p. 654, no. 12).

83 De Boüard I, p. 18.

84 '*Deinde ipsa gagia eis solvat more Regiorum Stipendiariorum, atque
florenis aureis ad rationem florenorum 5 pro uncia*' (Author's translation: 'Then he pays them their wages as is the custom with the royal
mercenaries, that is gold florins at a ratio of 5 florins to the ounce'),
Syllabus membranarum ad Regiae Siclae Archivium Pertinentium,
vol. I (Naples: Ex Regia Typographia, 1824), p. 153, no. 10.

85 The commune of Florence also paid Guy de Montfort, Charles's vicar-
general in Tuscany, with 4,000 gold florins for another military venture a few years later, on 5 December 1270, namely, the destruction
of Poggibonsi; Terlizzi, *Documenti*, p. 147, no. 251.

86 Barone, 'Ratio', pp. 433–4 (26 March 1282).

87 Stephan R. Epstein, *An Island for Itself: Economic Development
and Social Change in Late Medieval Sicily* (Cambridge: Cambridge
University Press, 1992), p. 52.

88 The winter period occurred between 1 October and 31 March; Egidi,
'Carlo d'Angiò e l'abbazia', p. 754.

89 To get a sense of the history of payments to mercenaries in the Italian peninsula before 1300, see Daniel Waley, 'The Army of the Florentine Republic from the Twelfth to the Fourteenth Century', in N. Rubinstein (ed.), *Florentine Studies. Politics and Society in Renaissance Florence* (London: Faber & Faber, 1968), pp. 70–108; Daniel Waley, '*Condotte* and *Condottieri* in the Thirteenth Century', *Proceedings of the British Academy* 61 (1975), 337–71. Although they are dated, these works are not always reliable when it comes to describing military wages: for example, Waley writes that in 1260, the monthly pay of a mercenary cavalryman was 8 'florins', as documented in the *Libro di Montaperti*, and 11 'florins' in 1277, according to a *condotta* contract from that year; Waley, 'The Army', pp. 78 and 86, respectively. Yet, he does not specify that those were not gold florins but *florinorum parvorum* or 'little Florentine deniers', the standard Florentine money of account, as also recorded in the original documents; see Cesare Paoli, *Il libro di Montaperti (An. MCCLX)* (Florence: G. P. Vieusseux, 1889), pp. 46–7, 86, 370–1, and 373–4; ASF, Diplomatico, Firenze, Adespote (coperte di libri), 1277 Maggio 5, online at www.archiviodigitale.icar.beniculturali.it/it/185/ricerca/detail/7776, accessed 20 September 2024.

90 It was expressly recorded that all payments to the military were to be made in gold florins, each worth s. 30 of Bologna ('*Et si paga fieri dabuerit ad florinos aureos pro quolibet florino computetur eis treginta solidi Bon' et non ultra vel minus*'); Waley, '*Condotte*', p. 339 no. 9, p. 361.

91 See Spufford, *Handbook*, for a list of contemporary exchange rates.

92 *RCA* XX, p. 39, no. 35.

93 *MEC* 14, p. 205.

94 The lack of written sources regarding the activity of the Angevin mint does not allow us to be more specific in this regard.

95 '*Pro bono populi propter fraudem quam committebant campsores in aliis monetis recipiendi et expendendis*' (Author's translation: 'For the good of the people on account of the fraud that moneychangers committed in receiving and spending other coins'), Sambon, *Sulle monete*, p. 144.

96 *RCA* XX, pp. 81–2, nos 26–7; Alfredo M. Santoro, 'Diffusione di grossi veneziani in Italia meridionale durante il regno di Carlo I d'Angiò: tra archeologia e archeometria', in R. Fiorillo and P. Peduto (eds), *III Congresso nazionale di archeologia medievale: Castello di Salerno, Complesso di Santa Sofia, Salerno 2–5 ottobre 2003* (Florence: All'Insegna del Giglio, 2003), pp. 115–21 (at p. 115); Travaini, 'Romesinas, provesini, turonenses', p. 125.

97 Sambon, *Sulle monete*, p. 147.
98 '*En charlois d'or ou en augustales ou en florins*' (Author's translation: 'In gold *carlini* or in *reali/augustales* or in florins'), De Boüard II, p. 289, no. 267.
99 Rinaldo Comba (ed.), *Gli Angiò nell'Italia nord-occidentale (1259–1382)* (Milan: Unicopli, 2006), especially the contribution by Paolo Grillo, 'Un dominio multiforme. I comuni dell'Italia nord-occidentale soggetti a Carlo I d'Angiò', pp. 31–101.
100 For further details on those pacts, see Patrizia Merati, 'Fra donazione e trattato. Tipologie documentarie, modalità espressive e forme autenticatorie delle sottomissioni a Carlo d'Angiò dei comuni dell'Italia settentrionale', in Comba (ed.), *Gli Angiò*, pp. 333–61.
101 Patrizia Mainoni, 'Il governo del re. Finanza e fiscalità nelle città angioine (Piemonte e Lombardia al tempo di Carlo I d'Angiò)', in Comba (ed.), *Gli Angiò*, pp. 103–37; Riccardo Rao, 'Gli Angiò e la gestione delle finanze in Piemonte e Lombardia', in S. Morelli (ed.), *Périphéries financières angevines. Institutions et pratiques de l'administration de territoires composites (XIIIᵉ–XVᵉ siècle) / Periferie finanziarie angioine. Istituzioni e pratiche di governo su territori compositi (sec. XIII–XV)* (Rome: École Française de Rome, 2018), pp. 271–90, online at https://books.openedition.org/efr/3564, accessed 20 September 2024.
102 Stefano Locatelli, 'Florins and Ducats in the Kingdom of Sicily-Aragon: The Syracuse Hoard (1313–c.1369)', *NC* 179 (2019), 299–340.

4

The florin and the papacy

The thirteenth century represented a crucial moment for the Holy See in its definition and deployment of a centralised financial system that fostered the movement of money and the development of capital transactions at an international level.[1] The origins of this phenomenon can be traced back to the history of the financing of the crusades in Italy, which is 'at its widest, the history of papal finance generally in the thirteenth and fourteenth centuries', as Norman Housley put it.[2]

In the final years of the twelfth century, the papacy began to levy special and extraordinary income taxes to render pecuniary assistance to the crusaders fighting the infidels in the Holy Land. While originally conceived as a temporary and extraordinary measure, papal income taxes soon proved to be an asset for the finances of the papal court, which did not hesitate to rely on them on many subsequent occasions and not solely for the crusades. In 1228, Pope Gregory IX (1227–41) asked the clergy of the ecclesiastical provinces not controlled by Emperor Frederick II to grant him a tenth of their revenues to raise an army against the Swabian, who had invaded the papal territories.[3] According to William E. Lunt, this was the first time a tithe was levied for a purpose other than a crusade.[4] The episode set a precedent, and from that moment on, the collection of the tithe became the standard way for the Catholic Church to fund either the crusades or its policy of expansion throughout the thirteenth century.[5]

To properly administer the flow of money moving from the periphery of the Christian world to the Apostolic Chamber (*Camera Apostolica*), i.e., the papal treasury in Rome, the papacy had to introduce new measures into its fiscal system. By the end of the twelfth century, operations such as the transfer of papal funds and the safeguarding of deposits began to be delegated more frequently to merchant bankers of different Italian cities and less to the knightly orders of the Templars and Hospitallers, which had previously been responsible for those matters. They possessed an organisational structure that encouraged the conveyance and protection of substantial sums of money, although fighting remained their main activity.[6]

The Holy See's economic relations with the Italian mercantile companies in the thirteenth century have been the object of a fair number of studies, although some of them are now quite dated.[7] The majority are mainly concerned with the development of these relations, their mutual benefits and political implications, as well as their effect on the economy of the time. Yet, from a monetary perspective, they largely fail to assess the beneficial effects that the papacy, with its financial system and wide network of merchant bankers, brought to the diffusion of contemporary innovations, including the gold florin of Florence.

So far, the circulation of the Florentine coin in the finances of the papal court has only been partly examined by John Day.[8] Day offered a systematic and statistical account of the coins paid to the collectors of the tithe of 1296 in the dioceses of Tuscany as part of the three triennial tithes ordered by Pope Boniface VIII in 1295–1304.[9] His research revealed that by the end of the century, the florin had made up almost 40 per cent of the total value of the tithe collected on that occasion. Yet, Day's analysis focused on a chronological period, the 1290s, when the adoption of the florin in several milieus had already occurred. In other words, his findings add little to discussions on the dynamics that led the Florentine gold coin to achieve such a strong presence in papal finances, the possible role played by the papacy in the rise of that currency, and the extent to which the florin represented an asset for the political projects of the popes.

This chapter aims to answer these questions by investigating the diffusion of the florin in the financial system of the papal court in the early decades following its introduction. It opens with an overview of the relations between the popes and the merchant bankers of Florence to show that for most of the century, the Florentines did not enjoy any privileged position but were just one group of the many Italian merchant bankers providing similar financial services to the papal court. Being appointed *mercatores papae* in the early 1260s certainly boosted their efforts to monopolise or at least get hold of significant chunks of papal business and finance; this in turn helped promote the spread of the florin. Yet, it was only under the pontificate of Boniface VIII that the gold coin came to act as a 'unique selling proposition' enabling the Florentine merchant bankers to outcompete other companies and gain almost full control of papal finances.

Nevertheless, the analysis of a remarkable set of hitherto neglected registers in the *Collectoriae* series of the *Archivio Apostolico Vaticano* covering the first four years (1274–78) of the collection of the sexennial tithe of Pope Gregory X in southern Italy proves that the florin was already being extensively collected in those territories, representing one-third of the total value of the tithe, with no significant rivals among the other gold, silver, and billon coins documented in the registers. This significant employment of the florin in papal collections in the early years of its life is a completely new aspect,[10] which does not seem to have depended on a direct order coming from the popes.

Finally, the study of papal expenditure related to the tithe money will shed new light on the mutual contributions and benefits of the papacy and the florin. While the papacy significantly enhanced the diffusion of the florin by adopting the currency to finance its major political projects, the florin acted as both an economic tool and a political instrument through which the popes could project their power and assert their authority.

The papacy and the Florentine merchant bankers

The earliest references to merchants of Florence pursuing their interests in Rome date back to the last decades of the twelfth and the early years of the thirteenth century. Pierre Toubert claimed that Florentines were already performing banking activities with the papacy as early as 1177.[11] In 1193, the Florentine Rainuncino Tedaldini was recorded in the *palatio sancti Adriani* in Rome, acting as a witness in a dispute between Gregorio, abbot of the monastery of Passignano (Florence), and two merchants of Siena regarding certain cloths the abbot had acquired from them but never paid for.[12] Given the object of the dispute, Robert Davidsohn regarded Rainuncino as another merchant.[13] In 1204, Tinioso Lamberti, consul of the oft-mentioned *Arte del Cambio*, was sent to appease Pope Innocent III regarding the dispute between the city of Florence and the bishop of Fiesole.[14] The appointment of guild consuls as civic emissaries to carry out diplomatic actions was a common habit at that time, not necessarily an effect of a special relationship between Florence, its merchant bankers, and the popes. And while these three cases suggest an early Florentine involvement in the economic network of the papacy, the sporadic references in the extant documentation do not demonstrate how close and strong those ties were at that stage.

In the first quarter of the thirteenth century, the recourse of the papal court to Florentine merchants became more frequent. In 1219, under the pontificate of Honorius III, Arengerio of Florence was entrusted by the papal Camerlengo, namely, the official appointed to administer the revenues of the Holy See, to collect the tributes from the castles of Carpi and Monte Baranzone that the commune of Modena owed to the papacy.[15] In the same year, the Florentines Gualtero Manerio and Angelo Cathelino were mentioned together with a group of Roman merchants and a Jewish one in a dispute over a loan originally contracted at the Roman Curia in favour of Walter, bishop of Chartres, which had not yet been repaid.[16] A similar partnership is also documented a few years later, in 1224, when Godfrey of Crowcombe and Stephen de Lucy, ambassadors of the English Crown, borrowed 500 marks from Giovanni Gualfredi of Florence and Giovanni Nicolai of Rome at the papal court.[17] In 1226, it was the king himself, Henry III of England, who ordered his treasurers to return the amount of 90 marks to Manerio Dedy, Guascone, Mannello, and Cambio, four merchants of Florence who operated in his kingdom, for certain loans their associates had granted at the Roman Curia to his representative, Master Philip of Hadham.[18]

It was in these same years that the merchants of Florence began to collect and transfer funds for the papacy while operating at the Holy See, as well as to exchange money or lend it to clerics or rulers in need. Yet, they were not alone in this. The same services were also being performed by many other merchants from different

Italian cities, whose relations with the Holy See were more fluid and less structured than they would become in the second half of the century.[19] In the registers of Pope Honorius III, for instance, there are several references to merchants of Pavia, Lucca, and Siena associated with the Romans in similar money-lending business.[20] The Florentines were just one of those groups and one of the poorer documented, presumably due to their lesser importance. Up to the 1240s–50s, the largest number of transactions remained in the hands of a few companies of Rome, joined in the 1230s by merchant bankers from Siena. Indeed, as they were all from Rome or the surrounding area, it is not surprising that the popes from Clement III (1187–91) to Gregory IX (1227–41) preferred to do business with their fellow citizens.[21]

Although documented, the companies of Florence continued to play a minor role under the pontificate of Gregory IX. On 3 February 1234, the Florentine Teobaldo stood with the Roman brothers Ottone and Stefano Mannetti, his commercial partners, against another member of the mercantile company, a certain Tinioso, who had depleted all the shared capital by contracting debts in England, France, and Rome.[22] On 22 December of the same year, Uberto, Guglielmo Clarissimi, Salvio, Scaltano, and other *mercatores* of Florence were responsible for a loan of more than 1,000 marks sterling given to the bishop of Glasgow with the authorisation of the papal court.[23] In 1241, other Florentines loaned 40 marks sterling to Milone, canon of the diocese of Orange (France), for the costs of an inquisitorial proceeding (*'pro negotio inquisitionis'*) he was pursuing against the bishop of the same diocese.[24]

It is incorrect to consider these and other operations between merchants of Florence and the papal court as the result of any privileged relationship. At this stage, no Florentine merchant had yet been granted the official title of *campsor domini papae*, literally 'exchanger of the lord pope'.[25] These were professional merchant bankers engaged in all aspects of the contemporary money exchange and trade, directly appointed by the pope to carry out specific assignments of different durations, including loans to prelates at the papal court, the collection and transfer of funds from other territories to Rome, or the exchange of money at the request of the Apostolic Chamber.[26] They operated on behalf and in the employ of the papal court but were not part of its organisation. For these years, archival sources record only Sienese or Roman merchants in this role, such as Angelerio Angiolieri, also called '*Solaficus*' (1228–29), Montanino (1233), *Raynucius* (1239) of Siena, and the Roman Bobo of Giovanni Bobone (1232).[27] Except for these individuals, the only ones who managed to establish a personal and privileged bond with the popes, the papacy continued to rely on a number of different companies from a wide range of Italian cities; Florence was just one among many.[28]

William E. Lunt speculated that some merchants of Florence were acting as papal agents as early as 1233.[29] On that occasion, King Henry III of England ordered his treasury to pay 1,000 marks to the Florentine Bonaccorso Ingelesk (*sic*), Aimerio Cosse, and their partners for the royal tribute due to the papal court.[30] However, while transporting papal revenues from England was a task normally entrusted to the pope's *campsores*, the lack of the specific title in the official documentation does not seem to support Lunt's thesis. Other factors may have influenced the papal decision to rely on Florentine merchants for that business. Certainly, the well-documented position of power occupied by the Florentine companies in England at that time would justify their participation. For example, members of the Scali, dal Borgo, and Pulci-Rimbertini companies had been operating there since the early 1220s as both wool traders and creditors of the English Crown.[31] In the eyes of the papal court, Florentine companies involved in the economic and financial affairs of the English kingdom would therefore have offered the best deals, terms, and conditions, having a competitive advantage in handling payment transactions to and from those territories. Thus, for its own gain, the Holy See considered it more convenient to rely, in this particular case, on those merchants rather than its own *campsores*. The same dynamic also applied to the Sicilian business of Pope Alexander IV (1254–61) and King Henry III in the 1250s, as will be discussed below.

On occasion, however, Pope Gregory IX took direct action to protect and promote the interests of the merchant bankers of Florence. In September 1235, at the request of Florentines lending money in France, he prohibited the four-year deferment of payment granted by crusade preachers to debtors that joined the holy army, as these deferments made it impossible for the merchants of Florence to recover their money in a reasonable time.[32] In the same month, Gregory entrusted the abbot of St Geneviève in Paris with the protection of the merchants of Florence operating at the Champagne Fairs by ordering that, in the dioceses of Paris, Meaux, Châlons, and Langres, the Florentines could only be put on trial by means of papal letters.[33] In November, the same privilege was granted to some merchants of Siena in the dioceses of Sens, Troyes, and Langres and then again to other Florentines in the dioceses of Rheims, Arras, and Paris.[34] The fact that merchants of Siena and Florence were enjoying equal benefits might be seen as evidence of the latter's growing importance in their relationship with the papacy. This seems to be confirmed by the special measures that the pope adopted two years later exclusively for the Florentines in France, acting almost like an informal overlord.

In February 1237, Gregory sent his secretary Benedetto de Guarcino to France to require the payment of all the debts that clergymen, laymen, and crusaders contracted with the companies of Florence.[35] The order came after several Florentines had gone bankrupt owing to the significant sums of money that had been borrowed from them and never repaid. To guarantee their reimbursement, the pope also appealed to Louis IX, King of France (1226–70), his bailiffs, and Theobald I, King of Navarre (1234–53) and Count of Champagne, where the Florentines then had a strong presence.[36] His initial request did not have the desired effect, so Gregory was forced to write again to those authorities a year later, in 1238, at which point the Florentines finally got their money back.[37]

Under the pontificate of Innocent IV (1241–55), references to Florentine merchants within the papal registers grow in number, and from 1243, they appear to offer loans to clergy all around Europe. Papal letters document transactions with the dioceses of Cambrai (1243), Utrecht (1246), Poitiers (1248), Palencia (1249), Lyon and Cologne (1250), and York and Cordoba (1253).[38] The contemporary decline of the merchant bankers of Rome significantly contributed to this result. In the 1240s, many of the Roman families previously involved in the financial market of the time lost their status, prestige, and power, and thus their relations with the papal court. As Marco Vendittelli points out, this was probably also due to the lack of support that the previous popes, Innocent III, Honorius III, and Gregory IX, all of Roman origin, had granted to the merchant bankers of their hometown, who were now unable to exercise direct control over the economic life of the city due to the internal crisis between its political parties.[39] This situation inevitably led to a higher level of involvement of Tuscan merchant bankers. The *Magna Tavola* of Orlando Bonsignori of Siena, the *campsores domini pape par excellence*, also called *mercatores camere* or *mercatores domini pape* from the 1260s, retained the monopoly of the financial operations of the papal court, but soon the companies from Florence began to rise in importance.[40]

The first qualitative leap in their relations with the papacy occurred in the 1250s. Under Alexander IV (1254–61), the Dal Borgo, the Scali, the Ghiberti-Bellindotti, and the Pulci-Rimbertini companies provided extensive loans to Henry III of England for the conquest of the Kingdom of Sicily, alongside the Sienese Bonsignori.[41] In this case, too, the decision of the papacy to rely on the Florentine companies primarily depended on the long records of financial relations that those firms – and similarly, the Bonsignori of Siena – already had with the English Crown. This time, however, the Florentines found themselves playing a more significant role, directly appointed to control the entire flow of capital that took place around the Sicilian venture of the English king. At the request of the pope, they anticipated significant loans to the monarchy on the promise of being repaid with the revenues of the special tithe that Pope Alexander established to fund Henry's military efforts.[42] This episode marked the first massive involvement of companies of Florence in papal financial operations but was rather unfortunate, as the military expedition never took place, not least due to the internal political crisis involving the king and his barons.

A second key moment in the participation of Florentine merchants in the financial affairs of the papacy occurred a few years later, under the pontificates of Urban IV (1261–64) and Clement IV (1265–68) when the papacy supported Charles of Anjou's victorious campaign against Manfred. On that occasion, the companies of Florence were able to establish strong and direct ties with both the Angevin Crown and the Holy See, especially at the expense of Sienese merchants, as noted. In return, not only did they obtain from the new king a whole series of tax exemptions and benefits to trade in southern Italy, but many Florentine companies in business with the Holy See, such as the Pulci-Rimbertini, the Scali, the Mozzi, the Frescobaldi, the Cerchi, and the Bardi, were also granted the privileged status of '*mercatores camere*', resulting in greater involvement in papal affairs. This title, however, was also attributed to the Riccardi, the Battosi, and the Cardellini of Lucca, and to the Ammannati and the Chiarenti of Pistoia.[43] Under Pope Gregory X (1271–76), the Scotti of Piacenza also joined this cohort of companies. Just like the Florentines, all these firms offered financial assistance to the popes, albeit to varying degrees and at different times, but equally sharing risks and without holding a monopoly on any transaction. This was the policy of the Holy See until the last decade of the century when it abruptly changed after the election of Pope Boniface VIII (1294–1303).[44]

Unlike all his predecessors, Boniface assigned the full administration of papal finances to just three companies, which acted as official treasurers of the papacy: the Spini and the Mozzi of Florence, and the Chiarenti of Pistoia. According to Robert Davidsohn and, more recently, Armand Jamme, it is only from this moment onward, that is, when the Florentines finally outnumbered the firms of other cities, that one can rightly speak of the 'Florentinisation' of the mercantile companies in the service of the papacy.[45]

Indeed, interpersonal relations and political alliances between the pope and those firms played a pivotal role in Boniface's decision. The Spini, for instance, were the leaders of the Florentine Black Guelphs' party supported by the pope, while the Chiarenti had been serving him since he was a cardinal at Anagni.[46] Yet, it is hard to believe that the economic situation of the time, and more precisely, the contemporary fall of two of the most powerful companies of the period, the Bonsignori of Siena and the Ricciardi of Lucca, direct competitors of the Florentine firms at the Holy See, played a minor role.

During the 1290s, the outbreak of new wars, such as the conflict between King Philip IV of France and King Edward I of England and the Aragonese-Angevin war in southern Italy, suddenly generated an urgent need for large sums of money. Neither the Bonsignori nor the Ricciardi were able to meet the growing demand for loans while simultaneously returning all their deposits to their customers, including the papacy.[47] Due to the severe liquidity crisis affecting their finances, both companies soon went bankrupt. Boniface's ultimate decision to limit his financial relations to just three banking companies may thus also have been dictated by the need for stability in the papal financial system. As Ignazio del Punta convincingly pointed out, the choice fell on the Mozzi, the Spini, and the Chiarenti, quite possibly because these firms had previously been less involved in heavy loans to political and ecclesiastical authorities. This, in return, would have made them 'more reliable and more solid' in the eyes of the pope.[48]

Against this backdrop, the very fact that the Florentines could rely on the gold florin might have eventually tipped the balance of the pope's decision firmly towards them. At that time, the florin represented one of the most stable and reliable gold coins in circulation, challenged only by the Venetian ducat minted from 1285 onward. As seen above, the Florentine currency was also already well-established in several milieus, including long-distance commerce and war markets, acting both as actual coin and money of account. As emphasised by Gino Arias, moreover, one must not forget that, as the makers of the florin, the Florentines could adjust its value on the market if necessary and sell it at a lower price than other firms in the event the pope asked for the coin.[49] For all these reasons, it is therefore very likely that the florin, by acting as what in today's economic jargon is called a 'unique selling proposition', that is, the crucial factor that differentiated the Florentines from any other competitor and enabled them to win the existing competition ahead of the other companies, increased the creditworthiness of Florentine companies and added value to the pope's choice.

Unfortunately, the lack of documentation makes it impossible to establish which one of these reasons, whether economic, political, or interpersonal, was given the most weight in Boniface's final decision. Assuming that the florin did actually play an important role in his choice, none of this would have been possible if the papacy were not already familiar with the coin, its features, and its advantages. The following analysis of the movement of capital around the papal court generated by the collection of the sexennial tithe of 1274, here covering part of the Kingdom of Sicily, offers a clear picture of the spread of the florin through papal finances. It shows that, at least in southern Italy, the florin was the most prevalent coin used to cover the largest portion of the value of the tithe collected by the papal agents. Before proceeding, however, a brief overview of the tithe, its importance in the financial system of the thirteenth-century Curia, and of the primary sources used in the following analysis will be presented.

The tithe in the papal finances of the thirteenth century

The clerical tenth or tithe was a special income tax levied by the papal court on the revenues of all clergy and, in theory, corresponded to one-tenth of the value of their annual revenues. Linked with the monetary needs of the crusades, the tenth was paid for religious purposes and under ecclesiastical obligations. The first pope to levy an income tax of this kind to provide a more solid financial basis to the imminent Fourth Crusade (1204) was Innocent III (1198–1216) with his fortieth of 1199.[50] This tax was assessed by the payers, and its collection was entrusted to local bishops, who were expected to deliver the money to local crusaders or directly to the Holy Land. This use of income taxes was not entirely new, as something similar already existed among the lay rulers of the time. In 1147, King Louis VII of France decreed a special tax on all his subjects, both lay and religious, in support of the Second Crusade. In 1188–89, both King Henry II of England and King Philip II of France ordered their subjects to pay a one-tenth tax assessed by the dioceses and known as the 'Saladin tithe' for the preparation of a new crusade after the capture of Jerusalem by the Muslim army (1187). Conversely, in 1199, Pope Innocent III introduced a new form of taxation that, despite the secular antecedents, 'was imposed solely by the will of the pope and paid by the clerical estate only'.[51]

The combination of tithes and crusades continued to prove its worth throughout the thirteenth century. The success of this formula was also due to the popes' ability to present their monetary needs in terms of holy wars for the defence of the faith, thus making it easier for them to justify the fiscal burden generated by the extraordinary collection of money.[52]

Three main changes were introduced under the pontificate of Gregory IX.[53] First, the amount requested by Gregory in 1228 was one-tenth of ecclesiastical revenues, and this became the portion usually demanded by the papacy from all clergy on subsequent occasions. Second, the tenth was not levied to provide financial aid to the crusaders only but also to fund the contemporary war of the papacy against Emperor Frederick II. Third, the assessment and collection of the new tenth were placed in the hands of dedicated officers directly nominated by the pope and responsible for the appointment of their own deputies. From that moment, the same principles were applied to many subsequent tithes levied either for the crusades or in support of the political interests of the papacy.[54] Nevertheless, new and crucial measures in the procedure for the collection of money were introduced by Pope Gregory X (1271–76) in 1274, which was a 'turning-point in the development of the papal fiscal system'.[55]

On 7 May 1274, Gregory X opened the fourteenth ecumenical council of the Catholic Church, also known as the Second Council of Lyon. Since his inaugural sermon, the pope sought to awaken the enthusiasm of the 300 or so bishops and archbishops attending the Council, along with King James I of Aragon (1230–76) and numerous royal messengers, for a new crusade in the Holy Land and to persuade everyone to make sacrifices in its name. After lengthy negotiations, his proposal succeeded in gaining the consent of the laymen and clergymen participating in the Council. Gregory obtained the imposition of a new one-tenth income tax upon all the profits of Christendom for the duration of six years, from 1274 to 1280.[56] The so-called 'sexennial tithe' began on 24 June 1274, and the annual payment was split into equal portions in two different instalments: the first on 25 December, Christmas day, the second on 24 June, the day of the nativity of St John the Baptist. To ensure that money would arrive on a regular basis and to strengthen papal control from the centre to the periphery, the entire territory of the Catholic Church was divided into twenty-six collectorates or *collectoriae*, territorial constituencies deputed to the collection of the tithe and formed by one or more ecclesiastical provinces extending from Norway to Sicily and from Portugal to Jerusalem. Except for the collectorates of the city of Rome and the Kingdom of Jerusalem, the others were under the responsibility of a general collector appointed by the pope.[57] It was Gregory himself who instructed these agents on the assessment and the collection of the tithe.[58] For the purposes of our inquiry, three main aspects are worth noting here.

First, the pope expressly ordered that all the payments throughout the six years had to be done solely in the money current in the territory where the tithe had been levied, without recourse to exchange transactions, while no payments in kind were allowed.[59] This disposition, the only one referring to the money collected, is a clear indication that at least all the coins recorded in our sources were part of the monetary circulation of those years, although the preference for payments in one currency over another might have depended on several factors, such as the reputation of that currency in a given area and at a specific time.[60] Second, not all people were required to pay the tithe. Exemptions were granted to the collectors and their deputies, to religious persons such as nuns or clerks with poor incomes or benefits, and to certain religious buildings like hospitals helping the poor and invalids.[61] Third, clearly, no negotiations between the collectors and the payers were allowed, and excommunication was the punishment for any misconduct. Each collector was responsible for the appointment of his own deputies or sub-collectors (*subcollectores*), normally from two to four per diocese, who had to serve under oath.[62] They were expected to collect the money and record all the sums received in their own registers (*Rationes decimarum*), usually one per semester. Those registers were sent to the relevant collector, who would compile the general account (*Ratio*) to be delivered to the papal *Camera* once the tithe was over.

In previous versions of the tithe, it was customary to deposit the proceeds in safe places, such as monasteries or cathedrals, while waiting to be donated to those kings leading the new crusade on the day of their departure. In the case of the sexennial tithe, however, probably also due to a series of cases of misconduct, the deposits were often assigned to companies of merchant bankers, who would award the money only at the request of the papacy.[63] Due to its volume, the unique geographical extension with no parallel in previous manifestations, and the complex machinery created by the papal court for the collection of money, scholars of papal finance have referred to this tithe as the first 'universal' tenth of the thirteenth century.[64]

Nevertheless, only a fragment of the financial accounts recorded either by the collectors or the sub-collectors during the sexennial tithe is still available today. The remaining documentation is preserved in the *Collectoriae* collection of the *Archivio Apostolico Vaticano*, a series of registers that the papal *Camera* stored to keep track of the work of its tax-agents.[65] As reported by Pietro Guidi, only twelve of the twenty-four *Rationes* compiled by the collectors are still preserved; complete or partial registers of the sub-collectors are documented for only six collectorates.[66] Part of this material was published in five of the fourteen volumes forming the series of the *Rationes Decimarum Italiae* and specifically in those covering the regions of Tuscia, Apulia-Lucania-Calabria, Sicily, Umbria, and Lazio.[67] However, up until now, far too little attention has been paid to this documentation from a monetary perspective. This may also be related to the issues affecting this kind of source and its interpretation.

Only on rare occasions did the collectors leave us either with a detailed description of the actual coins paid to them or with both a clear itemisation of the monetary specie received and the relative values in money of account. It is only in those circumstances that one can assess how much of each currency was paid and calculate their value as a portion of the total of the tithe in a specific year. Within the published documentation of the sexennial tithe, similar conditions apply only to the material in the Umbria and Lazio volumes.[68] In both cases, however, information is too scarce and fragmentary to allow a comprehensive study of the money collected over a continuous period of years. The still unpublished volume 217 in the *Collectoriae* collection of the *Archivio Apostolico Vaticano* related to the sexennial tithe levied in southern Italy represents an exception in this regard.

The florin and the sexennial tithe in southern Italy

Volume 217 consists of a series of registers of the sums collected (*quaterni decimarum*) and one register of deposits (*quaternus depostitorum*) belonging to two collectorates of southern Italy: the collectorate of the Kingdom of Sicily 'with the exclusion of Sicily and Calabria' (*'in Regno Syciliae exceptis Sycilia et Calabria'*), which was assigned to the collector Pietro da Ferentino, bishop of Sora in 1274 and of Rieti from 1278, and the collectorate of Calabria and Sicily, to which was appointed Marco d'Assisi, bishop of Cassano.[69]

In 1937, Domenico Vendola defined this material as being 'of little use' in tracking the religious bodies involved in the payment of the tithe in Apulia.[70] He noticed that the way payments were listed in those accounts, usually in the form of a single total amount for all sums collected from the bishop, the clergy, and the monasteries of a given diocese, was 'too schematic' to help calculate how much had been levied upon each individual religious body. Since then, historians have lost interest in this material.[71] Through a new and careful analysis, however, it is now possible to reassess the role of this documentation, which provides unique details regarding the movement of capital around the papal court, generated by the collection of the tithe and the diffusion of the florin within papal finances.

The focus here is on five registers that Bishop Pietro da Ferentino prepared once the sexennial tenth was over in 1280 and then delivered to the Apostolic Chamber in Rome.[72] These registers offer a full account of the sums paid by each diocese, often with the double entry of the actual money paid and the money of account. Also, more importantly, they document the collection of the tithe for four consecutive years of the six planned by Gregory: Year One (1274–75), Year Two (1275–76), Year Three (1276–77), and Year Four (1277–78). This is a crucial aspect that Vendola failed to notice, but which makes those registers an exceptional source, as they record the diffusion of the florin within papal finances with a degree of continuity over the years.

The number of dioceses and archdioceses those registers cover is 111, and this is also likely to be the total number for the Kingdom of Sicily in the years 1274–78 if we exclude those of Calabria and Sicily.[73] However, there are differences in how payments were recorded in these five registers, particularly between the first *quaternus* referring to Year One and the remaining four.

The first register is the only one to list payments for each of the 111 dioceses, and it appears to be more schematic and better organised than the others. It opens with the amounts paid by the dioceses 'directly subject' to the jurisdiction of the Holy See, or *immediate subiecte*, followed by the payments of those archdioceses and dioceses *mediate subiecte*, or 'subject through a mediated way', organised by ecclesiastical province.[74] These were ecclesiastical administrative districts formed by a group of suffragan dioceses governed by their own bishops, but all under the ecclesiastical jurisdiction of a metropolitan bishop or archbishop based in the archdiocese. Excluding the regions of Calabria and Sicily, there were fourteen ecclesiastical provinces in the Kingdom of Sicily at that time.[75]

Table 4.1 The five registers of bishop Pietro and their composition

Years	References (fos)	Titles	No. of dioceses
Year One (1274–75)	1r.–14v.	*Quaternus decimarum ad Terre Sancte subsidium*	111/111
	33r.–37v.	*Quaternus decimarum ad Terre Sancte subsidium particularium receptorum sive extraordinariorum*	53/111
Year Two (1275–76)	38r.–44v.	*Quaternus decimarum ad Terre Sancte subsidium particularium receptorum sive extraordinariorum*	56/111
Year Three (1276–77)	45r.–51v.	*Quaternus decimarum ad Terre Sancte subsidium particularium receptorum sive extraordinariorum*	55/111
Year Four (1277–78)	52r.–54v.	*Quaternus decimarum ad Terre Sancte subsidium particularium receptorum sive extraordinariorum*	11/111

All the payments recorded in the first register are exactly in the form described by Vendola, thus one single amount per diocese with no possibility of knowing how much was paid by each religious institution involved in the tithe that year. However, this is not the case for the other four registers. As illustrated in Table 4.1, they contain detailed accounts of the partial and extraordinary payments ('*particularium receptorum sive extraordinariorum*') made from year to year by individual religious bodies in different dioceses and archdioceses, which are thus specified.[76] The first of these registers refers to Year One, and it adds data to the sums from the previous *quaternus*; the others provide details up to Year Four. None of them, however, include payments for every single body or for each of the 111 dioceses and archdioceses forming the collectorate. The final register, for example, only records payments for eleven dioceses out of 111, thus providing a limited and fragmentary picture of the monetary circulation generated by the tithe in that year.

Owing to space limitations, it is impossible to report all the accounts for every single diocese of the 111 documented in the registers here.[77] The following analysis is based upon the totals calculated for every ecclesiastical province by aggregating the data available for each suffragan diocese and the relative archdiocese in each year.[78] In so doing, it has been possible not only to reduce the number of samples to a reasonable quantity without losing the distinctiveness of the different dioceses but also to provide a more comprehensive view of the circulation of money while identifying any possible pattern throughout the sexennial tithe. Table 4.2 provides a list of the fourteen ecclesiastical provinces, with details of the archdioceses and their suffragan dioceses as documented in volume 217.[79]

As for the money involved in payment transactions, a wide range of gold, silver, and billon coins is documented.[80] For gold, along with Florentine florins and *reali* of Charles of Anjou (identified here as *augustales*, as explained above), *auro fracto* (literally 'broken gold') is also recorded.[81] This is an unusual expression if it refers to any actual coin: it may include hackgold, namely fragments of gold items used as currency by weight, as well as gold taris '*spezzati*' of Sicily that, due to their irregularities (being often cut, fragmented, even similar to broken gold ingots) were normally spent by weight.[82] Written evidence of their existence appears in Villani's chronicle, when Charles entered Naples and took possession of Manfred's treasure, which was said to be made 'almost entirely' of taris *spezzati*.[83] Further confirmation of their diffusion comes from the limited archaeological material available for the period. For instance, the Benevento hoard, which was concealed around 1278, thus during the collection of the sexennial tithe, consists of 100 Hohenstaufen and Charles I gold taris, together with an unrecorded number of *spezzati*.[84] Yet, their use in these years has never been as well-documented as it appears in those registers.

Silver coins include English sterlings, French *gros tournois*, Italian *grossi* of Venice and Florence, and *aquilini* of Pisa. Both the old *grossi* of the Roman Senate issued in 1265 and worth, respectively, XV (15) or XVI (16) *provisini* by 1274 (*romanini veteres de XV or XVI proveniensibus*) make their appearance in the transactions,

Table 4.2 The ecclesiastical provinces forming the collectorate of bishop Pietro

No.	Province	*Archdioceses* and suffragan dioceses	Total
1	Acerenza	*Acerenza*, Anglona, Gravina, Potenza, Tricarico, Venosa	6
2	Amalfi	*Amalfi*, Capri, Lettere, Minori, Scala	5
3	Bari	*Bari*, Bitetto, Bitonto, Canne, Conversano, Giovinazzo, Lavello, Minervino, Molfetta, Polignano, Ruvo	11
4	Benevento	*Benevento*, Alife, Ariano, Ascoli Satriano, Avellino, Boiano, Bovino, Civitate, Dragonara, Fiorentino, Frigento, Guardialfiera, Larino, Lesina, Lucera, Montecorvino, Monte Marano, S. Agata de' Goti, Telese, Termoli, Tertiveri, Trevico, Trivento, Volturara	24
5	Brindisi	*Brindisi*, Ostuni	2
6	Capua	*Capua*, Caiazzo, Calvi, Carinola, Caserta, Isernia, Sessa Aurunca, Teano, Venafro	9
7	Conza	*Conza*, Bisaccia, Lacedonia, Monteverde, Muro Lucano, Sant'Angelo de' Lombardi, Satriano	7
8	Naples	*Naples*, Acerra, Ischia, Nola, Pozzuoli	5
9	Otranto	*Otranto*, Castro, Gallipoli, Lecce, Leuca, Ugento	6
10	Salerno	*Salerno*, Acerno, Capaccio, Marsico Nuovo, Nusco, Policastro, Sarno	7
11	Siponto	*Siponto*, Salpi, Vieste	3
12	Sorrento	*Sorrento*, Castellamare di Stabia, Massa Lubrense, Vico Equense	4
13	Taranto	*Taranto*, Castellaneta, Mottola	3
14	Trani	*Trani*, Andria, Bisceglie	3
		Total:	95[a]

[a] The total sum of 111 dioceses shall be calculated by adding the sixteen dioceses *immediate subiecte*: according to the registers, those were the dioceses of Aquila, Aquino, Aversa, Chieti, Fondi, Gaeta, Marsi, Melfi, Monopoli, Penne-Atri, Rapolla, Ravello, Sora, Teramo, Troja, and Valva-Sulmona.

along with the newer and heavier ones (*rinforciati*) worth XXI (21) *provisini* minted between 1274 and 1282.[85] These *provisini* must be regarded as copies of the deniers of Provins of the Counts of Troyes and Champagne issued by the Senate of Rome from the last decades of the twelfth century onwards.[86] They appear together with many other billon coins, including *denari* of Florence, Siena, Volterra, and Ravenna (also called *pistaculi* or pistachios) and *deniers tournois*, all made of an alloy of silver and copper, with a majority of base metal content.[87]

Payments in the registers were made in any of those coins and were recorded according to this format: unless counted by the piece, the o.t.gr. system of account was used for gold currencies and the £.s.d. ones for silver and billon coins. To compare the many currencies recorded and work out the values of the tithe, all the amounts in the following tables are provided in o.t.gr., the standard accounting system of the Kingdom of Sicily. This required the conversion of all the sums originally recorded in £.s.d., which was made possible by the exchange rates documented in the same records (Table 4.3).[88]

All these exchange rates bear witness to an active and diversified monetary circulation at the time of the sexennial tithe, which combined relatively stable coins of high intrinsic value, such as the Florentine gold florins or the Italian silver *grossi*, with billon pieces of low value, like the deniers of Volterra and Ravenna. Despite the large number of different denominations involved in the payments, the largest portion of the sexennial tithe in the collectorate of Bishop Pietro was paid in gold florins of Florence.

It appears that at least o. 785 t. 23 gr. 13 out of o. 2548 t. 17 gr. 16 1/4 collected by Bishop Pietro and his agents in the four-year period were actually paid in gold florins (Table 4.4 IV).[89] This corresponds to about one-third (30.83 per cent) of the value of the sexennial tithe of the collectorate of the Kingdom of Sicily – with the exception of Sicily and Calabria – recorded in the registers under consideration. This is the most striking aspect, especially considering that there is nothing like this ratio in the 'overall' percentages of Tables 4.4 I–III for the other coins, which were too small in quantity to play a role of much significance in the tithe.

Table 4.3 Exchange rates for the years 1274–78 as documented in the registers

Currencies	Exchange rates	Other rates
Gold coins		
Florins of Florence	1 Florin = t. 6 = gr. 120	o. 1 = 5 Florins
Reali/Augustales	1 *Reale/Aug.* = t. 7 gr. 10 = gr. 150	o. 1 = 4 *Reale/Aug.*
Silver coins		
Gros tournois	1274–76 1 *Gros tournois* = gr. 13 ⅓ 1276–78 1 *Gros tournois* = gr. 13[a]	1274–76 t. 2 = 3 *Gros tournois*[b] o. 1 = 45 *Gros tournois*[c] 1276–78 o. 1 = 46 *Gros tournois*[d]
Romanini of XXI *provisini*	1 *Rom.* XXI *pr.* = gr. 12[e]	–
Romanini of XVI *provisini*	1 *Rom.* XVI *pr.* = gr. 10	–
Romanini of XV *provisini*	1 *Rom.* XV *pr.* = gr. 9 ½[f]	–
Aquilini of Pisa	1 *Aquil.* = gr. 8[g]	–
Grossi of Venice	1 *Grosso* Ven. = gr. 6 ⅔[h]	t. 1 = 3 *Grossi* Ven.[i]
Grossi of Florence	1 *Grosso* Fl. = gr. 6	–
Sterlings	1 Sterl. = gr. 4	–

Currencies	Exchange rates	Other rates
	Billon coins	
Denari of Florence	1 *Den.* Fl. = gr. 3 ¾[j]	1 *Den.* Fl. = 6 *prov.*
Deniers tournois	1 *Den. tour.* = gr. 1[k]	–
Provisini	1 *Prov.* = gr. 0.625	o. 1 = £4 *Prov.*[l]
Denari of Volterra & Ravenna	1 *Den.* Vol./Rav. = gr. 0.35	–
Denari of Siena	1 *Den.* Si. = gr. 0.3125	1 *Den.* Si. = ½ *Prov.*[m]

[a] AAV, Collectoria 217, fol. 24v.
[b] AAV, Collectoria 217, fol. 2v. Exception: Teano, t. 2 = 3 *Gros* and 1 *Den. tournois*, see AAV, Collectoria 217, fol. 4v.
[c] Exception: Caiazzo, o. 1 = 46 *Gros tournois*; see AAV, Collectoria 217, fol. 4r.
[d] Exception: o. 1 = 46 *Gros* and 1 *Den. tournois*; AAV, Collectoria 217, fol. 24v.
[e] AAV, Collectoria 217, fol. 29r.
[f] AAV, Collectoria 217, fol. 2v.
[g] Ratio extrapolated from payment transactions of the early 1280s; see AAV, Collectoria 217, fols. 29r and 53r. However, a similar value (gr. 8.1) can be obtained if we calculate the rates between the gold ounces of Naples and the deniers of Pisa, and then between the deniers and the silver *aquilini* for the years 1271–72 according to the values in Baldassarri, *Zecca*, pp. 437 and 459.
[h] Only in the dioceses of Bitonto and Molfetta 1 *Grosso* Ven. is said to be worth gr. 6 ½ in 1274; AAV, Collectoria 217, fols. 11v–12r.
[i] AAV, Collectoria 217, fol. 2v.
[j] AAV, Collectoria 217, fol. 4v.
[k] AAV, Collectoria 217, fols. 29r. and 53r. This value corresponds to what also Charles of Anjou ordered: '*Soluta est pecunia in tornensis parvulis ad rationem tornensium 20 pro tareno (Tempore Caroli primi ab anno 2 Indict. usque ad ann. 6 Indict.)*'; Camillo Minieri Riccio, *Studi storici su' Fascicoli Angioini dell'archivio della Regia Zecca di Napoli* (Naples: presso Alberto Detken Piazza del Plebiscito, 1863), p. 23; Achille Giuliani and Davide Fabrizi, *Le monete degli Angioini in Italia meridionale: indagine archivistica sulla politica monetaria e analisi critica dei materiali* (Roseto degli Abbruzzi: Edizioni D'Andrea, 2014), p. 80 and note 216.
[l] AAV, Collectoria 217, fol. 2r.
[m] Ratio extrapolated from totals reported at the bottom of AAV, Collectoria, fols. 46v. and 48v.

Table 4.4 I–IV Revenues of the sexennial tithe per ecclesiastical province as documented in the registers

I.

No.	Provinces		Florins	Gold coins		
					Reali/Aug.	Auro fracto
1	Acerenza	o. t. gr.	o. 34 t. 15		t. 7 gr. 9	t. 11 gr. 3
		%	22.809			0.246
2	Amalfi	o. t. gr.	o. 7 t. 3 gr. 5			
		%	8.740			
3	Bari	o. t. gr.	o. 65 t. 21		t. 7 gr. 9	t. 12 gr. 2
		%	36.914		0.140	0.227
4	Benevento	o. t. gr.	o. 77 t. 20 gr. 16		o. 2 t. 7 gr. 10	o. 2 t. 6 gr. 15
		%	18.670		0.541	0.535
5	Brindisi	o. t. gr.	o. 15 t. 6			
		%	14.125			
6	Capua	o. t. gr.	o. 213 t. 20 gr. 2		o. 1 t. 7 gr. 10	o. 5 t. 11 gr. 2
		%	66.141		0.387	1.662
7	Conza	o. t. gr.	o. 22 t. 1 gr. 10		t. 7 gr. 10	o. 3 t. 14
		%	43.934		0.498	6.907

8	Naples	o. t. gr.	o. 76 t. 24 gr. 5	t. 22 gr. 10	o. 3 t. 22 gr. 10
		%	23.784	0.232	3.581
9	Otranto	o. t. gr.	o. 19 t. 6	t. 22 gr. 10	o. 2 t. 19 gr. 13
		%	18.337	0.716	0.501
10	Salerno	o. t. gr.	o. 165 t. 3 gr. 5	o. 2 t. 11 gr. 5	
		%	31.152	0.448	
11	Siponto	o. t. gr.	o. 29 t. 12	t. 7 gr. 10	
		%	50.063	0.426	
12	Sorrento	o. t. gr.	o. 25 t. 21 gr. 12		
		%	78.956		
13	Taranto	o. t. gr.	o. 23 t. 18 gr. 18	t. 3 gr. 15	t. 25 gr. 15
		%	20.579	0.109	0.747
14	Trani	o. t. gr.	o. 10	o. 2 t. 11 gr. 5	
		%	12.947	3.075	
	Overall	o. t. gr.	o. 785 t. 23 gr. 13	o. 10 t. 18 gr.14	o. 19 t. 3
		%	30.832	0.417	0.749

(*Continued*)

Note: for coin abbreviations, refer to Table 4.3

Table 4.4 (Cont.)

II.

					Silver coins				
No.	Provinces		Gros tournois	Rom. XXI pr.	Rom. XVI pr.	Aquil.	Grossi Ven.	Grossi Fl.	Sterl.
1	Acerenza	o. t. gr.	t. 22 gr. 4 1/3		t. 8 gr. 5		t. 16 gr. 13 1/3	gr. 6	gr. 4
		%	0.490		0.182		0.367	0.007	0.004
2	Amalfi	o. t. gr.	t. 25 gr. 12 1/3		t. 1		gr. 13 1/3		
		%	1.050		0.041		0.027		
3	Bari	o. t. gr.	o. 1 t. 18 gr. 2 2/3			t. 2. gr. 16	o. 9 t. 28		
		%	0.901			0.052	5.581		
4	Benevento	o. t. gr.	o. 11 t. 26 gr. 9	gr. 12	t. 1 gr. 10	gr. 8	o. 1 t. 14 gr. 13 1/3		
		%	2.855	0.005	0.012	0.003	0.358		
5	Brindisi	o. t. gr.	o. 9 gr. 17				t. 3		
		%	0.305				0.093		
6	Capua	o. t. gr.	o. 11 t. 10 gr. 19 1/3	t. 2 gr. 8	o. 6 t. 21		t. 11 gr. 6 2/3		
		%	3.518	0.025	2.074		0.117		

#	Place		o. t. gr. / %		
7	Conza	o. t. gr.	o. 8 t. 10 gr. 15	t. 1 gr. 13 1/3	
		%	16.654	0.111	
8	Naples	o. t. gr.	t. 10 gr. 8		
		%	0.107		
9	Otranto	o. t. gr.	t. 9 gr. 19 2/3	o. 5 t. 13 gr. 16 2/3	gr. 8
		%	0.318	5.216	0.013
10	Salerno	o. t. gr.	o. 5 t. 2 gr. 10	gr. 13 1/3	
		%	0.959	0.004	
11	Siponto	o. t. gr.	o. 6 t. 2 gr. 3 1/3	gr. 13 1/3	
		%	10.340	0.038	
12	Sorrento	o. t. gr.	t. 1 gr. 6		
		%	0.133		

(Continued)

Table 4.4 (Cont.)

II.

No.	Provinces		Gros tournois	Rom. XXI pr.	Rom. XVI pr.	Aquil.	Grossi Ven.	Grossi Fl.	Sterl.
							Silver coins		
13	Taranto	o. t. gr.	t. 7 gr. 18 1/3				t. 27 gr. 1		
		%	0.230				0.785		
14	Trani	o. t. gr.	t. 8 gr. 9				t. 12 gr. 6 2/3		
		%	0.365				0.532		
	Overall	o. t. gr.	o. 47 t. 16 gr. 14	t. 3	o. 7 t. 1 gr. 15	t. 3 gr. 4	o. 19 t. 10 gr. 11	gr. 6	gr. 12
		%	1.866	0.004	0.277	0.004	0.759	0.000	0.001

Note: for coin abbreviations, refer to Table 4.3

III.

No.	Provinces		Billon coins				General references
			Den. Fl.	Den. tour.	Prov.	Den. Vol./Rav.	Gold ounces
1	Acerenza	o. t. gr.		gr. 9			o. 114 t. 23 gr. 9
		%		0.010			75.886
2	Amalfi	o. t. gr.		t. 2 gr. 12			o. 73 t. 6 gr. 17 1/2
		%		0.107			90.036
3	Bari	o. t. gr.		t. 3 gr. 13			o. 99 t. 26 gr. 5
		%		0.068			56.116
4	Benevento	o. t. gr.		t. 22 gr. 18	gr. 5	t. 6 gr. 4	o. 319 t. 16 gr. 8
		%		0.183	0.002	0.050	76.787
5	Brindisi	o. t. gr.		g. 10			o. 91 t. 28 gr. 19
		%		0.015			85.461
6	Capua	o. t. gr.	t. 2 gr. 1 1/4	t. 15 gr. 16	gr. 3 3/4		o. 83 t. 19 gr. 2 1/2
		%	0.021	0.163	0.002		25.890
7	Conza	o. t. gr.		t. 6 gr. 4			o. 15 t. 24 gr. 1
		%		0.412			31.484
8	Naples	o. t. gr.		t. 19 gr. 14			o. 244 t. 11 gr. 7 1/2
		%		0.203			75.673

(Continued)

Table 4.4 (Cont.)

III.

No.	Provinces		Billon coins				General references
			Den. Fl.	Den. Tour.	Prov.	Den. Vol./Rav.	Gold ounces
9	Otranto	o. t. gr.		t. 1 gr. 14			o. 75 t. 4 gr. 7
		%		0.054			71.766
10	Salerno	o. t. gr.		gr. 10			o. 354 t. 22 gr. 9 1/2
		%		0.003			66.933
11	Siponto	o. t. gr.		t. 4 gr. 1	gr. 1 1/4		o. 22 t. 25 gr. 7
		%		0.230	0.004		38.901
12	Sorrento	o. t. gr.		gr. 2			o. 6 t. 24 gr. 5
		%		0.010			20.900
13	Taranto	o. t. gr.		gr. 4			o. 89 t. 1 gr. 5
		%		0.006			77.544
14	Trani	o. t. gr.		t. 1 gr. 12			o. 64 t. 3 gr. 10
		%		0.069			83.012
Overall		o. t. gr.	t. 2 gr. 1 1/4	o. 2 t. 19 gr. 19	gr. 10	t. 6 gr. 4	o. 1655 t. 27 gr. 13
		%	0.003	0.105	0.001	0.008	64.974

Note: for coin abbreviations, refer to Table 4.3

IV.

No.	Provinces		Totals
1	Acerenza	o. t. gr. %	o. 151 t. 7 gr. 13 2/3
2	Amalfi	o. t. gr. %	o. 81 t. 10 gr. 1/6
3	Bari	o. t. gr. %	o. 177 t. 29 gr. 7 2/3
4	Benevento	o. t. gr. %	o. 416 t. 4 gr. 8 1/3
5	Brindisi	o. t. gr. %	o. 107 t. 18 gr. 6
6	Capua	o. t. gr. %	o. 323 t. 1 gr. 11 1/2
7	Conza	o. t. gr. %	o. 50 t. 5 gr. 13 1/3
8	Naples	o. t. gr. %	o. 322 t. 28 gr. 4 1/2

(Continued)

Table 4.4   (Cont.)

IV.

No.	Provinces		Totals
9	Otranto	o. t. gr.	o. 104 t. 21 gr. 5 1/3
		%	
10	Salerno	o. t. gr.	o. 530 gr. 5 5/6
		%	
11	Siponto	o. t. gr.	o. 58 t. 21 gr. 15 11/12
		%	
12	Sorrento	o. t. gr.	o. 32 t. 17 gr. 5
		%	
13	Taranto	o. t. gr.	o. 114 t. 24 gr. 16 1/3
		%	
14	Trani	o. t. gr.	o. 77 t. 7 gr. 2 2/3
		%	
Overall		o. t. gr.	o. 2548 t. 17 gr. 16 1/4
		%	

Nevertheless, it must be noted that the notary who prepared those registers was not always entirely clear when it came to describing the sums collected. In several entries, mainly concentrated in the first register, the notary quite frequently used the vague expression 'gold ounces' as a term of accounting, which does not specify the actual coins paid to papal agents. On a few occasions, moreover, the notary reported that the sum was given '*in diversis monetis*', namely using different coins, sometimes indicating their types but not the respective quantities (i.e., florins and *gros tournois*, or florins and *grossi* of Venice). In these cases, it then becomes impossible to assess in what proportion each currency represented in the sum collected.

Unfortunately, these generic references to money, which are listed in the last column of Table 4.4 III, prevent us from knowing the nature of the coins used to pay *c.* 65 per cent of the total value of the tithe collected and recorded. We can only base our analysis on the remaining 35 per cent, for which we have precise information. In this regard, the fact that 30.83 per cent of the tithe was paid in florins, while all the other coins, whether they be gold, silver, or billon, contributed to only 4.19 per cent of that 35 per cent gives a clear indication of the significant penetration of the Florentine gold coin in the papal tithe from southern Italy.

Certainly, this result may depend on many factors and primarily on the number of transactions documented for each diocese and the quality of the information provided. Yet, the representation of the amounts collected per year suggests an even more widespread use of gold florins than the 30.83 per cent here documented (Figure 4.1).

For Year One and Year Four, respectively, 75.70 and 91.13 per cent of payment transactions were recorded in 'gold ounces' or *diversis monetis*. This makes it difficult to know the correct proportions of the different currencies involved. A different situation appears in Year Two and Year Three. In these cases, the total amounts of gold ounces/*diversis monetis* are estimated at 27.12 and 40.13 per cent, respectively. This implies that, at least for 73.35 and 59.87 per cent of the total values of those two years, we can produce a more accurate evaluation of the composition of the tithe since we know exactly which coins were used.

Year 1

Year 2

Year 3

Year 4

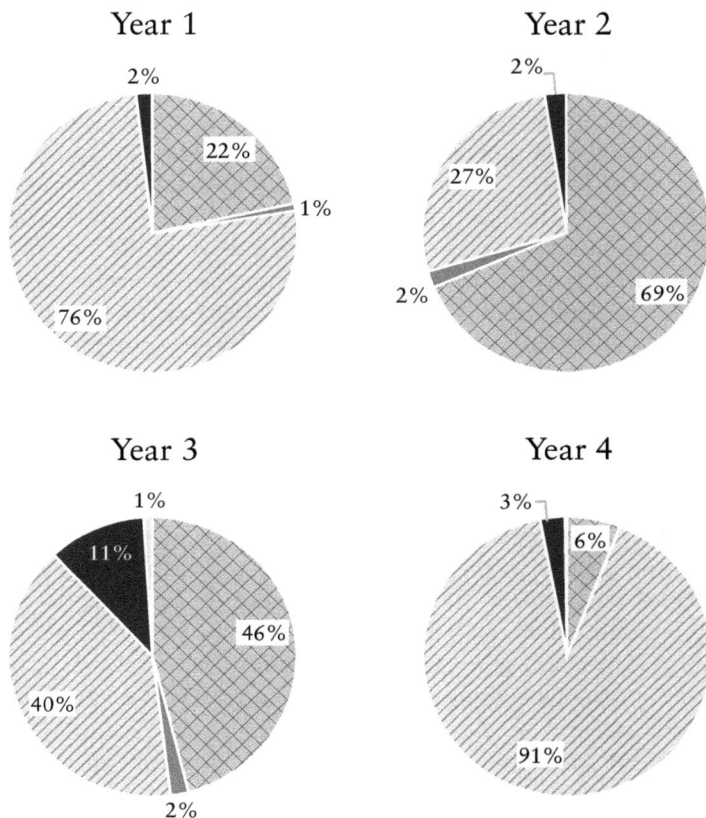

Florins ▨ Augustales/Auro fracto ▧ Gold Ounces ▨ Silver Coins ■ Billon Coins

Figure 4.1 Percentages of coins collected from the ecclesiastical provinces between 1274 (Year One) and 1278 (Year Four).

Year Two presents a higher percentage of gold florins, which contributed to 68.73 per cent of the value of the tithe collected that year, compared to the 45.95 per cent in Year Three. In this year, silver coins (10.73 per cent) and *augustales/auro fracto* (2.49 per cent) show higher percentages than in any other period, but still low compared to the florins, which remained the predominant money collected. Accordingly, it can be assumed that the 64.97 per cent recorded as gold ounces/*diversis monetis* in the 'totals' row of Table 4.4 includes a large proportion of gold florins, had the notary been clearer in his registration.

The greater involvement of florins also becomes evident if we look in more detail at those dioceses for which we have records of payment transactions documented for every single year of the period 1274–78. This is only possible for six of them (out of 111), namely the '*immediate subiecte*' dioceses of Marsi, Penne, and Valva-Sulmona, and the '*mediate subiecte*' dioceses of Capaccio, Siponto, and Trivento. The most interesting aspect here is that, on average, gold florins account for 38.89 per cent of the value of the tithe produced in those six dioceses, a percentage that almost matches the one registered by John Day in his study on the Tuscan tithe of 1296 (*c.* 40 per cent). This is an additional confirmation of the predominance of the florin in the papal tithe of southern Italy in the 1270s.

A final piece of evidence hints at the possibility that the florin played the same role also in other collectorates of the period. On 18 May 1279, in the diocese of Fiesole (Tuscany), *dominus* Benigno, *camerarius* of the Abbey of Passignano, paid the amount of £79 s. 12 *denari* of Pisa to the sub-collector Bernardo, prior of the rectory of San Donato in Citille (Greve in Chianti), which corresponded to the sum that the monastery still owed for Year Four of the sexennial tithe (1277–78). The notary Attaviano, who recorded the transaction, specified that those *denari* were actually received in gold florins of Florence.[90]

The florin in papal spending and the role of the papacy

The analysis has shown that throughout the 1270s, thousands of gold florins were being collected through the papal tithe, thus forming a substantial part of the wealth of the Holy See. This was well before the Florentines overcame competition from other banking companies and ended up dominating papal finances under Pope Boniface VIII. It would therefore be unreasonable to link such a massive presence of the florin in the papal coffers to a hypothetical, although undocumented, exclusive relationship between the Curia and the merchant bankers of Florence before that time. What remains to be seen is (i) how all those florins were used in the actual expenditure of the papacy, (ii) whether such a significant involvement was the effect of a direct request for florins coming from the Apostolic Chamber, (iii) in what ways the papacy contributed to the diffusion of the Florentine gold coin, and likewise (iv) how the florin benefited the papacy.

Let us begin by looking at how the popes spent the money collected. As noted, the sexennial tithe imposed on all the benefices of Christendom in 1274 was conceived – as were many other tithes before – to finance a new crusade to recover the Holy Land. In particular, the revenues of this tithe were to be granted to those rulers who would take the cross and fight the infidels. Thus, when King Charles of Anjou expressed his intention to join the crusade, Pope Gregory X granted him all the sums collected for six years in the Kingdom of Sicily, as well as those from the counties of Provence and Forcalquier, both part of his French dominions.[91] It was also agreed that if Charles did not embark on a crusade, the yield of the tithe would revert to his son and heir, Charles of Salerno, who would join the expedition as a crusader. Considering that the florin made up at least one-third of the income of the tithe collected in southern Italy and given the demand for florins coming from the military market, as illustrated in Chapter 3, there is little doubt that a good portion of the sum granted to Charles on that occasion would have been in gold florins.

Nevertheless, following the death of Pope Gregory in 1276, the crusade never took place, and the rest of the money collected was redistributed in Italy in subsequent years.[92] For example, the Italian Franciscan friar and chronicler Salimbene di Adam (1221–88) informs us that the papacy was leading a very costly fight against the Ghibellines in Romagna in 1282. For the expenses of that war, he wrote, Pope Martin IV (1281–85) paid the total sum of '14 times 100,000 gold florins' ('*XIIII vicibus centum millia florinos aureos*') or 1,400,000 gold florins that, in the words of Salimbene, 'originally formed the sexennial tithe ordered by Pope Gregory X to rescue the Holy Land'.[93]

New sums of gold florins were also collected through the triennial tithe of 1285–88, originally ordered by Pope Martin IV in 1284 and later confirmed by Pope Honorius IV (1285–87) to support the new war that King Charles was waging against the Aragonese dynasty to recover Sicily after the Sicilian Vespers of 1282. On 9 January 1288, in particular, the sub-collectors for the diocese of Arezzo, namely Guglielmo, abbot of the monastery of Santa Flora, and Leonardo, prior of the church of San Michele, deposited the sum of 900 gold florins '*bonos et legales*' with the Florentine merchants Mascio and Cione sons of Ruggero Minerbetti and Lapo Accursi. This is what amounted to the revenues collected in that diocese in the second year of that triennial tithe.[94]

According to these examples, gold florins were therefore used to cover the costs of the papacy's political projects, for which financing wars was a central component. As pointed out by Robert Davidsohn, under the pontificate of Martin IV, the florin was also adopted as a common money of account in the fiscal registers produced at the Curia.[95] If confirmed, this would further corroborate the success of the Florentine gold coin in the papal finances.

Nevertheless, the written sources at our disposal do not seem to support the hypothesis that the popes specifically requested or desired florins. In the case of the sexennial tithe, as seen, papal collectors were simply instructed to accept the currencies in circulation in their collectorate; no denomination was indicated in Gregory's dispositions. As a result, gold florins were being gathered along with many other gold, silver, and billon coins. This was because the papacy was in great need of money, but unlike the Angevin Crown, it did not need a precise currency. The popes would accept any coin to fund their projects as long as it was 'valid' at the time, that is, in circulation and commonly accepted and exchanged. One may argue that collecting florins would have been more profitable for the popes, as this would not have entailed additional transaction costs when exchanging money for future operations, given that florins were already broadly accepted in several milieus. Yet, since the popes could always count on the plethora of merchant bankers surrounding their Curia, they could relatively easily obtain florins when they needed them. In other words, it would be a mistake to think that collecting florins was a necessity for the papacy in the way that it was for Charles of Anjou. The strong presence of gold florins in the finances of the papacy is instead the result of their large diffusion in the Kingdom of Sicily, which is a reflection of the contemporary success of the Florentine gold coins in those territories.

The apparent lack of a specific demand for florins does not mean that we cannot clarify how the papacy contributed to the diffusion of this currency and, likewise, the beneficial role of the florin for the popes. The analysis seems to confirm the dynamics already encountered in the case of the Angevin Crown. In particular, the fact that the popes also adopted the florin to fund their political projects undoubtedly gave a major boost to the spreading of the currency in the early years of its life, allowing the Florentine coin to circulate beyond the circuit of long-distance trade and conquer new sections of the contemporary monetary market, including the papal finances. Papal connections with merchant bankers proved essential to this end.

As seen, the latter received in deposit the sums collected by the Church officials and stored the tithe money until the popes or their collectors requested it. The surviving register of deposits (*quaternus depostitorum*) written during the collection of the sexennial tithe in the collectorate of the bishop Pietro confirms that hundreds of gold florins were actually deposited with merchants belonging to a number of different companies from Lucca and Pistoia, but also Rieti, Ferentino, and Benevento.[96] All these merchants received a minor payment for the transport of the sums, although there was no profit related to the custody of the money collected through the tithe.[97] This means that if one excludes the patronage given by the popes, the actual profit for all those firms could only be derived from the use they would make of the money delivered to them. And by reinvesting florins, they would further enhance the diffusion and adoption of the gold coin.

Finally, the Florentine currency would eventually represent an important instrument in the hands of the popes for the deployment and consolidation of their power. Certainly, other coins were being collected and paid, yet the gold florin of Florence far outweighed all of them. Being the major currency collected and spent to fund political projects and military ventures through which the Holy See sought to establish or maintain its sovereignty over strategic territories (e.g., crusades and the East, the Kingdom of Sicily), the florin served as the primary means by which the papacy bolstered its authority and asserted its position as the main political institution of the time, especially given the simultaneous crisis of the Holy Roman Empire.

Conclusions

Throughout the 1270s, and thus in little more than twenty years since its apparent creation, the florin was accumulating significantly in the coffers of the papal court through the collection of the tithe, the favourite financial instrument in the hands of thirteenth-century popes to cover the high costs of their policies. This is what has emerged from the study of five unpublished registers for the collection of the sexennial tithe of Pope Gregory X in southern Italy between 1274 and 1278. On average, florins represented one-third of the total value of the money raised in the fourteen ecclesiastical provinces forming the collectorate of Bishop Pietro da Ferentino. This is an exceptional feature, especially considering that this percentage seems to rise whenever the sources are clearer about the actual coins paid to the papal collectors.

This significant involvement of the Florentine florin in papal finances was not a direct consequence of either the existing relations between the popes and the merchant bankers of Florence or the explicit demand for florins coming from the papacy or its agents. By looking at the papal expenditure related to the tithe money, it appears that, contrary to the Angevin ruler who desperately needed florins and explicitly ordered for them to be used in soldiers' pay, there was never a command or legal obligation made by the popes to pay the papal tithe in gold florins. These naturally flowed back into the coffers of the papal collector because of their ubiquitous presence.

Indeed, the involvement of Florentine merchants in the financial affairs of the Holy See throughout the thirteenth century helped promote the spread of the florin. This represented a mutually beneficial deal: the Curia could draw upon an impressive range of expertise and assets accumulated by the Florentine merchant community since the twelfth century in their late but nonetheless stellar emergence, rise, and predominance in the 'Commercial Revolution'; the Florentines could regulate the currency and its value at their behest, thus serving the popes with favourable exchange rates, and get in return a significant chunk of what was arguably one of the biggest financial businesses of the time, that is, remittances of all sorts of papal income to the Holy See in Rome. Yet, surviving documentation has shown that it was not until the pontificate of Boniface VIII that the florin would assist the Florentine companies in establishing their control over papal finances, although political reasons may have produced such a result. Once collected, the florin could further expand its role, as all the amounts received formed the capital of the papal court, which was normally invested to sustain its political plans. It was therefore also thanks to popes that the Florentine gold coin could conquer new milieus by acting as both a financial and political instrument in their hands.

We can get a final sense of the importance and popularity that the florin came to enjoy among the clergy from that point on if we look at the sermon *De peccato usure*. This was written in the early fourteenth century by Remigio de' Girolami, a distinguished preacher appointed as lector at the Florentine convent of S. Maria Novella, and includes a pompous 'eulogy of the florin' within its pages. In this sermon, while criticising the contemporary struggles for economic power among the Florentines, Remigio pays tribute to the gold florin as the second of seven holy gifts that God offered to the city of Florence (*'Deus autem contulit isti civitati septem bona quasi singularia'*). Despite being a member of the mendicant order of Dominicans, who were meant to live in poverty and depend directly on charity for their livelihood as did Jesus and the Apostles, Remigio praises the florin as a noble coinage (*nobilis monete*) for three main reasons: its material (*materie*), as it was 'made of the best gold', its iconography (*sculpture*), and its wide circulation (*cursus*) 'all over the world, also among the Saracens'.[98] Another contemporary of Remigio, Pope Clement V (1305–14), believed in the special virtues of the florin to the point that he used to add small fillings of its gold to his soup, especially for the prophylactic properties of both the purity of its metal and the image of St John.[99] Yet, Remigio warned the reader that if used improperly, the Florentine coin could blind people with 'false pride'.

Nevertheless, as illustrated in this chapter, the papacy's utilisation of the florin in the early years of its life clearly valorised the currency and helped frame it more as a gift than a sin. Yet, one wonders whether Cieo, a leather-worker from the Santo Spirito neighbourhood in Florence, also felt the same way when, in 1293, he had to return thirteen gold florins to Bene Bencivenni, who had paid a fine of £25 to the city treasurers (*chamarlinghi*) for all the blasphemies against God and the saints that his son Simone had shouted in public.[100]

Notes

1 See, for example, Adolf Gottlob, *Die päpstlichen Kreuzzugs-Steuern des 13. Jahrhunderts: ihre rechtliche Grundlage, politische Geschichte und technische Verwaltung* (Heiligenstadt: Cordier, 1892); Gino Arias, *Studi e documenti di storia del diritto* (Florence: Le Monnier, 1902), especially pp. 75–113; Luigi Nina, *Le finanze pontificie nel medioevo*, 3 vols (Milan: F.lli Treves, 1929–32); Mario Chiaudano, *Studi e documenti per la storia del diritto commerciale italiano nel secolo XIII* (Turin: Presso l'Istituto Giuridico della R. Università, 1930); William E. Lunt, *Papal Revenues in the Middle Ages*, 2 vols (New York: Columbia University Press, 1934); William E. Lunt, *Financial Relations of the Papacy with England to 1327* (Cambridge, MA: The Mediaeval Academy of America, 1939); Bruno Dini, 'I mercanti-banchieri e la sede apostolica (XIII–prima metà del XIV secolo)', in Centro Italiano di Studi di Storia e d'Arte (ed.), *Gli spazi economici della chiesa nell'Occidente mediterraneo (secoli XII–metà XIV), Pistoia, 16–19 maggio 1997* (Pistoia: Presso la sede del Centro, 1999), pp. 42–62; Marco Vendittelli, 'I primi "campsores domini papae"', in A. Serra (ed.), *Humanitas. Studi per Patrizia Serafin* (Rome: Universitalia, 2015), pp. 409–31; Thomas W. Smith, *Curia and Crusade. Pope Honorius III and the Recovery of the Holy Land 1216–1227* (Turnhout: Brepols, 2017), especially chapter 8.

2 Housley, *The Italian Crusades*, p. 173.

3 *Grégoire IX*, vol. I, p. 152, no. 249*ff*.

4 Lunt, *Financial Relations*, p. 247.

5 Further examples in *ibid.*, pp. 250 and 256.

6 They were still operating under the pontificate of Honorius III (1216–27); Vendittelli, 'I primi', p. 418; Smith, *Curia and Crusade*, p. 312*ff*; Thomas W. Smith, 'Pope Honorius III, the Military Orders and the Financing of the Fifth Crusade: A Culture of Papal Preference?', in J. Schenk and M. Carr (eds), *The Military Order Vol. 6.1* (London: Routledge, 2016), pp. 54–61.

7 In addition to the works in note 1, see also Edouard Jordan, *De mercatoribus camerae apostolicae saeculo XIII* (Condate Rhedonum: apud Oberthur Typographum, 1909); Glenn Olsen, 'Italian Merchants and the Performance of Papal Banking Functions in the Early Thirteenth Century', *Explorations in Economic History* 7:1 (1969), 43–63; Ignazio Del Punta, 'Tuscan Merchant-Bankers and Moneyers and their Relations with the Roman Curia in the XIIIth and Early XIVth Centuries', *Rivista di Storia della Chiesa in Italia* 64:1 (2010), 39–53; and the dedicated section in Agostino Paravicini Bagliani, *Il papato nel*

secolo XIII. Cent'anni di bibliografia (1875–2009) (Florence: SISMEL Edizioni del Galluzzo, 2010).

8 John Day, 'La circulation monétaire en Toscane en 1296', *Annales. Histoire, Sciences Sociales* 23:5 (1968), 1054–68, translated as John Day, 'The Monetary Circulation in Tuscany in the Age of Dante', in John Day, *The Medieval Market Economy* (Oxford: Basil Blackwell, 1987), pp. 129–40. I will refer to the English version.

9 We know which coins were actually used to pay the collectors only for the year 1296; the rest of the registers report a generic sum in money of account; Day, 'The Monetary', p. 129.

10 This is quite the opposite of what Alan Stahl argued, that is, 'In papal collections of about 1275, the gold florin did not achieve the wide prominence that it would have by the end of the century'; Stahl, *Zecca*, p. 30.

11 Pierre Toubert, *Les structures du Latium médiéval: le Latium méridional et la Sabine du IXᵉ siècle à la fin du XIIᵉ siècle*, 2 vols (Rome: École Française de Rome, 1973), vol. I, p. 618. The author refers to a 'document of Anagni, arch. capit., I, X–XI, no. 466 of 1177' that unfortunately I was not able to examine myself.

12 ASF, Diplomatico, Passignano, S. Michele (badia, vallombrosani), 1193 Ottobre 24, online at www.archiviodigitale.icar.beniculturali.it/it/185/ricerca/detail/88343, accessed 20 September 2024.

13 *Storia* I, p. 954.

14 *Ibid.*, p. 1193.

15 Vendittelli, 'I primi', p. 412.

16 *Regesta Honorii Papae III*, vol. 1, ed. P. Pressutti (Rome: Ex Typographia Vaticana, 1888), p. 299, no. 1802.

17 Olsen, 'Italian Merchants', p. 54. On the role of the Italian merchant bankers in England, see also Marco Vendittelli, *'In partibus Anglie'. Cittadini romani alla corte inglese nel Duecento: la vicenda di Pietro Saraceno* (Rome: Viella, 2001). As for Godfrey of Crowcombe, see David A. Carpenter, 'The Career of Godfrey of Crowcombe: Household Knight of King John and Steward of King Henry III', in C. Given-Wilson, A. Kettle, and L. Scales (eds), *War, Government and Aristocracy in the British Isles c. 1150–1500. Essays in honour of Michael Prestwich* (Woodbridge: Boydell Press, 2008), pp. 26–54.

18 *Rotuli litterarum clausarum in Turri londinensi asservati. Vol. II: ab anno MCCXXIV ad annum MCCXXVII*, ed. T. D. Hardy (London: George E. Eyre and Andrew Spottiswoode, 1844), pp. 128 and 141.

19 Vendittelli, 'I primi', p. 415.

20 Arias, *Studi*, p. 79.

21 Vendittelli, *'In partibus Anglie'*, p. 20.

22 *Grégoire IX*, vol. I, pp. 968–9, nos 1760–2; Marco Vendittelli, 'Mercanti romani del primo Duecento "in Urbe potentes" ', in C. Carbonetti Vendittelli *et al.* (eds), *Rome aux XIIIᵉ et XIVᵉ siècles. Cinq études réunies par Étienne Hubert* (Rome: École Française de Rome, 1993), pp. 97–135 (at p. 100).

23 *Grégoire IX*, vol. I, p. 1227, no. 2325.

24 *Ibid.*, vol. III, p. 339, no. 5333.

25 Goldthwaite claims that the first appearance of a Florentine officially identified as *campsor domini pape* dates to 1232; Goldthwaite, *Renaissance Florence*, p. 245. I could not find evidence in support of this information.

26 Further details on these figures can be found in Gottlob, *Die päpstlichen*, p. 251; Jordan, *De mercatoribus*, pp. 298–9; Agostino Paravicini Bagliani, 'Per una storia economica e finanziaria della corte papale preavignonese', in Centro Italiano di Studi di Storia e d'Arte (ed.), *Gli spazi economici della Chiesa nell'Occidente mediterraneo (secoli XII–metà XIV), Pistoia, 16–19 maggio 1997* (Pistoia: Presso la sede del Centro, 1999), pp. 19–24; Vendittelli, 'I primi', pp. 409–10.

27 Vendittelli, 'I primi', p. 416*ff.* A certain *Marcus campsor domini pape* is mentioned by Pope Innocent III in a document of 1199; Marco Vendittelli, 'Una nota sul primo campsor domini pape conosciuto', in M. Palma and C. Vismara (eds), *Per Gabriella. Studi in ricordo di Gabriella Braga*, 4 vols (Cassino: Università degli Studi di Cassino e del Lazio meridionale, 2013), vol. 4, pp. 1834–41.

28 Under Gregory IX, merchants from Bologna, Piacenza, Pistoia, Genoa, and Lucca are also documented; Arias, *Studi*, p. 80.

29 Lunt, *Financial Relations*, p. 146.

30 *Calendar of the Liberate Rolls Preserved in the Public Record Office: Henry III. Volume 1, 1226–1240* (London: H. M. Stationery Office, 1916), p. 196, no. 4. On the nature of the Peter's pence, see Lunt, *Financial Relations*, chapter 3.

31 Silvano Borsari, *Una compagnia di Calimala: gli Scali (secc. XIII–XIV)* (Macerata: Giardini, 1994).

32 *Grégoire IX*, vol. II, p. 165, no. 2765.

33 *Ibid.*, p. 164, no. 2764.

34 *Ibid.*, p. 204, no. 2842 (Sienese merchants), p. 211, no. 2857 (Florentine merchants).

35 *Ibid.*, p. 575, no. 3534.

36 *Ibid.*, p. 576, nos 3535–7, and p. 799, no. 3927. He also appealed to all the archbishops, bishops, and clerics of France; see *Ibid.*, pp. 744–6, nos 3842–5.

37 *Ibid.*, p. 932, no. 4180; p. 949, no. 4198; p. 952, no. 4202; p. 962, no. 4242; p. 972, no. 4264; Davidsohn, *Forschungen*, p. 6, no. 19; Schaube, *Storia*, pp. 434–5.

38 *Les Registres d'Innocent IV*, 4 vols, ed. É. Berger (Paris: E. Thorin/A. Fontemoing/E. De Boccard, 1884–1921), *ad indicem.*

39 Vendittelli, 'Mercanti romani', p. 92; Armand Jamme, 'De Rome à Florence, la curie et ses banquiers aux XIIᵉ et XIIIᵉ siècles', in W. Maleczek (ed.), *Die römische Kurie und das Geld. Von der Mitte des 12. Jahrhunderts bis zum frühen 14 Jahrhundert* (Ostfildern: Jan Thorbecke Verlag, 2018), pp. 167–204.

40 Paravicini Bagliani, 'Per una storia', pp. 22–3.

41 Lunt, *Financial Relations*, p. 600.

42 *Ibid.*, p. 255*ff.*, especially p. 267.

43 Del Punta, 'Tuscan Merchant-Bankers', p. 43; Dini, 'I mercanti-banchieri', pp. 54–5.

44 For a full description of the companies involved under each pope in the second half of the thirteenth century, see Arias, *Studi.*

45 *Storia* IV and VI, pp. 358 and 572, respectively; Jamme, 'De Rome', p. 198.

46 Del Punta, 'Tuscan Merchant-Bankers', pp. 45–6.

47 See, for example, Ignazio Del Punta, 'Il fallimento della compagnia Ricciardi alla fine del secolo XIII: un caso esemplare?', *ASI* 160:2 (2002), 221–68.

48 Del Punta, 'Tuscan Merchant-Bankers', p. 45.

49 Arias, *Studi*, pp. 24–5.

50 William E. Lunt, 'The Financial System of the Medieval Papacy in the Light of Recent Literature', *The Quarterly Journal of Economics* 23:2 (1909), 251–95 (at p. 280).

51 Lunt, 'Financial System', p. 280.

52 Housley, *The Italian Crusades*, p. 205.

53 See Lunt, *Financial Relations*, pp. 247–9; Lunt, 'Financial System', p. 281 for further details.

54 See, for instance, the tithe of 1245 decreed by the First Council of Lyon or the tithe associated with the Sicilian venture of King Henry III in Lunt, *Financial Relations*, pp. 250 and 256, respectively. In 1267, all the previous experience gathered in making valuations was summarised into a series of clear instructions that Pope Clement IV sent to the collectors in France for the assessment of a new three-year tithe; Lunt, *Papal Revenues*, vol. 1, p. 73.

55 William E. Lunt, 'A Papal Tenth Levied in the British Isles from 1274 to 1280', *The English Historical Review* 32:125 (1917), 49–89 (at p. 49). On Gregory's pontificate more generally, see Philip B. Baldwin, *Pope Gregory X and the Crusades* (Woodbridge: Boydell Press, 2014).

56 Further details on the Second Council of Lyon can be found in Sylvia Schein, *Fideles Crucis: The Papacy, the West, and the Recovery of the Holy Land, 1274–1314* (Oxford: The Clarendon Press, 1991).
57 For a complete list, see Gottlob, *Die päpstlichen*, p. 94*ff.*
58 Gregory's dispositions appear in full in Lunt, *Financial Relations*, pp. 314–17.
59 '*Pro decima supradicta non exigetur pecunia nisi illa que comuniter curret de mandato domini terre, cuius est moneta in locis, in quibus consistent fructus et redditus, unde decima persolvetur, nec aliqui pecuniam cambire cogentur eandem*' (Author's translation: 'For the aforementioned tithe, no money shall be exacted except that which commonly runs at the command of the lord of the land, to whom money belongs in the places, in which fruits and income consist, from which the tithe shall be paid, and no one shall be compelled to exchange money for the same'); Pietro Guidi, *Rationes decimarum Italiae nei secoli XIII e XIV: Tuscia. I: La decima degli anni 1274–1280* (Vatican City: Biblioteca Apostolica Vaticana, 1932), p. 323, no. 30.
60 Marcus Phillips, 'The Gros Tournois in the Mediterranean', in N. J. Mayhew (ed.), *The Gros Tournois. Proceedings of the Fourteenth Oxford Symposium on Coinage and Monetary History* (Oxford: Ashmolean Museum, Royal Numismatic Society, Société Française de Numismatique, 1997), pp. 280–337 (at p. 289); Baldassarri, *Zecca*, pp. 127 and 136. Phillips argues there was a tendency to pay the papal collectors in foreign coins, as they were often overvalued. That does not seem to be the case here, as the papal collectors would not have had any discretion to define the standard money for collection.
61 The revenues obtained from the pittances of monks or bequests to churches were also exempted from any sort of taxation; Lunt, *Financial Relations*, p. 314.
62 As regards their appointment and role, see Lunt, *Financial Relations*, pp. 313–17.
63 Ignazio Del Punta, *Mercanti e banchieri lucchesi nel Duecento* (Pisa: Pisa University Press, 2004), p. 194.
64 Gottlob, *Die päpstlichen*, 94*ff.*, Lunt, *Papal Revenues*, vol. 1, p. 73.
65 For a description of this series, see Lunt, 'A Papal Tenth', p. 49.
66 Guidi, *Tuscia*, pp. xiii–xvii (at p. xvii).
67 *Rationes Decimarum Italiae nei secoli XIII e XIV*, 12 vols (Vatican City: Biblioteca apostolica Vaticana, 1932–90).
68 For an initial but partial analysis of this material, see Marcus Phillips, 'References to the French Maille Tierce in Italian Accounts from 1278', *NC* 155 (1995), 283–8.

69 Further details on Pietro da Ferentino can be found in Stefano Locatelli, 'Gli strumenti del potere: per un'analisi della decima universale di papa Gregorio X nel Regno di Sicilia, 1274–1280', *Eurostudium3w* 56 (2021), 101–13 (at pp. 107–8); Kamp, *Kirche*, p. 104.

70 Domenico Vendola, 'Le Decime Ecclesiastiche in Puglia nel Sec. XIV', *Japigia* 8 (1937), 137–66 (at p. 138, note 1).

71 The alleged lack of exhaustiveness of the information contained in this source was reiterated by Kristjan Toomaspoeg in his *Decimae. Il sostegno economico dei sovrani alla Chiesa del Mezzogiorno nel XIII secolo* (Rome: Viella, 2009), p. 75. Hitherto unpublished fragments of the Collectoria 217 related to the Abruzzo region have recently appeared in Gianni Venditti, 'La decima sessennale del 1274 in Abruzzo', in A. Gottsmann, P. Piatti, and A. E. Rehberg (eds), *Incorrupta monumenta ecclesiam defendunt. Studi offerti a mons. Sergio Pagano, prefetto dell'Archivio Segreto Vaticano. II: Archivi, archivistica, diplomatica, paleografia* (Vatican City: Archivio Segreto Vaticano, 2018), pp. 909–22.

72 The expression '*per dominum Petrum episcopum reatinum tunc episcopum Soranum*' (Author's translation: 'for lord Pietro, bishop of Rieti, once bishop of Sora') in the title of each *quaternus* confirms that the registers were created at least after 2 August 1278, when Pietro left the diocese of Sora to move to Rieti; Kamp, *Kirche*, p. 104.

73 This uncertainty is due to discrepancies in the literature regarding the total number of dioceses of Sicily and southern Italy in the thirteenth century. Norbert Kamp listed 145 dioceses, and this number is the standard reference among historians today. However, in a more recent list of all the dioceses of the Kingdom of Sicily compiled from Angevin registers and papal sources, Kristjan Toomaspoeg gave a total of 144 dioceses for the years 1265–1325. If from 144 we deduct the numbers of documented dioceses for the regions of Calabria (23) and Sicily (10), we obtain the final figure of 111, which also corresponds to the number of dioceses recorded in our registers – thus in line with Toomaspoeg's data; Toomaspoeg, *Decimae*, p. 536.

74 For an overview of papal dominions in the late Middle Ages, see Sandro Carocci, 'Popes as Princes? The Papal State (1000–1300)', in A. Larson and K. Sisson (eds), *A Companion to the Medieval Papacy: Growth of an Ideology and Institution* (Leiden and Boston: Brill, 2016), pp. 66–84.

75 Konrad Eubel, *Hierarchia Catholica Medii Aevi sive Summorum Pontificum, S.R.E. Cardinalium, Ecclesiarum antistitum series, ab anno 1198 usque ad annum 1431 perductae documentis tabularii praesertim Vaticani collecta, digesta* (Munster: Sumptibus et typis librariae Regensbergianae, 1913), pp. 540–1.

76 The expression 'partial payments' usually covers payments result-ing from considerable arrears (*residui*) in paying the collector or his agents. Extraordinary payments could include spontaneous dona-tions or contributions from clergymen exempt from the tithe, as documented in the diocese of Sessa in Year One, where certain clerics '*qui non tenebantur ad decimam*' (Author's translation: 'who were not bound to tithe') donated 14 gold taris; AAV, Collectoria 217, fol. 35r.

77 For further details on this, see http://www.manchesterhive.com/florentine-florin-table-4-4

78 Unless specified otherwise, the sums paid by the sixteen '*immediate subiecte*' dioceses are not taken into account.

79 There are discrepancies between this list and those provided by Norbert Kamp and Konrad Eubel. Kamp included Aquino and Aversa among the suffragan dioceses of the ecclesiastical provinces of Capua and Naples, respectively. He argued that these remained directly subject to the Holy See only until the pontificate of Innocent III (1198–1216), who placed them under the jurisdiction of the respective archbishops; Kamp, *Kirche*, pp. 146 and 338. In our records, Aquino and Aversa are instead listed as *immediate subiecte* dioceses. Moreover, Kamp consid-ered Cuma as part of the province of Naples, but this is not mentioned in the registers in question, as it was suppressed in 1207; Toomaspoeg, *Decimae*, p. 59. As for Eubel, it is not clear why he did not add Sarno and Boiano in his list, when both are discussed in his volume; Eubel, *Hierarchia*, p. 140 (Boiano), p. 436 (Sarno), and p. 540. Instead, he included a couple of dioceses, such as Nocera dei Pagani (a diocese only from the fourteenth century) and Cattaro, which do not appear in our records; Eubel, *Hierarchia*, p. 177 (Cattaro), p. 314, note 1 (Nocera), and p. 540. A final interesting case is Salpi, which Eubel and Kamp ascribed to the province of Bari, whereas in the registers, it was part of the province of Siponto. This is an entirely new aspect that might suggest that the bishop of Salpi did not reside in his dio-cese at that time but had to take refuge in the neighbouring diocese of Siponto, which was vacant by then. Nevertheless, it is difficult to say whether all these discrepancies are due to mistakes by Pietro and his notary in the compilation of those usually accurate registers, or whether they are the effect of political claims by those dioceses, or even temporary changes in their status. We must stick to our sources here, leaving any further analysis to future research.

80 Many of the following coins were also being collected with the tithe from central Italy, yet in different percentages; Phillips, 'References', p. 284, note 7.

81 AAV, Collectoria 217, fol. 3v.

82 Lucia Travaini, *La monetazione dell'Italia normanna. Seconda versione con aggiornamento e ristampa anastatica con una appendice sui ritrovamenti 1995–2004 a cura di Giuseppe Sarcinelli* (Zurich and London: Numismatica ARS Classica NAC AG, 2016), pp. 137–41.

83 Villani, *Nuova cronica*, vol. 1, p. 425.

84 *MEC* 14, p. 415, no. 10.

85 *Rinforciati* also appear in Pegolotti's coin list as *romanini de peso*; Travaini, *Monete*, pp. 118–30. I am grateful to Adolfo Sissia for the correct interpretation of these coins.

86 Lucia Travaini, 'Roma', in Travaini (ed.), *Le zecche*, pp. 1077–117 and related bibliography.

87 Since in compiling these registers, notaries hardly ever distinguished between different issues of the same type, taking it for granted that they all had the same value, these *deniers tournois* could correspond either to those of the King of France or to feudal issues of Provence, Tours, or elsewhere; Phillips, 'References', p. 284, note 7.

88 It is difficult to provide a unified and clear picture of these ratios, as changes in value usually occurred from one year to the next or even between different places in the same year. These are therefore standard values, while exceptions are usually mentioned in the footnotes. Only the *gros tournois* has two different rates in the sources, one for the period 1274–76 (Year One and Year Two) and one for 1276–78 (Year Three and Year Four). The values of the *grossi* of Florence, the *aquilini* of Pisa, the English sterlings, and the *denari* of Volterra and Ravenna were derived by calculation from transactions in the early 1280s, due to the lack of any clear exchange rates for the years 1274–78 in our records. The ratios for the *romanini* of XVI and XXI *provisini* have been calculated by referring to the exchange rates documented for the *romanini* of XV *provisini*.

89 If we apply the exchange rates of five florins per ounce and six taris or 120 grains per florin to the sum of o. 785 t. 23 gr. 13, we obtain a remainder of t. 5 gr. 13. This could be the effect of the slight variations in the exchange rate of the florin, which was not always worth six taris during the years of the tithe.

90 ASF, Diplomatico, Passignano, S. Michele (badia, vallombrosani), 1279 Maggio 18, online at www.archiviodigitale.icar.beniculturali.it/it/185/ricerca/detail/91036, accessed 20 September 2024.

91 Augustus Potthast (ed.), *Regesta pontificum romanorum inde ab a. post Christum natum MCXCVIII ad a. MCCCIV*, 2 vols (Berlin: Rudolf de Decker, 1874–75), vol. II, p. 1700, no. 21082; Gottlob, *Die päpstlichen*, p. 112. The crusading tithe was also granted to Alfonso, King of Castile-Leon, and to Edward I, King of England.

92 Details can be found in Baldwin, *Gregory X*, p. 173.

93 'Haec fuit decima omnium ecclesiarum quam faciebat colligi Papa Gregorius decimus pro Terrae Sanctae succursu, quae taliter commutata fuit', in *Chronica Fr. Salimbene Parmensis ordinis minorum ex codice bibliothecae vaticanae nunc primum edita*, ed. A. Bertani (Parma: ex officina Pietri Fiaccadorii, 1867), p. 223. See also Gottlob, *Die päpstlichen*, p. 118, note 7. The nature of the source does not allow us to be sure about the sum recorded.

94 ASF, Diplomatico, Archivio Generale dei Contratti, 1287 Dicembre 15, online at www.archiviodigitale.icar.beniculturali.it/it/185/ricerca/detail/8968, accessed 20 September 2024.

95 *Storia* V, p. 253, note 2.

96 AAV, Collectoria 217, fols 19r.–29v.

97 Lunt, *Financial Relations*, p. 333.

98 Charles T. Davis, *Dante's Italy and Other Essays* (Philadelphia: University of Pennsylvania Press, 1984), pp. 205–7 (esp. p. 206, note 30).

99 Lucia Travaini, 'From the Treasure Chest to the Pope's Soup. Coins, Mints and the Roman Curia (1150–1305)', in W. Maleczek (ed.), *Die römische Kurie und das Geld. Von der Mitte des 12. Jahrhunderts bis zum frühen 14 Jahrhundert* (Ostfildern: Jan Thorbecke Verlag, 2018), pp. 27–64 (at p. 63).

100 Arrigo Castellani (ed.), *Nuovi testi fiorentini del Dugento con introduzione, trattazione linguistica e glossario. Tomo I* (Florence: G. C. Sansoni, 1952), p. 441 (52r.).

Conclusion

Venice, 31 October 1284. The Council of Forty, one of the highest governing bodies of the Republic, meets in the doge's palace to decide on an important measure that will transform Venetian monetary policy forever. On the agenda is the vote to introduce Venice's now-famous gold currency, the ducat. Curiously, only twenty-nine members of the Forty are present, joined by the doge and six councillors. The reason for this abstention is unknown. Yet, despite the low turnout, that day, with twenty-two members in favour and seven abstaining, marks both the birth of the florin's main competitor in the late medieval monetary scene and a fitting end for our story.[1]

Minted from March 1285, as pure as the florin (24 carats) but with a slightly heavier theoretical weight (3.54 g), as recorded in the surviving registers of the Great Council, the ducat represented the Venetian response to the well-established notoriety of the Florentine gold coin, and a successful one. As early as 1291, for example, thousands of gold ducats were already being carried to Egypt on Venetian ships often seized by the Arabs.[2] Such a significant export, supported by increasing mint output, was crucial in creating the critical mass of ducats in circulation that would soon allow the Venetian coin to replace the florin in the eastern Mediterranean. Other historical events with strong political implications also contributed to this, especially the destruction of the Pisan fleet by the Genoese at Meloria (1284), which deprived the city of Florence of its primary access to the sea through Pisa.[3] However, as Philip Grierson pointed out, it was as if two distinct but entangled 'monetary empires' had been established in the course of the fourteenth century: the ducat of Venice in the East and the florin of Florence in the West.[4] The simultaneous appearance of several ducat imitations, mainly of Aegean and Anatolian origins, further emphasises the popularity of the Venetian currency in those regions. The florin, for its part, maintained a predominant role in Europe where, from the early 1320s onwards, it became a standard benchmark for many imitative gold coins. Because of this, any study of the Florentine florin beyond 1284 implies the adoption of a comparative approach that takes into account the rivalry with the ducat, the appearance of gold imitations, and what this entailed from a monetary perspective, as well as the changing geopolitical conditions of the time. Yet, this goes beyond the scope of the present study.

This book set out to provide a comprehensive and complementary account of the florin's early life beyond the close and exclusive association with the world of long-distance trade and commercial business to which the Florentine coin has traditionally been confined. By investigating the contribution of political institutions and social agents to the birth and diffusion of the florin, not only has it been possible to gain a better appreciation of the 'return to gold' phenomenon in western Europe, which considered both the historical preconditions that led to the minting of gold and its aftermath, but also and above all a more holistic picture of the Florentine money as an economic, social, and political instrument with a pronounced cultural dimension and a strong identity.

Specifically, the analysis has shown that, on a macro level, the economic conditions that fostered the introduction of the florin were conventionally explained using modern and arguably anachronistic approaches, i.e., questions of the balance of trade and the gold–silver ratio. While these may hold some truth, the contours of those phenomena remain unclear. The same applies to the micro level – i.e., within Florence – where a lack of documentary evidence does not permit an unambiguous assessment of the economic conditions that fostered the introduction of the florin. Yet, the political context in which the gold coin was conceived and eventually minted is clear: the florin was part of the political reforms of the new government, the *Primo Popolo*, which had gained power following the death of Emperor Frederick II.

In this respect, the frequent refrain that the Florentine gold coin was minted at the request of merchants tells only one part of the story. Giovanni Villani created this myth during the heyday of the florin, when it regularly served in long-distance trade between northern European markets and the Levant, to the extent of becoming synonymous in Arabic (*ifrantī*) with Western gold coins.[5] Conversely, in mid-thirteenth century Florence, merchants were not just simple traders providing the necessary gold to the local mint. They were economic actors and policy-makers – the ones who conceived the coin and decided its iconography, administered the monetary policy of Florence, minted the new currency, and provided networks of circulation.

The fact that the florin is first documented by sources related to politics and only later by those of a purely mercantile nature (company accounts books, registers of notaries working for businessmen, minutes of corporate courts, and so on) depends, among other things, on archival contingencies. Yet, by focusing on the simultaneous diffusion of the florin in other non-commercial realms in the early years of its existence, namely the 'public finances' of the Angevin Crown and the papacy, an entirely new and hitherto unknown history of the currency comes to light.

Within the Angevin dominions, the florin was not only involved in the grain trade and the cloth market of the time but was also a political instrument deployed to further the king's power by financing Charles' political projects. The symbiotic relationship between the Crown and the coin fostered the circulation of the florin across wider regions, especially the Mediterranean, while establishing itself as a domestic currency in the Kingdom of Sicily. Through such involvement, the florin assisted the rise of Florentine merchants, who became necessary for the Angevin Kingdom and its military expenditure. Specifically, the fact that Charles depended directly on mercantile companies for the collection of gold florins (i.e., loans) for his expenses opened a unique opportunity for the Florentines, as creators of the florin, to interact with the monarchy while carving out a new position in the political sphere of the time. In other words, they gained political power through the financial power of their creation.

Conversely, the circulation of the florin in the papal coffers did not depend on either a legal obligation, a command, or an explicit request for florins coming directly from the Holy See. Nor was this the effect of the privileged status of the merchants of Florence in their relations with the papacy. In fact, it was only under the pontificate of Pope Boniface VIII that the florin, with its power and stability, would eventually act as a 'unique selling proposition', allowing the Florentines to increase their influence and displace other merchants, thus establishing themselves as official *mercatores pape*, especially in light of the serious financial crisis affecting other major banking companies. This would explain why, at the opening of the first jubilee in 1300, Boniface allegedly defined the Florentines as the 'fifth element' of the world, thus considering them as essential to life as earth, air, fire, and water.[6] Florins naturally flowed into the coffers of papal collectors mainly because of their near ubiquity. In the same way as for the Angevin Crown, the florin became an instrument of power, ascertaining papal authority in the political arena of the time, especially by financing the pope's projects and campaigns within and outside the Italian peninsula.

Taken together, the chapters have shown that the interplay between the different actors of the political, military, financial, and mercantile realms created a dynamic in which one factor of success depended on the other. The identification of one single element of success is perhaps moot, and it was instead the co-presence and convergence of several aspects that was crucial. Additionally, neither metallist nor chartalist approaches alone have fully captured the florin's complex and multifaceted nature. Chartalism, for instance, cannot explain the market dynamics that led the florin, conceived here as a commodity money with unique intrinsic value and features, to outperform the competition of the other – yet debased – gold coins. On the contrary, metallism does not help us understand the florin as a key element in the acquisition of power and as an instigator of social and political change. Only the combination of the two, or what Katsari has interestingly called 'fiscal metallism', makes it possible for us to fully grasp the early life of the florin in the historical context it inhabited.[7]

More generally, the analysis has revealed that money, whether in the form of goods (i.e., shells, pepper or stones), coins such as medieval Chinese strings of cash coins (*guàn*), modern *Reales de a ocho* (pieces of eight) of the Spanish Empire, or today's cryptocurrency, most notably Bitcoin, is not and never has been solely an economic artefact operating 'over and above social – and political – life'.[8] Money is and always has been a politically constructed object, created and shaped by historical contingencies and power relations, which cannot be ignored. In the case of the florin, in particular, our notions of economics and politics as entangled yet separate fields become blurred and untenable. While a separation between the political and financial spheres, and thus perhaps between politics and economics, characterised this period, the two realms remained deeply intertwined. In this context, the nature of the florin was two-fold. On the one hand, the gold coin succeeded as an economic vehicle in the big business of the time, which was state-controlled resource extraction (both the papacy and the Angevin Kingdom) and force projection (Sicily). On the other, it became a political agent of change not only as an occasional tool and manifestation of power. The florin made kings, enabled military victories and, in turn, benefitted its operators, especially the merchants of Florence who, as they orchestrated, sponsored, and profiteered from their new creation, saw their status enhanced by the 'political life' of the florin.

Notes

1 For a full account, see Stahl, *Zecca*, p. 28*ff.*
2 *Ibid.*, p. 212.
3 Locatelli, 'Florins and Ducats', pp. 307–8.
4 Philip Grierson, 'La moneta veneziana nell'economia mediterranea del Trecento e Quattrocento', in G. Pavone (ed.), *La civiltà veneziana del Quattrocento* (Florence: Sansoni, 1957), pp. 77–97 (at p. 93).
5 Eliyahu Ashtor, *Levant Trade in the Middle Ages* (Princeton: Princeton University Press, 1983), p. 138.
6 Claudia Tripodi, 'I fiorentini "quinto elemento dell'universo": L'utilizzazione encomiastica di una tradizione/invenzione', *ASI* 168: 625 (2010), 491–512.
7 Katsari, *The Roman Monetary System*, p. 253.
8 Nigel Dodd, 'The Social Life of Bitcoin', *Theory, Culture & Society* 35:3 (2018), 35–56.

Appendix

Tuscan monetary issues and their chronology, 1150s–1250s

Table A.1 details the monetary issues of mints active in Tuscany between the 1150s and 1250s. For each coin, it specifies the year or period when it was introduced and the mint responsible for its production. Variations in issues and style of the same coin within the same mint and their relative chronologies are not considered. This table is based on the most recent literature; however, some chronologies remain debated due to lack of information or ambiguities in the surviving archival records.

Table A.1 Tuscan monetary issues and their chronology, 1150s–1250s

Denari	
From the late 10th c.	Lucca
1155	Pisa
c. 1186	Siena
c. 1189	Volterra
c. 1256	Florence
1258	Arezzo
Half *denari* or *mezzaglie*	
First half of the 12th c.	Lucca
1155	Pisa
Silver *Grossi* (worth 1 *solidus*)	
1204/5–1216	Pisa

(Continued)

Table A.1   (Cont.)

1209–15	Lucca
1211/50	Siena
c. 1236	Florence
c. 1243	Arezzo
Gold coins	
1250–56	Lucca
1252	Firenze
Silver *Grossi* (worth 2 *solidi* or other multiples)	
1254/56–1264	Pisa
1250–70	Arezzo

Bibliography

Unpublished archival sources

Florence, Archivio di Stato di Firenze, Diplomatico, Passignano, S. Michele (badia, vallambrosani), 1179 Febbraio 26, online at www.archivio digitale.icar.beniculturali.it/it/185/ricerca/detail/87871, accessed 20 September 2024.

Florence, Archivio di Stato di Firenze, Diplomatico, Passignano, S. Michele (badia, vallombrosani), 1193 Ottobre 24, online at www.archivio digitale.icar.beniculturali.it/it/185/ricerca/detail/88343, accessed 20 September 2024.

Florence, Archivio di Stato di Firenze, Diplomatico, Firenze, S.ma Annunziata (serviti), 1267 Dicembre 21, online at www.archivio digitale.icar.beniculturali.it/it/185/ricerca/detail/68658, accessed 20 September 2024.

Florence, Archivio di Stato di Firenze, Diplomatico, Adespote (coperte di libri), 1277 Maggio 5, online at www.archiviodigitale.icar.beniculturali. it/it/185/ricerca/detail/7776, accessed 20 September 2024.

Florence, Archivio di Stato di Firenze, Diplomatico, Passignano, S. Michele (badia, vallombrosani), 1279 Maggio 18, online at www.archivio digitale.icar.beniculturali.it/it/185/ricerca/detail/91036, accessed 20 September 2024.

Florence, Archivio di Stato di Firenze, Diplomatico, Archivio Generale dei Contratti, 1287 Dicembre 15, online at www.archiviodigitale.icar. beniculturali.it/it/185/ricerca/detail/8968, accessed 20 September 2024.

Lucca, Archivio Storico Diocesano di Lucca, Archivio Capitolare, Libro Segnato, LL no. 17, fos 17r., 30v.–31r., 87r.

Oxford, The Bodleian Libraries, MS. Laud. Or. 210, fo. 90r.

Pisa, Archivio di Stato di Pisa, Diplomatico, Primaziale, 1238 Agosto 30.

Vatican City, Archivio Apostolico Vaticano, Camera Apostolica, Collectoria 217.

Published primary sources

Alighieri, Dante, *Convivio*, ed. Giorgio Inglese (Milan: Biblioteca Universale Rizzoli, 1999).

Alighieri, Dante, *La Divina Commedia*, 3 vols, ed. Anna Maria Chiavacci Leonardi (Milan: Mondadori, 2005).

Arias, Gino, *I trattati commerciali della Repubblica fiorentina, vol. 1: secolo XIII* (Florence: Successori Le Monnier, 1901).

Arrighi, Gino (ed.), *Opera matematica. Libro di ragioni – Liber habaci. Codici Magliabechiani Classe XI, nn. 87 e 88 (sec. XIV) della Biblioteca Nazionale di Firenze* (Lucca: Maria Pacini Fazi editore, 1987).

Astuti, Guido, *Il libro dell'entrata e dell'uscita di una compagnia mercantile senese del secolo XIII (1277–1282)* (Turin: S. Lattes & C., 1934).

Caggese, Romolo (ed.), *Statuti della Repubblica Fiorentina*, 2 vols (Florence: Tip. Galileiana, [then] E. Ariani, 1910–21); new edition, G. Pinto, F. Salvestrini, and A. Zorzi (eds), *Statuti della Repubblica fiorentina editi a cura di Romolo Caggese*, 2 vols (Florence: L. S. Olschki, 1999).

Calendar of the Liberate Rolls Preserved in the Public Record Office: Henry III. Volume 1, 1226–1240 (London: H. M. Stationery Office, 1916).

Castellani, Arrigo (ed.), *Nuovi testi fiorentini del Dugento con introduzione, trattazione linguistica e glossario. Tomo I* (Florence: G. C. Sansoni, 1952).

Castellani, Arrigo (ed.), *La prosa italiana delle origini*, 2 vols (Bologna: Patron, 1982).

Chellini, Riccardo (ed.), *Chronica de Origine Civitatis Florentiae* (Rome: Palazzo Borromini, 2009).

Chronica Fr. Salimbene Parmensis ordinis minorum ex codice bibliothecae vaticanae nunc primum edita, ed. A. Bertani (Parma: ex officina Pietri Fiaccadorii, 1867).

Davidsohn, Robert, *Forschungen zur Geschichte von Florenz III* (Berlin: Ernst Siegfried Mittler und Sohn, 1901).

De Boüard, Alain, *Documents en française des archives angevines de Naples (regne de Charles Ier)*, 2 vols (Paris: E. De Boccard, 1933).

Dellacasa, Sabina (ed.), *I libri iurium della Repubblica di Genova, Vol. I/4* (Genoa: Società Ligure di Storia Patria, 1998).

Eubel, Konrad, *Hierarchia Catholica Medii Aevi sive Summorum Pontificum, S.R.E. Cardinalium, Ecclesiarum antistitum series, ab anno 1198 usque ad annum 1431 perductae documentis tabularii praesertim Vaticani collecta, digesta* (Munster: Sumptibus et typis librariae Regensbergianae, 1913).

Evans, Allan (ed.) *Francesco Balducci Pegolotti. La Pratica della Mercatura* (Cambridge, MA: The Mediaeval Academy of America, 1936).

Falco, Giorgio and Geo Pistarino (eds), *Il cartulario di Giovanni di Giona di Portovenere (sec. XIII)* (Turin: Istituto grafico Bertello, 1955).

Ferretto, Arturo, *Codice Diplomatico delle Relazioni fra la Liguria, la Toscana, la Lunigiana ai Tempi di Dante (1265–1321). Parte prima: dal 1265 al 1274* (Rome: Tipografia Artigianelli di San Giuseppe, 1901).

Gherardi, Alessandro, *Le consulte della Repubblica fiorentina dall'anno MCCLXXX al MCCXCVIII*, 2 vols (Florence: G. C. Sansoni, 1898).

Guidi, Pietro, *Rationes decimarum Italiae nei secoli XIII e XIV: Tuscia. I: La decima degli anni 1274–1280* (Vatican City: Biblioteca Apostolica Vaticana, 1932).

Hall-Cole, M. V., H. C. Krueger, R. G. Reinert, and R. L. Reynolds (eds), *Giovanni di Guiberto (1200–1211)*, vol. 1 (Genoa: Deputazione di Storia Patria, 1939).

Hartwig, Otto, *Quellen und Forschungen zur ältestern Geschichte der Stadt Florenz* (Marburg: N. G. Elwert'sche Verlasbuch Haundlung, 1875).

I registri della Cancelleria angioina riscostruiti da Riccardo Filangieri con la collaborazione degli archivisti napoletani, 50 vols (Naples: Academia Pontaniana, 1950–2010).

Idrīsī, *La première géographie de l'Occident*, ed. H. Bresc and A. Nef (Paris: Flammarion, 1999).

Imperiale di Sant'Angelo, Cesare, *Annali Genovesi di Caffaro e de' suoi continuatori dal MCCLI al MCCLXXIX*, vol. 4 (Rome: Tipografia del Senato Palazzo Madama, 1926).

Imperiale di Sant'Angelo, Cesare, *Codice Diplomatico della Repubblica di Genova dal DCCCLVIII al MCLXIII*, vol. 1 (Rome: Tipografia del Senato, 1936).

Johnson, Charles (ed.), *Dialogus de Scaccario: The Course of the Exchequer by Richard Fitz Nigel and Constitutio Domus Regis. The Establishment of the Royal Household* (Oxford: Clarendon Press, 1983).

Knipping, Richard (ed.), *Die Regesten der Erzbischöfe von Köln im Mittelalter III, 1205–1304* (Düsseldorf: Droste, 1985).

Krueger, Hilmar C. and Robert L. Reynolds (eds), *Lanfranco 1202–1206, Vol. II* (Genoa: Società Ligure di Storia Patria, 1951).

Les Registres d'Innocent IV, 4 vols, ed. É. Berger (Paris: E. Thorin/A. Fontemoing/E. De Boccard, 1884–1921).

Les Registres de Grégoire IX, 4 vols, ed. L. Auvray, S. Clémencet, and L. Carolus-Barré (Paris: A. Fontemoing/E. De Boccard, 1896–1955).

Minieri Riccio, Camillo, *Studi storici su' Fascicoli Angioni dell'archivio della Regia Zecca di Napoli* (Naples: presso Alberto Detken Piazza del Plebiscito, 1863).

Monaci, Ernesto (ed.), *Crestomazia italiana dei primi secoli* (Città di Castello: S. Lapi, 1912).

Morozzo della Rocca, Raimondo and Attilio Lombardo, *Documenti del commercio veneziano nei secoli XI–XIII*, 2 vols (Rome: Regio Istituto Storico Italiano per il Medio Evo, 1940).

Paoli, Cesare, *Il libro di Montaperti (An. MCCLX)* (Florence: G. P. Vieussex, 1889).

Paoli, Cesare and Enea Piccolomini (eds), *Lettere volgari del secolo XIII scritte da senesi* (Bologna: G. Romagnoli, 1871).

Pieri, Paolino, *Croniche della città di Firenze*, ed. C. Coluccia (Rome: Pensa Multimidia, 2013).

Pinto, Giuliano, *Il libro del biadaiolo: carestie e annona a Firenze dalla metà del '200 al 1348* (Florence: L. S. Olschki, 1978).

Potthast, Augustus (ed.), *Regesta pontificum romanorum inde ab a. post Christum natum MCXCVIII ad a. MCCCIV*, 2 vols (Berlin: Rudolf de Decker, 1874–75).

Predelli, Riccardo (ed.), *Il Liber Communis detto anche Plegiorum del R. Archivio Generale di Venezia: Regesti* (Venice: Tipografia del commercio di Marco Visentini, 1872).

Rationes Decimarum Italiae nei secoli XIII e XIV, 12 vols (Vatican City: Biblioteca apostolica Vaticana, 1932–90).

Regesta Honorii Papae III, vol. 1, ed. P. Pressutti (Rome: Ex Typographia Vaticana, 1888).

Rodolico, Niccolò (ed.), *Cronaca Fiorentina di Marchionne di Coppo Stefani* (Città di Castello: S. Lapi, 1903).

Rotuli litterarum clausarum in Turri londinensi asservati. Vol. II: ab anno MCCXXIV ad annum MCCXXVII, ed. T. D. Hardy (London: George E. Eyre and Andrew Spottiswoode, 1844).

Santini, Pietro, *Documenti dell'antica costituzione del comune di Firenze* (Florence: G. P. Vieussuex, 1895).

Santini, Pietro, *Documenti dell'antica costituzione del comune di Firenze: appendice* (Florence: L. S. Olschki, 1952).

Schneider, Fedor (ed.), *Regestum Volaterranum: Regesten der Urkunden von Volterra (778–1303)* (Rome: E. Loescher & Co., 1907).

Syllabus membranarum ad Regiae Siclae Archivium Pertinentium, vol. 1 (Naples: Ex Regia Typographia, 1824).

Terlizzi, Sergio, *Documenti delle relazioni tra Carlo d'Angiò e la Toscana (1265–1285)* (Florence: L. S. Olschki, 1950).

Villani, Giovanni, *Nuova cronica*, 3 vols, ed. Giuseppe Porta (Parma: Fondazione Pietro Bembo/U. Guanda, 1990–91).

Wicksteed, Philip H. (ed.), *Villani's Chronicle: Being Selections from the First Nine Books of the Chroniche Fiorentine of Giovanni Villani*, trans. R. E. Selfe (London: Archibald Constable & Co., 1906), online at www.elfinspell.com/VillaniBk6b.html#sect53, accessed 20 September 2024.

Secondary sources

Abulafia, David, *The Two Italies: Economic Relations Between the Norman Kingdom of Sicily and the Northern Communes* (Cambridge: Cambridge University Press, 1977).

Abulafia, David, 'Southern Italy and the Florentine Economy, 1265–1370', *Economic History Review* New ser. 34:3 (1981), 377–88, reprinted in David Abulafia, *Italy, Sicily and the Mediterranean 1100–1400* (London: Variorum, 1987), chapter 6.

Abulafia, David, 'Crocuses and Crusaders: San Gimignano, Pisa and the Kingdom of Jerusalem', in B. Z. Kedar, H. E. Mayer, and R. C. Smail (eds), *Outremer: Studies in the History of the Crusading Kingdom of Jerusalem Presented to Joshua Prawer* (Jerusalem: Yad Izhak Ben-Zvi Institute, 1982), pp. 227–43, reprinted in David Abulafia, *Italy, Sicily and the Mediterranean 1100–1400* (London: Variorum, 1987), chapter 14.

Abulafia, David, 'Maometto e Carlomagno: le due aree monetarie dell'oro e dell'argento', *Storia d'Italia, Annali 6* (1983), 223–70; reprinted in David Abulafia, *Italy, Sicily and the Mediterranean 1100–1400* (London: Variorum, 1987), chapter 4.

Abulafia, David, 'A Tyrrhenian Triangle: Tuscany, Sicily, Tunis 1276–1300', in C. Violante (ed.), *Studi di storia economica toscana nel Medioevo e nel Rinascimento in memoria di Federigo Melis* (Pisa: Biblioteca del bollettino storico pisano, 1987), pp. 53–75; reprinted in David Abulafia, *Commerce and Conquest in the Mediterranean, 1100–1500* (London: Variorum, 1993), chapter 7.

Abulafia, David, 'The Levant Trade of the Minor Cities in the Thirteenth and Fourteenth Centuries: Strengths and Weaknesses', *Asian and African Studies* 22 (1988), 183–202; reprinted in David Abulafia, *Commerce and Conquest in the Mediterranean, 1100–1500* (London: Variorum, 1993), chapter 11.

Abulafia, David, *The Western Mediterranean Kingdoms 1200–1500: The Struggle for Dominion* (London: Longman, 1997).

Aime, Marco, *La carovana del sultano. Dal Mali alla Mecca: un pellegrinaggio medievale* (Turin: Einaudi, 2023).

Albanese, Gabriella, Bruno Figliuolo, and Paolo Pontari, 'Dei notai, cartolai e mercanti attorno al *Liber Dantis* di Giovanni Villani e del modo di leggere i documenti antichi', *Studi danteschi* 84 (2019), 285–385.

Allen, Martin, 'Currency Depreciation and Debasement in Medieval Europe', in D. Fox and W. Ernst (eds), *Money in the Western Legal Tradition: Middle Ages to Bretton Woods* (Oxford: Oxford University Press, 2016), pp. 41–52.

Arias, Gino, *Studi e documenti di storia del diritto* (Florence: Le Monnier, 1902).

Arrighi, Gino, 'Due trattati di Paolo Gherardi matematico fiorentino. I codici magliabechiani cl. XI, nn. 87 e 88 (prima metà del Trecento) della Biblioteca Nazionale di Firenze', in F. Barbieri, R. Franci, and L. Toti Rigatelli (eds), *Gino Arrighi. La matematica dell'età di mezzo. Scritti scelti* (Pisa: Edizioni ETS, 2004), pp. 81–98.

Ashtor, Eliyahu, *Les métaux précieux et la balance des payements du Proche-Orient a la Basse Époque* (Paris: SEVPEN, 1971).

Ashtor, Eliyahu, *Levant Trade in the Middle Ages* (Princeton: Princeton University Press, 1983).

Asolati, Michele, 'Nota preliminare sul gruzzolo di dinar fatimidi rinvenuto in Piazza della Signoria a Firenze (1987–88)', in *Simposio Simone Assemani sulla monetazione islamica. Padova, II Congresso Internazionale di Numismatica e Storia Monetale. Padova 17 maggio 2003, Musei Civici agli Eremitani-Museo Bottacin (Biblioteca)* (Padua: Esedra, 2005), pp. 127–35.

Baadj, Amar S., *Saladin, the Almohads and the Banū Ghāniya: The Contests for North Africa (12th and 13th Centuries)* (Leiden and Boston: Brill, 2015).

Baggott, Clare M., *Business, Politics and Family Ties. Three Case Studies: The Cerchi, dell'Antella and Portinari of Florence 1260–1360* (PhD dissertation, University of Keele, 1985).

Baldassarri, Monica, *Il tesoretto di Banchi. Un ripostiglio pisano di monete auree medievali* (Pontedera: Bandecchi e Vivaldi, 2000).

Baldassarri, Monica, *Zecca e monete del comune di Pisa: dalle origini agli inizi della seconda repubblica. XII secolo–1406*, vol. 1 (Ghezzano: Felici, 2010).

Baldassarri, Monica, 'Coniazioni ed economia monetaria del Comune di Genova: dalle origini agli inizi del Trecento', *Quaderni Ticinesi di Numismatica e Antichità Classiche* 45 (2016), 283–306.

Baldassarri, Monica, 'Miliarenses and Silver Grossi in the Western Mediterranean: New Documents and Perspectives', in M. Caccamo Caltabiano (ed.), *XV International Numismatic Congress Taormina 2015: Proceedings*, 2 vols (Rome and Messina: Arbor Sapientiae, 2017), vol. 2, pp. 1052–7.

Baldassarri, Monica, 'Zecche e monete nella Toscana bassomedievale tra passate e recenti ricerche', in M. Baldassarri (ed.), *Massa di Maremma e la Toscana nel basso Medioevo: zecche, monete ed economia* (Florence: All'Insegna del Giglio, 2019); pp. 19–36.

Baldassarri, Monica, *Le monete di Lucca. Dal periodo longobardo al Trecento* (Sesto Fiorentino: All'Insegna del Giglio, 2021).

Baldassarri, Monica, 'Tarì e altre monete normanno-sveve in area alto tirrenica: un quadro tra fonti scritte e materiali (X-XIII secolo)', in A. M. Santoro and L. Travaini (eds), *Il Tarì moneta del Mediterraneo. Atti del Convegno, Amalfi, 20–21 maggio 2022* (Amalfi: Presso la Sede del Centro, 2023), pp. 239–64.

Baldassarri, Monica and Daniele Ricci, 'I grossi d'argento e la monetazione di Genova tra Due e Trecento: nuovi dati e osservazioni per vecchi problemi', *Quaderni Ticinesi di Numismatica e Antichità Classiche* 42 (2013), 275–99.

Baldassarri, Monica et al., 'X-Ray Fluorescence Analysis of XII–XIV Century Italian Gold Coins', *Journal of Archaeology* (2014), 1–6.

Baldassarri, Monica and Stefano Locatelli, 'Genoa, Florence and the Mediterranean: New Perspectives on the Return to Gold in the 13th Century', *Revue Numismatique* 178 (2018), 433–75.

Baldwin, Philip B., *Pope Gregory X and the Crusades* (Woodbridge: Boydell Press, 2014).

Balestracci, Duccio, 'Quando Siena diventò guelfa. Il cambiamento di regime e l'affermazione dell'oligarchia novesca nella lettura di Giuseppe Martini', in G. Piccinni (ed.), *Fedeltà ghibellina, affari guelfi. Saggi e riletture intorno alla storia di Siena fra Duecento e Trecento*, 2 vols (Ospedaletto: Pacini editore, 2008), vol. 1, pp. 363–83.

Balestracci, Duccio, *La battaglia di Montaperti* (Bari: Laterza, 2017).

Bandelj, Nina, Frederick F. Wherry, and Viviana A. Zelizer (eds), *Money Talks: Explaining How Money Really Works* (Princeton and Oxford: Princeton University Press, 2017).

Barone, Nicola, 'La Ratio Thesaurariorum della Cancelleria angioina', *Archivio Storico per le Province Napoletane* 10:3–4 (1885), 413–34 and 653–64.

Barton, Simon, 'Traitors to the Faith? Christian Mercenaries in al-Andalus and the Maghreb, *c.* 1100–1300', in R. Collins and A. Goodman (eds), *Medieval Spain: Culture, Conflict, and Coexistence. Studies in Honour of Angus MacKay* (Basingstoke: Palgrave Macmillan, 2002), pp. 23–45.

Bell, Stephanie, 'The Role of the State and the Hierarchy of Money', *Cambridge Journal of Economics* 25:2 (2001), 149–63.

Benvenuti, Anna, 'Il sovramondo delle arti fiorentine. Tra i santi delle corporazioni', in *Arti fiorentine. La grande storia dell'artigianato, I – Il Medioevo* (Florence: Giunti, 1998), pp. 103–28.

Benvenuti, Marco *et al.*, 'Studying the Colline Metallifere Mining Area in Tuscany: An Interdisciplinary Approach', *IES Yearbook* (2014), 261–87.

Bernocchi, Mario, *Le monete della Repubblica fiorentina*, 5 vols (Florence: L. S. Olschki, 1974–85).

Bird, Jessalyn, Edward Peters, and James M. Powell (eds), *Crusade and Christendom: Annotated Documents in Translation from Innocent III to the Fall of Acre, 1187–1291* (Philadelphia: University of Pennsylvania Press, 2013).

Biscione, Giuseppe, *Statuti del Comune di Firenze nell'Archivio di Stato: tradizione archivistica e ordinamenti* (Rome: MiBAC, 2009).

Blanchard, Ian, *Mining, Metallurgy and Minting in the Middle Ages. Vol 3: Continuing Afro-European Supremacy, 1250–1450* (Stuttgart: Franz Steiner Verlag, 2005).

Blaydes, Lisa, Justin Grimmer, and Alison McQueen, 'Mirrors for Princes and Sultans: Advice on the Art of Governance in the Medieval Christian and Islamic Worlds', *The Journal of Politics* 80:4 (2018), 1150–67.

Bloch, Marc, 'Le problème de l'or au moyen age', *Annales d'histoire économique et sociale* 5:19 (1933), 1–34; translated by J. E. Anderson as Marc Bloch, 'The Problem of Gold in the Middle Ages', in *Land and Work in Medieval Europe: Selected Papers* (London: Routledge and Kegan Paul, 1967), pp. 186–229.

Blomquist, Thomas, 'The Second Issuance of a Tuscan Gold Coin: The Gold Groat of Lucca, 1256', *Journal of Medieval History* 13:4 (1987), 317–25.

Bocchi, Andrea. 'L'avventura di un filologo. Le carte dei Cicci di Fucecchio', in V. Formentin (ed.), *Letteratura e Filologia. Voci da un Seminario* (Padua: Cleup, 2023), pp. 11–78.

Bolton, Jim L., *Money in the Medieval English Economy: 973–1489* (Manchester: Manchester University Press, 2012).

Bompaire, Marc, 'Le Mythe du Bezant?', in *Mélanges Cécile Morrisson* (Paris: Association des Amis du Centre d'Histoire et Civilisation de Bysance, 2010), pp. 93–116.

Bompaire, Marc and Pierre-Joan Bernard, 'Le retour à l'or au treizième siècle: le cas de Montpellier (...1244–1246...)', in N. Holmes (ed.), *Proceedings of the XIVth International Numismatic Congress Glasgow 2009* (Glasgow: International Numismatic Congress, 2011), pp. 1392–400.

Bonar, James, 'Knapp's Theory of Money', *The Economic Journal* 32:125 (1922) 39–47.

Borghese, Gian Luca, *Carlo I d'Angiò e il Mediterraneo: politica, diplomazia e commercio internazionale prima dei Vespri* (Rome: École Française de Rome, 2008).

Borsari, Silvano, *Una compagnia di Calimala: gli Scali (secc. XIII–XIV)* (Macerata: Giardini, 1994).

Bourquelot, Louis F., *Études sur les foires de Champagne* (Paris: Imprimerie Imperiale, 1865).

Bovill, Edward W., *Golden Trade of the Moors* (London: Oxford University Press, 1958).

Buenger Robbert, Louis, 'Money and Prices in Thirteenth-Century Venice', *Journal of Medieval History* 20:4 (1994), 373–90.

Bulliet, Richard W., *The Camel and the Wheel* (Cambridge, MA: Harvard University Press, 1975).

Burström, Nanouschka M. and Gitte T. Ingvardson (eds), *Divina Moneta: Coins in Religion and Ritual* (London and New York: Routledge, 2017).

Cadier, Léon, *Essai sur l'administration du royaume de Sicile sous Charles Ier et Charles II d'Anjou* (Paris: E. Thorin, 1891).

Carocci, Sandro, 'Popes as Princes? The Papal State (1000–1300)', in A. Larson and K. Sisson (eds), *A Companion to the Medieval Papacy: Growth of an Ideology and Institution* (Leiden and Boston: Brill, 2016), pp. 66–84.

Carolus-Barré, Louis, 'Objets précieux et monnaies retrouvés dans le port de Trapani, en 1270, dont 21 écus d'or de Saint Louis', *Revue Numismatique* 6:18 (1976), 115–18.

Carpenter, David A., 'The Gold Treasure of King Henry III', in P. R. Coss and S. D. Lloyd (eds), *Thirteenth Century England I: Proceedings of the Newcastle-upon-Tyne Conference, 1985* (Woodbridge: The Boydell Press, 1986), pp. 61–88.

Carpenter, David A., 'Gold and Gold Coins in England in the Mid-Thirteenth Century', *The Numismatic Chronicle* 147 (1987), 106–13.

Carpenter, David A., 'The Career of Godfrey of Crowcombe: Household Knight of King John and Steward of King Henry III', in C. Given-Wilson, A. Kettle, and L. Scales (eds), *War, Government and Aristocracy in the British Isles c. 1150–1500. Essays in Honour of Michael Prestwich* (Woodbridge: Boydell Press, 2008), pp. 26–54.

Caskey, Jill, *Art and Patronage in the Medieval Mediterranean: Merchant Culture in the Region of Amalfi* (Cambridge: Cambridge University Press, 2004).

Centre National de Ressources Textuelles et Lexicales, 'Menu', online at www.cnrtl.fr/definition/menu, accessed 20 September 2024.

Chiaudano, Mario, *Studi e documenti per la storia del diritto commerciale italiano nel secolo XIII* (Turin: Presso l'Istituto Giuridico della R. Università, 1930).

Chorley, Patrick, 'The Cloth Exports of Flanders and Northern France during the Thirteenth Century: A Luxury Trade?', *Economic History Review* New ser. 40:3 (1987), 349–79.

Cipolla, Carlo M., *Money, Prices, and Civilization in the Mediterranean World: Fifth to Seventeenth Century* (Princeton: Princeton University Press, 1956).

Cipolla, Carlo M., 'Currency Depreciation in Medieval Europe', *Economic History Review* 2nd ser. 15:3 (1963), 413–22.

Cipolla, Carlo M., *Le avventure della lira* (Bologna: Il Mulino, 1975).

Cipolla, Carlo M., *Il fiorino e il quattrino. La politica monetaria a Firenze nel 1300* (Bologna: Il Mulino, 1982).

Comba, Rinaldo (ed.), *Gli Angiò nell'Italia nord-occidentale (1259–1382)* (Milan: Unicopli, 2006).

Concioni, Graziano, 'Le coniazioni della zecca lucchese nel secolo XIII', *Rivista di archeologia, storia, costume* 23:3/4 (1995), 35–88.

Constable, Olivia, *Housing the Stranger in the Mediterranean World: Lodging, Trade, and Travel in Late Antiquity and the Middle Ages* (Cambridge: Cambridge University Press, 2003).

Conti, Elio, *La formazione della struttura agraria moderna nel contado fiorentino. I: Le campagne nell'età precomunale* (Rome: Istituto Storico Italiano per il Medio Evo, 1965).

Cook, Barrie J., 'The Bezant in Angevin England', *The Numismatic Chronicle* 159 (1999), 255–75.

Cook, Barrie, Stefano Locatelli, Giuseppe Sarcinelli, and Lucia Travaini (eds), *The Italian Coins in the British Museum. Vol. 1: South Italy, Sicily, Sardinia* (Bari: Edizioni D'Andrea, 2020).

Cordero di San Quintino, Giulio, *Della zecca e delle monete di Lucca nei secoli di mezzo. Discorsi.* Memorie e documenti per servire alla storia di Lucca. Tomo XI (Lucca: Tipografia di Giuseppe Giusti, 1860).

Cornish, Alison, *Vernacular Translation in Dante's Italy: Illiterate Literature* (Cambridge: Cambridge University Press, 2011).

Coss, Peter, *The Aristocracy in England and Tuscany* (Oxford: Oxford University Press, 2020).

Crusafont, Miguel, Anna M. Balaguer, and Philip Grierson, *Medieval European Coinage, with a Catalogue of the Coins in the Fitzwilliam Museum Cambridge, 6: The Iberian Peninsula* (Cambridge: Cambridge University Press, 2013).

Cuozzo, Enrico, 'Le investiture cavalleresche', in G. Musca (ed.), *Le eredità normanno-sveve nell'età angioina. Persistenze e mutamenti nel Mezzogiorno* (Bari: Dedalo, 2004), pp. 137–49.

Dameron, George, Review of *Firenze nell'età romanica (1000–1211). L'espansione urbana, lo sviluppo istituzionale, il rapporto con il territorio* by Enrico Faini, *Speculum*, 88:1 (2013), 288–9.

Danna, Raffaele, 'Figuring Out: The Spread of Hindu-Arabic Numerals in the European Tradition of Practical Mathematics (13th–16th Centuries)', *Nuncius* 36 (2021), 5–48.

Davidsohn, Robert, *Storia di Firenze*, 8 vols (Florence: Sansoni 1956–68).

Davis, Charles T., *Dante's Italy and Other Essays* (Philadelphia: University of Pennsylvania Press, 1984).

Day, John, 'La circulation monétaire en Toscane en 1296', *Annales. Histoire, Sciences Sociales* 23:5 (1968), 1054–68, translated as John Day, 'The Monetary Circulation in Tuscany in the Age of Dante', in John Day, *The Medieval Market Economy* (Oxford: Basil Blackwell, 1987), pp. 129–40.

Day, William R., Jr., 'The Monetary Reforms of Charlemagne and the Circulation of Money in Early Medieval Campania', *Early Medieval Europe* 6:1 (1997), 25–45.

Day, William R., Jr., *The Early Development of the Florentine Economy, c. 1100–1275* (PhD dissertation, London School of Economics, 2000).

Day, William R., Jr., 'Population Growth and Productivity: Rural–Urban Migration and the Expansion of the Manufacturing Sector in Thirteenth-Century Florence', in B. Blondé, E. Vanhaute, and M. Galand (eds), *Labour and Labour Markets between Town and Countryside (Middle Ages–19th Century)* (Turnhout: Brepols, 2001), pp. 82–110.

Day, William R., Jr., 'The Population of Florence before the Black Death: Survey and Synthesis', *Journal of Medieval History* 28 (2002), 93–129.

Day, William R., Jr., 'Early Imitations of the Gold Florin of Florence and the Imitation Florin of Chivasso in the Name of Theodore I Paleologus, Marquis of Montferrat (1306–1338)', *The Numismatic Chronicle* 164 (2004), 183–99

Day, William R., Jr., 'Fiorentini e altri italiani appaltatori di zecche straniere, 1200–1600: un progetto di ricerca', *Annali di Storia di Firenze* 5 (2010), 9–29.

Day, William R., Jr., 'Economy', in Z. Baranski and L. Pertile (eds), *Dante in Context* (Cambridge: Cambridge University Press, 2015), pp. 30–46.

Day, William R., Jr., 'Before the *Libro della Zecca*: Money and Coinage in Florence in the 12th and 13th Centuries, Part I (Petty Coinage)', *Archivio Storico Italiano* 175:3 (2017), 441–82.

Day, William R., Jr., 'Before the *Libro della Zecca*: Money and Coinage in Florence in the 12th and 13th Centuries, Part II (Silver and Gold Trade Coinages)', *Archivio Storico Italiano* 176:3 (2018), 431–84.

Day, William R., Jr. and Massimo De Benetti, 'The Willanzheim Hoard (1853) of Florentine Gold Florins', *Rivista Italiana di Numismatica e Scienze Affini* 119 (2018), 101–62.

Day, William R., Jr., Michael Matzke, and Andrea Saccocci, *Medieval European Coinage, with a Catalogue of the Coins in the Fitzwilliam Museum Cambridge, 12: Italy (I) (Northern Italy)* (Cambridge: Cambridge University Press, 2016).

Day, William R., Jr., Chiara Peroni, and Franca M. Vanni, 'Firenze (Toscana)', in L. Travaini (ed.), *Le zecche italiane fino all'Unità* (Rome: Istituto Poligrafico e Zecca dello Stato, 2011), pp. 667–702.

De Benetti, Massimo, *Il tesoro di Alberese: un ripostiglio di fiorini d'oro del XIII secolo* (San Benedetto del Tronto: Numismatica Picena, 2015).

De Benetti, Massimo, *I primi 100 anni del fiorino d'oro di Firenze (1251–1351): analisi e nuove prospettive di ricerca* (Rome: Istituto Poligrafico e Zecca dello Stato, 2024).

de Roover, Raymond, 'Discussion of Gras's paper "Capitalism: Concepts and History"', *Bulletin of the Business Historical Society* 16 (1942), 34–9.

de Roover, Raymond, 'The Cambium Maritimum Contract according to the Genoese Notarial Records of the Twelfth Centuries', *Explorations in Economic History* 7:1 (1969), 15–33.

De Rosa, Daniela, *Alle origini della Repubblica fiorentina: dai consoli al 'primo popolo' (1172–1260)* (Florence: Arnaud, 1995).

de Villard, Ugo Monneret, 'La tessitura palermitana sotto i Normanni e i suoi rapporti con l'arte bizantina', in *Miscellanea Giovanni Mercati III* (Vatican City: Biblioteca Apostolica Vaticana, 1946), pp. 464–89.

Del Punta, Ignazio, 'Il fallimento della compagnia Ricciardi alla fine del secolo XIII: un caso esemplare?', *Archivio Storico Italiano* 160:2 (2002), 221–68.

Del Punta, Ignazio, *Mercanti e banchieri lucchesi nel Duecento* (Pisa: Pisa University Press, 2004).

Del Punta, Ignazio, *Guerrieri, Crociati, Mercanti. I Toscani in Levante in età pieno-medievale (secoli XI–XIII)* (Spoleto: Fondazione centro italiano di studi sull'alto Medioevo, 2010).

Del Punta, Ignazio, 'Tuscan Merchant-Bankers and Moneyers and their Relations with the Roman Curia in the XIIIth and Early XIVth Centuries', *Rivista di Storia della Chiesa in Italia* 64:1 (2010), 39–53.

Desan, Christine, *Making Money: Coin, Currency, and the Coming of Capitalism* (Oxford: Oxford University Press, 2014).

228   *Bibliography*

Despy, Georges, *Les tarifs de tonlieux* (Turnhout: Brepols, 1976).

Devisse, Jean, 'Routes de commerce et échanges en Afrique occidentale en relation avec la Méditerranée. Un essai sur le commerce africain médiéval du XIe au XVIe siècle', *Revue d'histoire économique et sociale* 50:1 (1972), 42–73.

Diacciati, Silvia, *Popolani e magnati: società e politica nella Firenze del Duecento* (Spoleto: Fondazione centro italiano di studi sull'alto Medioevo, 2010).

Dini, Bruno, 'I mercanti-banchieri e la sede apostolica (XIII–prima metà del XIV secolo)', in Centro Italiano di Studi di Storia e d'Arte (ed.), *Gli spazi economici della chiesa nell'Occidente mediterraneo (secoli XII–metà XIV), Pistoia, 16–19 maggio 1997* (Pistoia: Presso la sede del Centro, 1999), pp. 42–62.

Dodd, Nigel, *The Sociology of Money: Economics, Reason and Contemporary Society* (London: Continuum International Publishing Group, 1994).

Dodd, Nigel, *The Social Life of Money* (Princeton and Oxford: Princeton University Press, 2015).

Dodd, Nigel, 'The Social Life of Bitcoin', *Theory, Culture & Society* 35:3 (2018), 35–56.

Dunbabin, Jean, 'The Household and Entourage of Charles I of Anjou, King of the Regno, 1266–85', *Historical Research* 77:197 (2004), 313–36.

Dunbabin, Jean, *The French in the Kingdom of Sicily, 1266–1305* (Cambridge: Cambridge University Press, 2011).

Dunbabin, Jean, *Charles I of Anjou: Power, Kingship, and State-Making in Thirteenth Century Europe* (London and New York: Routledge, 2014).

Duplessy, Jean, 'La circulation des monnaies arabes en Europe occidentale du VIIIe au XIIIe siècle', *Revue Numismatique* 5:18 (1956), 101–63.

Egidi, Pietro, 'Carlo d'Angiò e l'abbazia di S. Maria della Vittoria presso Scurcola', *Archivio Storico per le Province Napoletane* 34:2 (1909), 732–67.

Eich, Stefan, *The Currency of Politics: The Political Theory of Money from Aristotle to Keynes* (Princeton and Oxford: Princeton University Press, 2022).

Epstein, Stephan R., *An Island for Itself: Economic Development and Social Change in Late Medieval Sicily* (Cambridge: Cambridge University Press, 1992).

Fabbri, Lorenzo, 'Calimala e l'Opera di San Giovanni: il governo del Battistero di Firenze fra autorità ecclesiastica e potere civile', in F. Guerrieri (ed.), *Battistero di San Giovanni. Conoscenza, Diagnostica, Conservazione. Atti del Convegno Internazionale Firenze, 24–25 Novembre 2014* (Florence: Mandragora, 2017), pp. 73–85.

Face, Richard D., 'Techniques of Business in the Trade Between the Fairs of Champagne and the South of Europe in the Twelfth and Thirteenth Centuries', *Economic History Review* New ser. 10:3 (1958), 427–38.

Face, Richard D., 'Secular History in Twelfth-Century Italy: Caffaro of Genoa', *Journal of Medieval History* 6 (1980), 169–84.

Faini, Enrico, 'Il convito del 1216. La vendetta all'origine del fazionalismo fiorentino', *Annali di Storia di Firenze* 1 (2006), 9–36.

Faini, Enrico, *Firenze nell'età romanica (1000–1211). L'espansione urbana, lo sviluppo istituzionale, il rapporto con il territorio* (Florence: L. S. Olschki, 2010).

Faini, Enrico, 'Prima del fiorino. Le origini del decollo economico di Firenze', in T. Verdon (ed.), *Firenze prima di Arnolfo: retroterra di grandezza. Atti del ciclo di conferenze (Firenze, 14 gennaio–24 marzo 2015)* (Florence: Mandragora, 2016), pp. 89–100.

Faini, Enrico, 'I notai e la costruzione dell'identità fiorentina entro il 1260: prime indagini', in G. Pinto, L. Tanzini, and S. Tognetti (eds), *Notariorum itinera. Notai toscani del basso medioevo tra routine, mobilità e specializzazione* (Florence: L. S. Olschki, 2018), pp. 15–25.

Fantacci, Luca, 'The Dual Currency System of Renaissance Europe', *Financial History Review* 15:1 (2008), 55–72.

Fauvelle, François-Xavier, *The Golden Rhinoceros: Histories of the African Middle Ages* (Princeton and Oxford: Princeton University Press, 2018).

Felten, Sebastian, *Money in the Dutch Republic: Everyday Practice and Circuits of Exchange* (Cambridge: Cambridge University Press, 2022).

Finetti, Angelo, *La zecca e le monete di Perugia nel medioevo e nel rinascimento* (Perugia: Volumnia, 1997).

Fiumi, Enrico, *Volterra e San Gimignano nel medioevo*, ed. G. Pinto (Siena: Grafica Pistolesi, 1983).

Franceschi, Franco, '1252. Il fiorino di Firenze, il dollaro della crescita medievale', in A. Giardina (ed.), *Storia Mondiale dell'Italia* (Bari: Laterza, 2017), pp. 258–62.

Franceschi, Franco, 'La crescita economica dell'Occidente medievale: un tema storico non ancora esaurito. Introduzione', in Centro Italiano di Studi di Storia e d'Arte (ed.), *La crescita economica dell'Occidente medievale: un tema storico non ancora esaurito, Pistoia, 14–17 maggio 2015* (Rome: Viella, 2017), pp. 1–24.

Fuiano, Michele, *Carlo I d'Angiò in Italia: studi e ricerche* (Naples: Liguori, 1974).

Gigli, Elisabetta, 'Operatori economici fiorentini a cavallo del primo popolo: intorno alla "societas filiorum Falconerii"', in L. Gatto and P. Supino Martini (eds), *Studi sulla società e le culture del Medioevo per Girolamo Arnaldi*, 2 vols (Florence: All'Insegna del Giglio, 2002), vol. 1, pp. 229–43.

Giuliani, Achille and Davide Fabrizi, *Le monete degli Angioini in Italia meridionale: indagine archivistica sulla politica monetaria e analisi critica dei materiali* (Roseto degli Abruzzi: Edizioni D'Andrea, 2014).

Glick, Thomas F., Steven J. Livesey, and Faith Wallis (eds), *Medieval Science, Technology, and Medicine: An Encyclopedia* (New York: Routledge, 2005).

Goldthwaite, Richard A., 'Schools and Teachers of Commercial Arithmetic in Renaissance Florence', *Journal of European Economic History* 1:2 (1972), 418–33.

Goldthwaite, Richard A., *The Economy of Renaissance Florence* (Baltimore: Johns Hopkins University Press, 2009).

Goldthwaite, Richard A. and Giulio Mandich, *Studi sulla moneta fiorentina: secoli XIII–XIV* (Florence: L. S. Olschki, 1994).

Gondonneau, Alexandra and Maria F. Guerra, 'The Circulation of Precious Metals in the Arab Empire: The Case of the Near and the Middle East', *Archaeometry* 44:4 (2002), 573–99.

Goodhart, Charles A. E., 'The Two Concepts of Money: Implications for the Analysis of Optimal Currency Areas', *European Journal of Political Economy* 14 (1998), 407–32.

Gordus, Adon A. and David M. Metcalf, 'Neutron Activation Analysis of the Gold Coinages of the Crusader States', in D. M. Metcalf and W. A. Oddy (eds), *Metallurgy in Numismatics I* (London: The Royal Numismatic Society, 1980), pp. 119–50.

Gottlob, Adolf, *Die päpstlichen Kreuzzugs-Steuern des 13. Jahrhunderts: ihre rechtliche Grundlage, politische Geschichte und technische Verwaltung* (Heiligenstadt: Cordier, 1892).

Green, Louis, *Chronicle into History: An Essay on the Interpretation of History in Florentine Fourteenth-Century Chronicles* (Cambridge: Cambridge University Press, 1972).

Green, Louis, 'Florence', in D. Abulafia (ed.), *The New Cambridge Medieval History Vol. 5: c. 1198–c. 1300* (Cambridge: Cambridge University Press, 1999), pp. 479–96.

Grierson, Philip, 'Oboli de Musc', *The English Historical Review* 66:258 (1951), 75–81.

Grierson, Philip, 'La moneta veneziana nell'economia mediterranea del Trecento e Quattrocento', in G. Pavone (ed.), *La civiltà veneziana del Quattrocento* (Florence: Sansoni, 1957), pp. 77–97.

Grierson, Philip, 'The President's Address: Session 1965–1966. The Interpretation of Coin Finds (I)', *The Numismatic Chronicle* 5 (1965), i–xvi.

Grierson, Philip, 'The Origins of Money', *Research in Economic Anthropology* 1 (1978), 1–35.

Grierson, Philip, *Later Medieval Numismatics (11th–16th Centuries)* (London: Variorum, 1979).

Grierson, Philip, 'The Weight of the Gold Florin in the Fifteenth Century', *Quaderni Ticinesi di Numismatica e Antichità Classiche* 10 (1981), 421–31.

Grierson, Philip, *The Coins of Medieval Europe* (London: Seaby, 1991).

Grierson, Philip, 'Il fiorino d'oro: la grande novità dell'Occidente medievale', *Rivista Italiana di Numismatica e Scienze Affini* 107 (2006), 415–19.

Grierson, Philip and Lucia Travaini, *Medieval European Coinage, with a Catalogue of the Coins in the Fitzwilliam Museum Cambridge, 14: Italy (III) (South Italy, Sicily, Sardinia)* (Cambridge: Cambridge University Press, 1998).

Grillo, Paolo, 'Un dominio multiforme. I comuni dell'Italia nord-occidentale soggetti a Carlo I d'Angiò', in R. Comba (ed.), *Gli Angiò nell'Italia nord-occidentale (1259–1382)* (Milan: Unicopli, 2006), pp. 31–101.

Grossi, Paolo, *L'ordine giuridico medievale* (Bari: Laterza, 2003).

Gualtieri, Piero, *Il comune di Firenze tra Due e Trecento. Partecipazione politica e assetto istituzionale* (Florence: L. S. Olschki, 2009).

Guidi, Pietro, 'Di alcuni maestri lombardi a Lucca nel sec. XIII (Appunti d'archivio per la loro biografia e per la storia dell'arte)', *Archivio Storico Italiano* 87:4 (1929), 209–31.

Guyer, Jane I. (ed.), *Money Matters: Instability, Values and Social Payments in the Modern History of West African Communities* (Portsmouth, NH: Heinemann, 1995).

Hart, Keith, 'Heads or Tails? Two Sides of the Coin', *Man* New ser. 21:4 (1986), 637–56.

Hazard, Harry W., *The Numismatic History of Late Medieval North Africa* (New York: American Numismatic Society, 1952).

Hebert, Raymond J., 'The Coinage of Islamic Spain', *Islamic Studies* 30:1/2 (1991), 113–28.

Hélary, Xavier, 'Les rois de France et la Terre Sainte de la croisade de Tunis à la chute d'Acre', *Annuaire-Bulletin de la Société de l'histoire de France* (2005), 21–104.

Hendy, Michael, *Coinage and Money in the Byzantine Empire 1081–1261* (Washington, DC: Dumbarton Oaks, 1969).

Hocquet, Jean Claude, *Le sel et le pouvoir: de l'an mil à la révolution française* (Paris: Albin Michel, 1985).

Hopley, Russel, 'Aspects of Trade in Western Mediterranean During the Eleventh and Twelfth Centuries: Perspectives from Islamic Fatwās and State Correspondence', *Mediaevalia* 13 (2011), 5–42.

Hoshino, Hidetoshi, *L'arte della lana in Firenze nel Basso Medioevo: il commercio della lana e il mercato dei panni fiorentini nei secoli XIII–XV* (Florence: L. S. Olschki, 1980).

Houlbrook, Ceri, *The Magic of Coin-Trees from Religion to Recreation: The Roots of a Ritual* (Cham: Palgrave Macmillan, 2018).

Housley, Norman, *The Italian Crusades: The Papal-Angevin Alliance and the Crusades against Christian Lay Powers, 1254–1343* (Oxford: Clarendon Press, 1982).

Housley, Norman, 'European Warfare, c. 1200–1320', in M. Keen (ed.), *Medieval Warfare: A History* (Oxford: Oxford University Press, 1999), pp. 113–36.

Høyrup, Jens, 'Mathematics Education in the European Middle Ages', in A. Karp and G. Schubring (eds), *Handbook on the History of Mathematics Education* (New York: Springer, 2014), pp. 109–24.

Hunt, Edwin S., *The Medieval Super-companies* (Cambridge: Cambridge University Press, 1994).

Hyde, John K., 'Some Uses of Literacy in Venice and Florence in the Thirteenth and Fourteenth Centuries', *Transactions of the Royal Historical Society* 29 (1979), 109–28.

Idris, Hady Roger, *La Barbérie orientale sous les Zīrīdes. X^e–XIIe*, 2 vols (Paris: Adrien-Maisonneuve, 1962).

Ingham, Geoffrey, *The Nature of Money* (Cambridge and Malden: Polity Press, 2004).

Jacobi, Lauren, 'Reconsidering the World-system: The Agency and Material Geography of Gold', in D. Savoy (ed.), *Globalization of Renaissance Art: A Critical Review* (Leiden and Boston: Brill, 2017), pp. 131–57.

Jamme, Armand, 'De Rome à Florence, la curie et ses banquiers aux XIIe et XIIIe siècles', in W. Maleczek (ed.), *Die römische Kurie und das Geld. Von der Mitte des 12. Jahrhunderts bis zum frühen 14 Jahrhundert* (Ostfildern: Jan Thorbecke Verlag, 2018), pp. 167–204.

Jordan, Edouard, *De mercatoribus camerae apostolicae saeculo XIII* (Condate Rhedonum: apud Oberthur Typographum, 1909).

Jordan, Edouard, *Les origines de la domination angevine en Italie* (Paris: A. Picard fils, 1909).

Kamp, Norbert, *Kirche und Monarchie im Staufischen Königreich Sizilien, I: Prosopographische Grundlegung: Bistümer und Bischöfe des Königreichs 1194–1266, Teil I: Abruzzen und Kampanien* (Munich: Fink, 1973).

Katsari, Constantina, *The Roman Monetary System: The Eastern Provinces from the First to the Third Century AD* (Cambridge: Cambridge University Press, 2011).

Kaye, Joel, *Economy and Nature in the Fourteenth Century: Money, Market, Exchange, and the Emergence of Scientific Thought* (Cambridge: Cambridge University Press, 2004).

Kiesewetter, Andreas, 'La Cancelleria angioina', in *L'état angevin. Pouvoir, culture et société entre XIIIe et XIVe siècle. Actes du colloque international organisé par l'American Academy in Rome (Rome–Naples, 7–11 novembre 1995)* (Rome: École Française de Rome, 1998), pp. 361–415.

Kiesewetter, Andreas, 'L'acquisto e l'occupazione del litorale meridionale dell'Albania da parte di re Carlo I d'Angiò (1279–1283)', *Rassegna storica salernitana* 32:63 (2015), 27–62.

Kirshner, Julius, 'Civitas Sibi Faciat Civem: Bartolus of Sassoferrato's Doctrine on the Making of a Citizen', *Speculum* 48:4 (1973), 694–713.

Knapp, Georg Friedrich, *The State Theory of Money* (London: Macmillan & Company Limited, 1924).

Kool, Robert, 'A Thirteenth Century Hoard of Gold Florins from the Medieval Harbour of Acre', *The Numismatic Chronicle* 166 (2006), 301–20.

Kovacević, Desanka, 'Dans la Serbie et la Bosnie medievales: les mines d'or et d'argent', *Annales. Économies, Sociétés, Civilisations* 15:2 (1960), 248–58.

Kowalski, Heinrich, 'Die Augustalen Kaiser Friedrichs II', *Schweizerische Numismatische Rundschau* 55 (1976), 77–150.

Lambertini, Roberto, 'Mirrors for Princes', in H. Lagerlund (ed.), *Encyclopedia of Medieval Philosophy: Philosophy between 500 and 1500* (Dordrecht and London: Springer, 2010), pp. 791–7.

Lane, Frederic C. and Reinhold C. Mueller, *Money and Banking in Medieval and Renaissance Venice* (Baltimore and London: John Hopkins University Press, 1985).

Lasinio, Ernesto, 'Frammento di un quaderno di mandati dell'antica Camera del Comune di Firenze', *Archivio Storico Italiano* 35:238 (1905), 440–7.

Lau, Jeffrey Y. F. and John Smithin, 'The Role of Money in Capitalism', *International Journal of Political Economy* 32:3 (2002), 5–22.

Le Goff, Jacques, *Money and the Middle Ages: An Essay in Historical Anthropology* (Cambridge: Polity Press, 2012).

Lee, Geoffrey, 'The Oldest European Account Book: A Florentine Bank Ledger of 1211', *Nottingham Mediaeval Studies* 1:16 (1972), 28–60.

Lee, Geoffrey, 'The Florentine Bank Ledger Fragments of 1211: Some New Insights', *Journal of Accounting Research* 11:1 (1973), 47–61.

Lenzi, Luciano, 'Il grosso d'oro di Lucca: 1246?', *Memorie dell'Accademia Italiana di Studi Filatelici e Numismatici* 6:1 (1995), 73–91.

Léonard, Émile G., *Les Angevins de Naples* (Paris: Presses universitaires de France, 1954); trans. Renato Liguori, *Gli Angioini di Napoli* (Milan: Dall'Oglio, 1967).

Leonard, Robert D., 'The Effects of the Fourth Crusade on European Gold Coinage', in T. F. Madden (ed.), *The Fourth Crusade: Events, Aftermath, and Perceptions* (Burlington: Ashgate, 2008), pp. 75–88.

Levtzion, Nehemia, *Ancient Ghana and Mali* (London: Methuen, 1973).

Lisini, Alessandro, 'Le monete e le zecche di Volterra, Montieri, Berignone e Casole', *Rivista Italiana di Numismatica e Scienze Affini* 22 (1909), 266–7.

Locatelli, Stefano, 'Florins and Ducats in the Kingdom of Sicily-Aragon: The Syracuse Hoard (1313–c.1369)', *The Numismatic Chronicle* 179 (2019), 299–340.

Locatelli, Stefano, 'Gli strumenti del potere: per un'analisi della decima universale di papa Gregorio X nel Regno di Sicilia, 1274–1280', *Eurostudium3w* 56 (2021), 101–13.

Locatelli, Stefano and Lucia Travaini, 'Objects for History: The Coins of South Italy, Sicily and Sardinia in the British Museum', in B. Cook,

S. Locatelli, G. Sarcinelli, and L. Travaini (eds), *The Italian Coins in the British Museum. Vol. 1: South Italy, Sicily, Sardinia* (Bari: Edizioni D'Andrea, 2020), pp. 23–53.

Lopez, Roberto S., 'Un "consilium" di giuristi torinesi nel Dugento', *Bollettino Storico-bibliografico Subalpino* 38:1–2 (1936), 143–50.

Lopez, Roberto S., 'The Dollar of the Middle Ages', *The Journal of Economic History* 11:3 (1951), 209–34.

Lopez, Roberto S., 'Settecento anni fa: il ritorno all'oro nell'Occidente due-centesco', *Rivista Storica Italiana* 65 (1953), 19–55 and 161–98.

Lopez, Roberto S., 'Back to Gold, 1252', *Economic History Review* New ser. 9:2 (1956), 219–40.

Lopez, Roberto S., *The Commercial Revolution of the Middle Ages, 950–1350* (Englewood Cliffs, NJ: Prentice Hall, 1971).

Lopez, Roberto S. and Irving W. Raymond, *Medieval Trade in the Mediterranean World: Illustrative Documents* (New York: Columbia University Press, 1995).

Lunt, William E., 'The Financial System of the Medieval Papacy in the Light of Recent Literature', *The Quarterly Journal of Economics* 23:2 (1909), 251–95.

Lunt, William E., 'A Papal Tenth Levied in the British Isles from 1274 to 1280', *The English Historical Review* 32:125 (1917), 49–89.

Lunt, William E., *Papal Revenues in the Middle Ages*, 2 vols (New York: Columbia University Press, 1934).

Lunt, William E., *Financial Relations of the Papacy with England to 1327* (Cambridge, MA: The Mediaeval Academy of America, 1939).

Luzzati, Michele, 'Falconieri', in *Dizionario Biografico degli Italiani*, vol. 44 (Rome: Istituto della Enciclopedia Italiana, 1994), pp. 369–71, online at www.treccani.it/enciclopedia/falconieri_(Dizionario-Biografico), accessed 20 September 2024.

Mac Cracken, J., 'The Dedication Inscription of the Palazzo del Podestà Dating from the Period of the First Democracy (1250–1260) Probably Composed by Brunetto Latini', *Rivista d'Arte* 30 (1955), 183–205.

Mainoni, Patrizia, 'Il governo del re. Finanza e fiscalità nelle città angioine (Piemonte e Lombardia al tempo di Carlo I d'Angiò)', in R. Comba (ed.), *Gli Angiò nell'Italia nord-occidentale (1259–1382)* (Milan: Unicopli, 2006), pp. 103–37.

Maire Vigueur, Jean-Claude (ed.), *I podestà dell'Italia comunale. Parte I: Reclutamento e circolazione degli ufficiali forestieri (fine XII sec.– metà XIV sec.)* (Rome: Istituto Storico Italiano per il Medio Evo–École Française de Rome, 2000).

Manzalaoui, Mahmoud, 'The Pseudo-Aristotelian "Kitāb Sirr al-Asrār". Facts and Problems', *Oriens* 23/24 (1974), 147–257.

Massagli, Domenico, *Introduzione alla storia della zecca e delle monete lucchesi. Memorie e documenti per servire alla storia di Lucca*. Tomo XI, parte seconda (Lucca: Tipografia Giusti, 1870).

Mathews, Karen Rose, Silvia Orvietani Bush, and Stefano Bruni (eds), *A Companion to Medieval Pisa* (Leiden and Boston: Brill, 2022).

Mayhew, Nicholas J., 'Modelling Medieval Monetisation', in R. H. Britnell and B. M. S. Campbell (eds), *A Commercialising Economy: England 1086–1300* (Manchester: Manchester University Press, 1995), pp. 55–77.

McIntosh, Susan K., 'A Reconsideration of Wangara/Palolus, Island of Gold', *The Journal of African History* 22 (1981), 145–58.

Merati, Patrizia, 'Fra donazione e trattato. Tipologie documentarie, modalità espressive e forme autenticatorie delle sottomissioni a Carlo d'Angiò dei comuni dell'Italia settentrionale', in R. Comba (ed.), *Gli Angiò nell'Italia nord-occidentale (1259–1382)* (Milan: Unicopli, 2006), pp. 333–61.

Messier, Ronald A., 'The Almoravids: West African Gold and the Gold Currency of the Mediterranean Basin', *Journal of Economic and Social History of the Orient* 17:1 (1974), 31–47.

Metcalf, David M., *Coinage of the Crusades and the Latin East in the Ashmolean Museum Oxford* (London: Royal Numismatic Society, 1995).

Meyer, Andreas, 'Organisierter Bettel und andere Finanzgeschäfte des Hospitals von Altopascio im 13. Jahrhundert', *Pariser Historische Studien* 57 (2007), 55–105.

Milani, Giuliano, 'Monete, cambiatori e popolo. Un tentativo di riforma monetaria bolognese nel 1264', *Annali dell'Istituto Italiano di Numismatica* 57 (2011), 131–56.

Milani, Giuliano, 'Uno snodo nella storia dell'esclusione. Urbano IV, la crociata contro Manfredi e l'avvio di nuove diseguaglianze nell'Italia bassomedievale', *Mélanges de l'École Française de Rome – Moyen Âge* 125:2 (2013), online at https://journals.openedition.org/mefrm/1278, accessed 20 September 2024.

Miskimin, Harry A., 'Money and Movements in France and England at the End of the Middle Ages', in J. F. Richards (ed.), *Precious Metals in the Later Medieval and Early Modern Worlds* (Durham, NC: Carolina Academic Press, 1983), pp. 79–96.

Miskimin, Harry A., 'The Enforcement of Gresham's Law', in A. Vannini Marx (ed.), *Credito, banche e investimenti, secoli XIII–XX. Atti della quarta Settimana di studio (Prato, 14–21 aprile 1972), Istituto Internazionale di Storia Economica 'F. Datini'* (Florence: Felice le Monnier, 1985), pp. 147–161, reprinted in Harry A. Miskimin, *Cash, Credit and Crisis in Europe, 1300–1600* (London: Variorum, 1989), chapter 9.

Montagano, Alessio, *Monete italiane regionali: Firenze* (Pavia: Numismatica Varesi, 2008).

Morrisson, Cécile, 'Byzantine Money: Its Production and Circulation', in A. E. Laiou (ed.), *The Economic History of Byzantium: From the Seventh through the Fifteenth Century* (Washington, DC: Dumbarton Oaks, 2002), pp. 909–66.

Murray, Alexander, *Reason and Society in the Middle Ages* (Oxford: Oxford University Press, 1978; reprinted 2002).

Naismith, Rory, 'The Social Significance of Monetization in the Early Middle Ages', *Past & Present* 223 (2014), 3–39.

Naismith, Rory (ed.), *Money and Coinage in the Middle Ages* (Leiden and Boston: Brill, 2018).

Naqar, 'Umar Al-, 'Takrur: The History of a Name', *The Journal of African History* 10:3 (1969), 365–74.

Nassar, Magdi A. M., *Le monete di Arezzo* (Leipzig: Numismatica-Mente, 2018).

Nassar, Magdi A. M., *Le monete di Volterra. Vol. II: Il Medioevo e l'Età Moderna* (Pavia: Edizioni Numismatica Varesi, 2021).

Nina, Luigi, *Le finanze pontificie nel medioevo*, 3 vols (Milan: F.lli Treves, 1929–32).

Oberländer-Târnoveanu, Ernest, 'Les hyperpères de type Jean III Vatatzès. Classification, chronologie et évolution du titre (à la lumière du trésor d'Uzunbair, dép. de Tulcea)', in M. Iacob, E. Oberländer-Târnoveanu, and F. Topoleanu (eds), *Istro-Pontica, Muzeul Tulcean la a 50–a Aniversare 1950–2000* (Tulcea: Consiliul Judeţean, 2000), pp. 499–562.

Olsen, Glenn, 'Italian Merchants and the Performance of Papal Banking Functions in the Early Thirteenth Century', *Explorations in Economic History* 7:1 (1969), 43–63.

Paganelli, Jacopo, *Dives episcopus. La signoria dei vescovi di Volterra nel Duecento* (Rome: Viella, 2021).

Paravicini Bagliani, Agostino, 'Per una storia economica e finanziaria della corte papale preavignonese', in Centro Italiano di Studi di Storia e d'Arte (ed.), *Gli spazi economici della Chiesa nell'Occidente mediterraneo (secoli XII–metà XIV), Pistoia, 16–19 maggio 1997* (Pistoia: Presso la sede del Centro, 1999), pp. 19–24.

Paravicini Bagliani, Agostino, *Il papato nel secolo XIII. Cent'anni di bibliografia (1875–2009)* (Florence: SISMEL Edizioni del Galluzzo, 2010).

Parsons, Jotham, *Making Money in Sixteenth-Century France: Currency, Culture, and the State* (Ithaca and London: Cornell University Press, 2014).

Percy, William A., Jr., *The Revenues of the Kingdom of Sicily under Charles of Anjou 1266–1285 and their Relationship to the Vespers* (PhD dissertation, Princeton University, 1964).

Pesce, Giovanni and Giuseppe Felloni, *Le monete genovesi. Storia, arte ed economia nelle monete di Genova dal 1139 al 1814* (Genoa: Cassa di Risparmio di Genova e Imperia, 1975).

Petralia, Giuseppe, 'I toscani nel Mezzogiorno medievale. Genesi ed evoluzione trecentesca di una relazione di lungo periodo', in S. Gensini (ed.), *La Toscana nel secolo XIV: caratteri di una civiltà regionale* (Pisa: Pacini, 1988), pp. 289–336.

Phillips, Marcus, 'References to the French Maille Tierce in Italian Accounts from 1278', *The Numismatic Chronicle* 155 (1995), 283–8.

Phillips, Marcus, 'The Gros Tournois in the Mediterranean', in N. J. Mayhew (ed.), *The Gros Tournois: Proceedings of the Fourteenth Oxford Symposium on Coinage and Monetary History* (Oxford: Ashmolean Museum, Royal Numismatic Society, Société Française de Numismatique, 1997), pp. 280–337.

Phillips, Marcus, 'The Monetary Use of Uncoined Silver in Western Europe in the Twelfth and Thirteenth Centuries', in M. Allen and N. J. Mayhew (eds), *Money and Its Use in Medieval Europe: Three Decades On. Essays in Honour of Professor Peter Spufford* (London: Royal Numismatic Society, 2017), pp. 1–18.

Plesner, Johan, *L'emigrazione dalla campagna alla città libera di Firenze nel XIII secolo* (Monte Oriolo: F. Papafava, 1979).

Poloni, Alma, 'Firenze prima di Firenze: Poloni legge Faini', *Storica* 51 (2011), 121–37.

Pratellesi, Guido, *Studio giacimentologico delle mineralizzazioni argentifere della zona di Massa Marittima – Montieri (Grosseto)* (Unpublished dissertation, Università degli Studi di Firenze, 1984).

Pryor, John H., 'The Origins of the Commenda', *Speculum* 52:1 (1977), 5–37.

Ramacciotti, Gaetano, *Gli archivi della reverenda fabbrica Camera Apostolica* (Rome: Camera Apostolica, 1961).

Randall Wray, Larry, 'From the State Theory of Money to Modern Money: An Alternative to Economic Orthodoxy', in D. Fox and W. Ernst (eds), *Money in the Western Legal Tradition: Middle Ages to Bretton Woods* (Oxford: Oxford University Press, 2016), pp. 631–52.

Rao, Riccardo, 'Gli Angiò e la gestione delle finanze in Piemonte e Lombardia', in S. Morelli (ed.), *Périphéries financières angevines. Institutions et pratiques de l'administration de territoires composites (XIIIᵉ–XVᵉ siècle) / Periferie finanziarie angioine. Istituzioni e pratiche di governo su territori compositi (sec. XIII–XV)* (Rome: École Française de Rome, 2018), pp. 271–90, online at https://books.openedition.org/efr/3564, accessed 20 September 2024.

Raveggi, Sergio, 'Siena nell'Italia dei Guelfi e dei Ghibellini', in G. Piccinni (ed.), *Fedeltà ghibellina, affari guelfi. Saggi e riletture intorno alla storia di Siena fra Duecento e Trecento*, 2 vols (Ospedaletto: Pacini editore, 2008), vol. 1, pp. 29–61.

Raveggi, Sergio, 'La vittoria di Montaperti', in G. Piccinni (ed.), *Fedeltà ghibellina, affari guelfi. Saggi e riletture intorno alla storia di Siena fra Duecento e Trecento*, 2 vols (Ospedaletto: Pacini editore, 2008), vol. 2, pp. 447–66.

Rohlfs, Gherard, *Grammatica storica della lingua italiana e dei suoi dialetti. Fonetica* (Turin: Einaudi, 1966).

Rolnick, Arthur J., Francois R. Velde, and Warren E. Weber, 'The Debasement Puzzle: An Essay on Medieval Monetary History', *Quarterly Review* (Fall 1997), 8–20.

Rössner, Philipp R., 'Money, Banking, Economy', in A. Classen (ed.), *Handbook of Medieval Culture: Fundamental Aspects and Conditions of the European Middle Ages. Volume 2* (Berlin and Boston: De Gruyter, 2015), pp. 1137–66.

Rössner, Philipp R., 'From the Black Death to the New World (*c.* 1350–1500)', in R. Naismith (ed.), *Money and Coinage in the Middle Ages* (Leiden and Boston: Brill, 2018), pp. 151–75.

Roux, Corinne and Maria F. Guerra, 'La Monnaie Almoravide: de l'Afrique à l'Espagne', *Revue d'Archéométrie* 24 (2000), 39–52.

Rubinstein, Nicolai, 'The Beginnings of Political Thought in Florence', *Journal of the Warburg and Courtauld Institutes* 5 (1942), 198–227.

Ryan, Magnus, 'Bartolus of Sassoferrato and Free Cities', *Transaction of the Royal Historical Society* 10 (2000), 65–89.

Salvatori, Erica, *Boni amici et vicini: le relazioni tra Pisa e le città della Francia meridionale dall'XI alla fine del XIII secolo* (Pisa: Edizioni ETS, 2002).

Salvestrini, Francesco, 'Giovanni Villani and the Aetiological Myth of Tuscan Cities', in E. Kooper (ed.), *The Medieval Chronicle II: Proceedings of the 2nd International Conference on the Medieval Chronicle, Driebergen/Utrecht 16–21 July 1999* (Amsterdam and New York: Rodopi, 2002), pp. 199–211.

Salvestrini, Francesco, 'Tra "civiltà" e "natura". La presenza del fiume nei contesti urbani, il caso toscano fra Medioevo e prima Età Moderna', in D. Canzian and R. Simonetti (eds), *Acque e territorio nel Veneto medievale* (Rome: Viella, 2012), pp. 133–46.

Sambon, Arthur, *Sulle monete delle provincie meridionali d'Italia dal XII al XV secolo*, ed. L. Lombardi (Terlizzi: Biblionumis, 2015).

Santini, Pietro, 'Frammenti di un libro di banchieri fiorentini scritto in volgare nel 1211', *Giornale storico della letteratura italiana* 10:28/29 (1887), 161–77.

Santini, Pietro, *Studi sull'antica costituzione del comune di Firenze: la città e le classi sociali in Firenze nel periodo che precede il primo popolo* (Rome: Multigrafica, 1972).

Santoro, Alfredo M., 'Diffusione di grossi veneziani in Italia meridionale durante il regno di Carlo I d'Angiò: tra archeologia e archeometria', in R. Fiorillo and P. Peduto (eds), *III Congresso nazionale di archeologia medievale: Castello di Salerno, Complesso di Santa Sofia, Salerno 2–5 ottobre 2003* (Florence: All'Insegna del Giglio, 2003), pp. 115–21.

Santoro, Alfredo M., *Circolazione monetaria ed economica a Salerno nei secoli XIII e XIV* (Florence: All'Insegna del Giglio, 2011), pp. 29–30.

Sartori, Andrew, 'Silver and the Social in Locke's Monetary Thought', *The Journal of Modern History* 93:3 (2021), 501–32.

Savigny, Friedrich K. von, *The History of the Roman Law during the Middle Ages, Vol. I* (Edinburgh: A. Black, 1829).

Savorelli, Alessandro, 'Giglio di Firenze', in M. M. Donato and D. Parenti (eds), *Dal Giglio al David. Arte civica a Firenze fra medioevo e rinascimento* (Florence and Milan: Giunti, 2013), p. 141.

Sbarbaro, Massimo, 'Circolazione di idee e di esperienze economiche nell'Italia del Duecento. La coniazione del ducato veneziano: scelta politica o economica?', in A. L. Trombetti Budriesi (ed.), *Cultura cittadina e documentazione. Formazione e circolazione di modelli. Bologna, 12–13 ottobre 2006* (Bologna: Clueb, 2009), pp. 59–72.

Schaube, Adolf, *Storia del commercio dei popoli latini del Mediterraneo sino alla fine delle Crociate* (Turin: Unione tipografico-editrice torinese, 1915).

Schein, Sylvia, *Fideles Crucis: The Papacy, the West, and the Recovery of the Holy Land, 1274–1314* (Oxford: The Clarendon Press, 1991).

Schlumberger, Gustave L., *Numismatique de l'Orient latin* (Paris: Ernest Leroux, 1878).

Schumpeter, Joseph A., *History of Economic Analysis* (London: Routledge, 1987).

Simpson, Alexander Carson, 'The Mint Officials of the Florentine Florin', *American Numismatic Society Museum Notes 5* (1952), 113–55.

Smith, Romney David, 'Calamity and Transition: Re-imagining Italian Trade in the Eleventh-Century Mediterranean', *Past & Present* 228 (2015), 15–56.

Smith, Thomas W., 'Pope Honorius III, the Military Orders and the Financing of the Fifth Crusade: A Culture of Papal Preference?', in J. Schenk and M. Carr (eds), *The Military Order Vol. 6.1* (London: Routledge, 2016), pp. 54–61.

Smith, Thomas W., *Curia and Crusade: Pope Honorius III and the Recovery of the Holy Land 1216–1227* (Turnhout: Brepols, 2017).

Soldani, Maria Elisa, 'Da Accettanti a Setantí: il processo di integrazione di una famiglia lucchese nella società barcellonese del Quattrocento', in C. Iannella (ed.), *Per Marco Tangheroni. Studi su Pisa e sul Mediterraneo medievale offerti dai suoi ultimi allievi* (Pisa: Edizioni ETS, 2005), pp. 209–33.

Spufford, Peter, *Handbook of Medieval Exchange* (London: Royal Historical Society, 1986).

Spufford, Peter, *Money and Its Use in Medieval Europe* (Cambridge: Cambridge University Press, 1988).

Spufford, Peter, 'The First Century of the Florentine Florin', *Rivista Italiana di Numismatica e Scienze Affini* 107 (2006), 421–36.

Spufford, Peter, 'Lapis, Indigo, Woad: Artists' Materials in the Context of International Trade before 1700', in J. Kirby, S. Nash, and J. Cannon (eds), *Trade in Artists' Materials: Markets and Commerce in Europe to 1700* (London: Archetype Publications, 2010), pp. 10–25.

Spufford, Peter, 'The Provision of Stable Moneys by Florence and Venice, and North Italian Financial Innovations in the Renaissance Period', in P. Bernholz and R. Vaubel (eds), *Explaining Monetary and Financial Innovation: A Historical Analysis* (Berlin: Springer, 2014), pp. 227–51.

Stahl, Alan, *Zecca: The Mint of Venice in the Middle Ages* (Baltimore and London: The Johns Hopkins University Press, 2000).

Stahl, Alan, 'Coinage and Money in the Latin Empire of Constantinople', *Dumbarton Oaks Papers 55* (2001), 197–206.

Stahl, Alan, 'The Mediterranean Melting Pot: Monetary Crosscurrents of the Twelfth through Fifteenth Centuries', in M. S. Brownlee and D. H. Gondicas (eds), *Renaissance Encounters: Greek East and Latin West* (Leiden and Boston: Brill, 2013), pp. 241–62.

Sthamer, Eduard, *L'amministrazione dei castelli nel Regno di Sicilia sotto Federico II e Carlo I d'Angiò* (Bari: Adda, 1995).

Sznura, Franek, *L'espansione urbana di Firenze nel Dugento* (Florence: La Nuova Italia, 1975).

Tangheroni, Marco, *Commercio e navigazione nel medioevo* (Rome: Laterza, 1996).

TLIO, 'Tesoro della Lingua Italiana delle Origini', online at http://tlio.ovi.cnr.it/TLIO/, accessed 20 September 2024.

Toch, Michael, 'Welfs, Hohenstaufen and Habsburgs', in D. Abulafia (ed.), *The New Cambridge Medieval History Vol. 5: c. 1198–c. 1300* (Cambridge: Cambridge University Press, 1999), pp. 375–404.

Tognetti, Sergio, 'Mercanti e libri di conto nella Toscana del basso medioevo: le edizioni di registri aziendali dagli anni '60 del Novecento a oggi', *Anuario de Estudios Medievales* 42:2 (2012), 867–80.

Tognetti, Sergio, 'Il Mezzogiorno angioino nello spazio economico fiorentino tra XIII e XIV secolo', in B. Figliuolo, G. Petralia, and P. F. Simbula (eds), *Spazi economici e circuiti commerciali nel Mediterraneo del Trecento. Atti del Convegno Internazionale di Studi, Amalfi, 4–5 giugno 2016* (Amalfi: Centro di cultura e storia amalfitana, 2017), pp. 147–70.

Toomaspoeg, Kristjan, *Decimae. Il sostegno economico dei sovrani alla Chiesa del Mezzogiorno nel XIII secolo* (Rome: Viella, 2009).

Toubert, Pierre, *Les structures du Latium médiéval: le Latium méridional et la Sabine du IXe siècle à la fin du XIIe siècle*, 2 vols (Rome: École Française de Rome, 1973).

Travaini, Lucia (ed.), *Moneta locale, moneta straniera: Italia ed Europa, XI–XV secolo/Local Coins, Foreign Coins: Italy and Europe 11th–15th Centuries, The Second Numismatic Symposium* (Milan: Società Numismatica Italiana, 1999).

Travaini, Lucia, 'Romesinas, provesini, turonenses...: monete straniere in Italia meridionale ed in Sicilia (XI–XV secolo)', in L. Travaini (ed.), *Moneta locale, moneta straniera: Italia ed Europa, XI–XV secolo/ Local Coins, Foreign Coins: Italy and Europe 11th–15th Centuries, the Second Numismatic Symposium* (Milan: Società Numismatica Italiana, 1999), pp. 113–33.

Travaini, Lucia, 'Monete, battiloro e pittori. L'uso dell'oro nella pittura murale e i dati della cappella degli Scrovegni. Coins, Gold-beaters and Painters. How Gold Was Used in Wall Paintings: Some Examples from the Scrovegni Chapel', *Bollettino d'Arte* (2005), 145–52.

Travaini, Lucia (ed.), 'Firenze 1252–2002: 750 anni del fiorino, Atti della Giornata celebrativa in ricordo del numismatico fiorentino Alberto Banti, Firenze, Palazzo Vecchio, Salone dei Cinquecento, 16 novembre 2002', *Rivista Italiana di Numismatica e Scienze Affini* 107 (2006), 397–469.

Travaini, Lucia, 'La quarta crociata e la monetazione nell'area mediterranea', in G. Ortalli, G. Ravegnani, and Peter Schreiner (eds), *Quarta crociata: Venezia, Bisanzio, Impero Latino* (Venice: Istituto veneto di scienze, lettere e arti, 2006), pp. 525–53.

Travaini, Lucia, 'Roma', in L. Travaini (ed.), *Le zecche italiane fino all'Unità* (Rome: Istituto Poligrafico e Zecca dello Stato, Libreria dello Stato, 2011), pp. 1077–117.

Travaini, Lucia, 'Le zecche italiane', in L. Travaini (ed.), *Le zecche italiane fino all'Unità* (Rome: Istituto Poligrafico e Zecca dello Stato, 2011), pp. 31–126.

Travaini, Lucia, *La monetazione dell'Italia normanna. Seconda versione con aggiornamento e ristampa anastatica con una appendice sui ritrovamenti 1995–2004 a cura di Giuseppe Sarcinelli* (Zurich and London: Numismatica ARS Classica NAC AG, 2016).

Travaini, Lucia, 'Sacra Moneta: Mints and Divinity: Purity, Miracles and Power', in N. M. Burström and G. T. Ingvardson (eds), *Divina Moneta: Coins in Religion and Ritual* (London and New York: Routledge, 2017), pp. 174–89.

Travaini, Lucia, 'From the Treasure Chest to the Pope's Soup: Coins, Mints and the Roman Curia (1150–1305)', in W. Maleczek (ed.), *Die römische Kurie und das Geld. Von der Mitte des 12. Jahrhunderts bis zum frühen 14 Jahrhundert* (Ostfildern: Jan Thorbecke Verlag, 2018), pp. 27–64.

Travaini, Lucia, *Monete mercanti e matematica. Le monete medievali nei trattati di aritmetica e nei libri di mercatura. Seconda edizione ampliata con nuove liste inedite* (Milan: Jouvence, 2020).

Travaini, Lucia, *The Thirty Pieces of Silver: Coin Relics in Medieval and Modern Europe* (Abingdon and New York: Routledge, 2022).

Travaini, Lucia and Matteo Broggini, 'San Giovanni sull'incudine. Fondatori cristiani e fondatori mitici sulle monete italiane medievali e moderne', in L. Travaini and G. Arrigoni (eds), *Polis, urbs, civitas: moneta e identità. Atti del Convegno di studio del Lexicon Iconographicum Numismaticae (Milano 25 ottobre 2012)* (Rome: Quasar, 2013), pp. 165–76.

Travaini, Lucia and Matteo Broggini (eds), *Il tesoro di Montella (Avellino): ducati e fiorini d'oro italiani e stranieri occultati nella metà del Trecento* (Rome: Quasar, 2016).

Travaini, Lucia and Namal Siedlecki, 'Branding Your Own Personal Offering: New Finds from the Trevi Fountain', *Quaderni Ticinesi di Numismatica e Antichità Classiche* 49 (2020), 359–83.

Trifone, Romualdo, *La legislazione angioina: edizione critica* (Naples: L. Lubrano, 1921).

Tripodi, Claudia, 'I fiorentini "quinto elemento dell'universo": L'utilizzazione encomiastica di una tradizione/invenzione', *Archivio Storico Italiano* 168:625 (2010), 491–512.

Trivellato, Francesca, 'Renaissance Florence and the Origins of Capitalism: A Business History Perspective', *Business History Review* 94 (2020), 229–51.

Ulivi, Elisabetta, 'Masters, Questions and Challenges in the Abacus Schools', *Archive for History of Exact Sciences* 69 (2015), 651–70.

Vendittelli, Marco, 'Mercanti romani del primo Duecento "in Urbe potentes"', in C. Carbonetti Vendittelli *et al.* (eds), *Rome aux XIIIᵉ et XIVᵉ siècles. Cinq études réunies par Étienne Hubert* (Rome: École Française de Rome, 1993), pp. 97–135.

Vendittelli, Marco, *'In partibus Anglie'. Cittadini romani alla corte inglese nel Duecento: la vicenda di Pietro Saraceno* (Rome: Viella, 2001).

Vendittelli, Marco, 'Una nota sul primo campsor domini pape conosciuto', in M. Palma and C. Vismara (eds), *Per Gabriella. Studi in ricordo di Gabriella Braga*, 4 vols (Cassino: Università degli Studi di Cassino e del Lazio meridionale, 2013), vol. 4, pp. 1834–41.

Vendittelli, Marco, 'I primi "campsores domini papae"', in A. Serra (ed.), *Humanitas. Studi per Patrizia Serafin* (Rome: Universitalia, 2015), pp. 409–31.

Venditti, Gianni, 'La decima sessennale del 1274 in Abruzzo', in A. Gottsmann, P. Piatti, and A. E. Rehberg (eds), *Incorrupta monumenta ecclesiam defendunt. Studi offerti a mons. Sergio Pagano, prefetto dell'Archivio Segreto Vaticano. II: Archivi, archivistica, diplomatica, paleografia* (Vatican City: Archivio Segreto Vaticano, 2018), pp. 909–22.

Vendola, Domenico, 'Le Decime Ecclesiastiche in Puglia nel Sec. XIV', *Japigia* 8 (1937), 137–66.

Waley, Daniel, 'The Army of the Florentine Republic from the Twelfth to the Fourteenth Century', in N. Rubinstein (ed.), *Florentine Studies: Politics and Society in Renaissance Florence* (London: Faber & Faber, 1968), pp. 70–108.

Waley, Daniel, '*Condotte* and *Condottieri* in the Thirteenth Century', *Proceedings of the British Academy* 61 (1975), 337–71.

Walker, Thomas, 'The Italian Gold Revolution of 1252: Shifting Currents in the Pan-Mediterranean Flow of Gold', in J. F. Richards (ed.), *Precious Metals in the Later Medieval and Early Modern Worlds* (Durham, NC: Carolina Academic Press, 1983), pp. 29–52.

Watson, Andrew, 'Back to Gold – and Silver', *Economic History Review* 2nd ser. 20:1 (1967), 1–34.

Werthmann, Katja, 'Gold Mining and Jula Influence in Precolonial Southern Burkina Faso', *The Journal of African History* 48:3 (2007), 395–414.

Wickham, Chris, 'The Sense of the Past in Italian Communal Narratives', in P. Magdalino (ed.), *The Perception of the Past in Twelfth-Century Europe* (London and Rio Grande: The Hambledon Press, 1992), pp. 173–89.

Wickham, Chris, *The Donkey and the Boat: Reinterpreting the Mediterranean Economy, 950–1180* (Oxford: Oxford University Press, 2023).

Woodhouse, Adam, 'Who Owns the Money? Currency, Property, and Popular Sovereignty in Nicole Oresme's *De moneta*', *Speculum* 92:1 (2017), 84–116.

Yver, Georges, *Le commerce et les marchands dans l'Italie méridional au XIIIᵉ et au XIVᵉ siècle* (Paris: Fontemoing, 1903).

Zabbia, Marino, 'Villani, Giovanni', in *Dizionario Biografico degli Italiani*, vol. 99 (Rome: Istituto della Enciclopedia Italiana, 2020), pp. 333–8, online at www.treccani.it/enciclopedia/giovanni-villani_%28Dizionario-Biografico%29/, accessed 24 September 2024.

Zelizer, Viviana A., *The Social Meaning of Money: Pin Money, Paychecks, Poor Relief, & Other Currencies* (New York: Basic Books, 1994).

Index

EU authorised representative for GPSR:
Easy Access System Europe, Mustamäe tee 50,
10621 Tallinn, Estonia
gpsr.requests@easproject.com

www.ingramcontent.com/pod-product-compliance
Ingram Content Group UK Ltd.
Pitfield, Milton Keynes, MK11 3LW, UK
UKHW021816010525
458091UK00006B/24